Robert Young

Proposed Emendations

Of the Metrical Version of the Psalms Used in Scotland

Robert Young

Proposed Emendations
Of the Metrical Version of the Psalms Used in Scotland

ISBN/EAN: 9783744784979

Printed in Europe, USA, Canada, Australia, Japan

Cover: Foto ©Lupo / pixelio.de

More available books at **www.hansebooks.com**

PROPOSED EMENDATIONS

OF THE

METRICAL VERSION OF THE PSALMS

USED IN SCOTLAND.

BY THE

REV. ROBERT YOUNG, M.A.

FORMERLY CLASSICAL TEACHER, GLASGOW ; LATTERLY FOR SOME TIME
MINISTER OF THE FREE CHURCH, CHAPELTON.

EDINBURGH :
THOMAS LAURIE, 92, PRINCES STREET.
1863.

EDINBURGH: T. CONSTABLE,
PRINTER TO THE QUEEN, AND TO THE UNIVERSITY

PREFATORY REMARKS.

THE reader, on looking at the title of the following attempt, will naturally ask, What is the character of the emendations here proposed to be made on our Metrical Version of the Psalms? The answer to this question will be given by glancing at the more prominent *faults* of our version as it now stands.

Of the merits of this version, which is believed to be chiefly, if not wholly, the production of Mr. Francis Rous, who resided in England, our neighbours in South Britain speak very contemptuously; at least many of them do so. Even Mr. James Montgomery, no mean poet, when lately in Scotland, and when far advanced in years, confessed that he was only then learning to relish our Scottish version of the Psalms. Had its merits been great, and easily seen, it is to be supposed that so good a man, and so good a judge of poetry, would have spoken of them in a different manner.

Rous's translation has the merit of being more literal than that of Buchanan, or than that of Brady and Tate; its style is simple, plain, and popular, and, as a translation, it is in *general* characterized by a faithful adherence to the inspired original. It cannot, however, claim high poetical merit. In *versification*,

A

it is far from accuracy or fluency; the *style*, though simple, is often bald and unpoetical, not even always grammatically correct; and the *translation*, though in general faithful in expressing the sense of the original, has yet, in some places, much need of emendation.

But in judging of our metrical version of the Psalms, and of the possibility of improving it, we must look at its *age*, as well as its merits. It was composed about the year 1646, and is consequently fully 200 years old. During this long period many changes have happened to our language, as well as to other living languages. Many words, many modes of expression, and many forms of construction then current, and deemed elegant, have since gone into disuse, and others have taken their place, just like the changes in dress, architecture, manners, and almost everything human. Our version of the Psalms is but thirty-five years later than the authorized version of the English Bible. Now, if Dr. Conquest judged 20,000 emendations needful to modernize all which had become obsolete, and to remove all which was otherwise objectionable in the phraseology of that version, we may reasonably suppose that our metrical version of the Psalms does not less require a renovating process, as it cannot be regarded equal in merit to the authorized version of the Bible.

Faults of Rous's Versification. In the version of the Psalms as given by Rous, there is much need of emendation in the translator's *versification*. In this department his faults are neither few nor small. His version

PREFATORY REMARKS. 3

is professedly regulated by the laws of measure; and as it is a specimen of *lyric* poetry intended to be sung in churches and in families, there was all the more need of exactness in the measure, so as to produce agreement between the poetry and the music. In many of the stanzas, however, this requisite exactness does not exist. Above 270 *lines* are either too long or too short, according as our language is *now* pronounced. Rous may not be responsible for all of these irregularities in the length of his lines, as a considerable part of them may be caused by those changes in pronunciation which have happened to our language since the time at which Rous composed his version. But for some of these anomalous lines Rous is responsible, such, for instance, as two in Ps. i., ii. :—

Above 270 lines faulty in measure.

  " near planted by a river,
   for his leaf fadeth never."

  " to be my King appointed,
   I have him King anointed."

In all these and many similar lines, which have an extra syllable, there can have been no change in pronunciation since the date of their composition, so that they must have been wrong composed in regard to measure.

In Ps. iii. is an instance of a line *defective* in measure by one syllable,—

  " Salvation doth appertain."

Many lines like that immediately above want *one* requisite syllable; some want *two*, as the following from Ps. lxxviii., cxxx. :—

"The nations of Canaan."
"And plenteous redemption."

Now, whether these lines were wrong made, or have since become defective, they and all such should now be amended, so as to make them unexceptionable in point of measure. The number requiring adjustment is above 270, as formerly hinted.

To complete the requisite number of syllables in his lines, Rous has recourse sometimes to a rather clumsy expedient, such as writing *Jehudah* for Judah, *thorough* for through, *commandement* for commandment, *rememberance* for remembrance. All such lines require emendation also.

But Rous's versification is often faulty in *rhyme* as well as in measure. About seventy of his stanzas have *no* rhyme. This may justly be said of all those stanzas which rhyme like the following, in Ps. lxxx., civ. :—

<small>About 70 stanzas without rhyme.</small>

"Turn us again, O Lord our God,
   and upon us vouchs*afe*
To make thy countenance to shine,
   and so we shall be *safe*."

"By them the fowls of heav'n shall have
   their habita*tion*,
Which do among the branches sing
   with delec*tation*."

Truly seventy such stanzas need emendation. In what English lyric poet, except Rous, shall we find seventy such stanzas?

But Rous's versification needs emendation not only in measure and rhyme, but also in regard to ruggedness, as the following specimen from Ps. xvii. :—

PREFATORY REMARKS.

Rugged lines. " *Thou prov'dst mine heart, thou visit'dst me.*"

Rous often, too, shows a want of skill in verse-building, such as a mason would show in house-building who should put very *small* stones in the *corner* of the house.

Of many existing examples, take the following one from Ps. lxxxvi. :—

" And like the works which thou hast done,
not any work is *there.*"

The word *there* in the second of these two lines is one of small importance in the sentence, and should not therefore occupy so prominent a place in the line.

Faults of Rous's style. These observations will show the need of emendations in Rous's versification. There is frequent occasion for emendations also in the department of *style.*

As the rules of grammar now stand, it would at least require *fifty* emendations to clear Rous's version of grammatical errors. It is not improbable that 200 years ago the laws of grammar might be somewhat different from what they are now. Be this as it may, existing errors ought now to be corrected. What are these errors? They are such as the following :—Thou hast *stroke*, for thou hast struck, Ps. iii. ; Thou *raz'd*, for thou raz'dst, Ps. ix. ; Thou *wastes*, for thou wastest, Ps. xxxix. ; Thou *took*, for thou took'st, Ps. lvi. ; Thou *caus'd*, for thou caus'dst, Ps. lxxvi. 8 ; Thou *raised*, for thou raisedst, Ps. cii., long metre ; Thou *said*, for thou saidst, Ps. civ. ; Thou *gare*, for thou gavest, Ps. cxix. 52 ; Thou art *acquaint*, for thou art acquainted, Ps. cxxxix., etc.

Grammatical errors.

A 2

There are errors not a few arising from *nominatives* without verbs. These it were long to enumerate. Take as a specimen two from Ps. x.,—

<blockquote>
"The wicked, through his pride of face,
on God <i>he</i> doth not call.
His ways <i>they</i> always grievous are."
</blockquote>

Redundant nominatives.

It may be pleaded by some in defence of Rous, that some of these sentences, objected to on the ground of having a redundant nominative, are to be regarded not as grammatical errors, but as specimens of the Hebraistic idiom, like the sentence in Job, "The fear of the Lord, *that* is wisdom."

In reply it may be said, that when a sentence has a redundant nominative in the original, the translator should be allowed to give a redundant nominative in his translation of that sentence. But it will never do to allow a translator to construct such sentences as often as he chooses, whether there be or be not a redundant nominative in the original. That Rous does take such liberties it were easy to prove by many examples. Take the following, for one, from Psalm cxix. 70:—

<blockquote>
"Their hearts through worldly ease and wealth,
as fat as grease <i>they</i> be."
</blockquote>

But other words may be redundant as well as nominatives. Examples:—

<blockquote>
"Because of (those) mine enemies." Ps. v.
"Instead of (those) thy fathers dear." Ps. xlv.
"But when (that) thou, O gracious God."—Ps. xxx.
"(The) wicked men estranged are."—Ps. lviii.
"Above all (other) gods thou art." Ps. xcvii.
</blockquote>

PREFATORY REMARKS.

The words within parentheses in these examples are considered redundant.

Obsolete words. Many emendations, at least forty, are needed to render modern what is *antiquated* in the style of our version of the Psalms, partly in words, partly in phrases; as *folk* for people; *sith* for since; *cunning* for skilful; *For why?* for because; *when as* for when; *spake* for spoke; *coin* for money; etc.

Some emendations are needed for such lines as the following:—

Unpoetical words.
"Froward thou *kyth'st*
unto the froward *wight*."— Ps. xviii.
" On his own *pate* shall come."—Ps. vii.
" The na-ti-ons of Ca-na-an."— Ps. lxxviii.

Very many emendations are needful to bring into agreement with present usage Rous's peculiarities of style in regard to the use of *relative pronouns.* Like other authors of his time, he often applies *which* when persons are meant. He is especially partial to the use of the word *that* as a relative. In the *Too frequent use of that as a relative pronoun.* first twenty of the Psalms, while he uses *who* nine times, and *which* fourteen times, he uses *that* as a relative forty-nine times, showing a striking preponderance in the use of a favourite word. If it be asked, What is improper in this, and why think of amending such passages? It may be replied, that since the word *that* in our language is used both as a *conjunction* and as a *demonstrative* pronoun, it is throwing needless obscurity over language to use it also so frequently as a *relative* pronoun. In proportion as any word is used in a greater *variety* of senses, the greater the chance of its being occasionally misunderstood by those not critically acquainted with language. It is probably to guard against the danger of such mistakes, that within the last fifty years the use of *that* as a relative pronoun has become much less common. If the Greeks with all their refinement were content with one *relative*, ὅς, ἥ, ὅ ; and the Romans with one, *qui, quæ, quod* ; the English may be satisfied with the use of *who* and *which*, without subjecting the word *that* to a worse than useless variety of duty. Nor should it be forgotten that the use of *that* as a relative more readily leads to mistakes in meaning than the use of *who* and *which* does ; for *that* has no distinction as *who* and *which* have. Dr. Conquest, accordingly, in his edition of the Bible with 20,000 emendations, has very often changed *that* as a relative into *who* or *which*.

Some emendations are needed to correct the occasional *tautology* of Rous's style ; such as *large* and *great*, Ps. lxxii. ; *slain* and *dead*, Ps. lxxix. ; *praise*, *laud*, Ps. c. ; *fear* and *dread*, *change* and *mutation*, Ps. cii. ; thy *endless* years do last *for aye*, etc. But many more emendations are required to rectify what is injudicious in the *arrangement* of his words. From

<small>Faulty in the arrangement of words.</small> a want of attention to arrangement, Rous's poetry is often far from elegant, and his meaning is sometimes obscure. See a proof of both in Ps. lv. 19 :

    " The Lord shall hear and them afflict,
       of old who hath abode."

The fault in the arrangement here is, that seven words

are unhappily put between the antecedent *Lord* and its relative *who*, thereby making it doubtful whether the relative *who* belongs to the word *Lord*, or to the word *them*. In other places of his version, Rous, by an unskilful arrangement, makes his lines less rhythmically fluent than they might be. One of many examples occurs in Psalm xlvi. 5 :—

> " Nothing shall her remove ;"

otherwise arranged—

> " Her nothing shall remove."

Giving Rous credit for the general plainness and simplicity of his style, it is yet true that not unfrequently it is unpoetical and bald. Take one from many instances, in the following stanzas from Ps. lxxiv. 5, 6 :—

Style often unpoetical

> 5 " A man was famous, and was had
>   in estimation.
>   According as he lifted up
>   his axe thick trees upon.
> 6   But all at once with axes now
>   and hammers they *go to*,
>   And down the carved work thereof
>   they break and quite undo."

Would the following proposed emendation improve the above stanzas ?—

> 5 In times of old was famed the man
>   who did utensils wield,
>   To cut and square the trees with which
>   thy dwelling-place was ceil'd.
> 6 But now in sacrilegious hands
>   the axe and hammer sound,
>   To break and spoil the carvèd work
>   which long thy temple crown'd.

PREFATORY REMARKS.

Having thus endeavoured to show that our metrical version of the Psalms requires emendations in its *versification*, and in its *style*, let us now see whether it needs emendation in some passages as a *translation*. The question here is, Can passages be pointed out in which the translator has failed to convey the precise meaning of the sacred original? In page 1 of these remarks, it was admitted that *in general* Rous's version of the Psalms is characterized by a faithful adherence to the original as to giving the sense of it. But even in *this* department there appears to be now and then need of emendations. In proof of this let us look at his translation of Ps. xlv. 7. This passage is first mentioned, not because it is the first which occurs, but because it seems a mistranslation of *very great importance*. In our authorized prose translation the verse is thus translated: "Thou lovest righteousness, and hatest wickedness: *therefore* God, thy God, hath anointed thee with the oil of gladness above thy fellows."

<small>Faults of Rous as a translator.</small>

<small>The meaning of a prophecy darkened or misinterpreted.</small>

Rous's version—

"Thou lovest right, and hatest ill : *for* God, thy God, most high," etc.

Our translators use the word *therefore*, Rous *for*, the former an inferential, the latter a causal conjunction—the former word is placed before the effect, the latter placed before the cause.

It is carefully to be noticed that this verse is part of a *prophecy concerning Christ's exaltation*. According to the *prose* version, he was exalted *because* he loved righteousness, and hated wickedness; Rous, on the

PREFATORY REMARKS.

contrary, says that Christ's love of righteousness, and his hatred of wickedness, was the *effect* of his being anointed by God. Cause and effect, light and darkness, differ not more from each other than does the rendering of our translators from that of Rous. Rous is evidently in error here; and it is the more wonderful, and the less excusable, that he erred so grossly, when, in the Epistle to the Hebrews, i. 9, he had, or might have had, in the apostle Paul an infallible guide to the right rendering of the verse in question.

The Apostle gives the sense as our translators have done, but directly contrary to the sense of Rous's version. In this verse, then, of Rous's version, a glaring error in an important prophecy about our Saviour has been for the long space of 200 years permitted to remain uncorrected, misleading, or at least calculated to mislead, all the millions who use our metrical version of the Psalms. Here then, surely, is greatly needed an emendation such as the following:—

> Thou lovest right, and hatest ill,
> hence God, thy God, most high, etc.

The change of *for* into *hence* rectifies the mistake.

Rous appears to give another instance of mistranslation in Ps. vii. 14, last clause, and falsehood *shall bring* forth, thereby differing from the prose translation, which renders it, and *brought* forth falsehood. In Rous we have here a *prophecy;* in the *prose* translation we have a historical fact stated.

In Ps. xi. 3, last clause, Rous has,

> " What hath the righteous done?"

Prose translation—
> "What *can* the righteous do?"

Rous's rendering leads us to ask, Of what fault have the righteous been guilty? whereas the prose translation leads to the question, What *resource* can the righteous have?

In Ps. xvii. 3, Rous has, "nothing *found'st*."—Prose translation has, "*shalt find* nothing."

In Ps. xxii. 31, last clause, Rous has,
> "*And* that he hath done this."

The *and* here is a supplement of Rous's own, and injures the meaning. The line should be,
> In that he hath done this.

In Ps. xliv. 2, last two lines, Rous writes thus:
> "Thou didst afflict the nations,
> but them thou didst increase."

Proposed emendation:—
> Thou, Lord, the nations didst afflict,
> and cast them from their place.

Where is Rous's authority for the *latter* of his two lines?

In Ps. xlviii. 2, last line, Rous has,
> "On her *north* side doth stand."

Proposed emendation:—
> On her *south* side doth stand.

Both Bishop Patrick and Henry agree in saying that Mount Sion stands on the *north* side of the city of Jerusalem; if so, how can the city, as Rous writes, stand on the north side of Mount Sion? See Patrick and Henry, *in loco;* see also Henry on Ps. lxxv. sect. 2.

In this same Psalm (xlviii. 6-8) Rous writes thus:—

PREFATORY REMARKS.

> 6 " Great terror there took hold on them,
>   they were possess'd with fear;
>   Their grief came like a woman's pain,
>   when she a child doth bear.
> 7 Thou Tarshish ships with east wind break'st:
> 8   As we have heard it told,
>   So, in the city of the Lord,
>   our eyes did it behold."

Proposed emendation,—

> 6 Fear—pain—they felt, as woman feels,
>   when she a child doth bear;
> 7 Despair—as Tarshish crews, whose ships
>   with east wind broken are.
> 8 As we have from our fathers learn'd
>   the wonders done of old,
>   So, in the city of the Lord,
>   our eyes did this behold.

In what part of ver. 6 in the original did Rous find authority for his words, "great terror," and "grief"?

In Ps. lv. 19, Rous writes thus :—

> 19 " The Lord shall hear, and them afflict,
>   of old who hath abode:
>   Because they never changes have,
>   therefore they fear not God."

Line 2, for a reason stated at the foot of p. 8, is *obscure*, and the word *therefore*, line 4, might be dispensed with.

Would the following proposed emendation remove the obscurity and improve the style?—

> The eternal God will them afflict,
>   and he my prayer will hear;
> Because they never changes have,
>   the Lord they do not fear.

In Ps. lviii. 2, Rous has another *obscure* sentence,—

2 "Yea, ev'n within your very hearts
ye wickedness have done;
*And ye the vi'lence of your hands
do weigh the earth upon.*"

Proposed emendation,—

You practise evil in your hearts,
then sin in open day,
Since o'er the land, in balance false,
you deeds and causes weigh.

Rous has no authority for *and* at the beginning of his third line; and as the violence complained of did not refer to the whole *earth*, but only to *Canaan*, the word *land* seems preferable. Rous's *fourth* line seems unintelligible.

In Ps. lxxiv. 14, Rous has a stanza which is *probably* mistranslated :—

14 "The leviathan's head thou brak'st
in pieces, and didst give
Him to be meat unto the folk
in wilderness that live."

As Bishop Patrick, Bishop Horne, and Mr. Job Orton explain this verse, we are to understand by it that the dead bodies of the drowned Egyptians were given for a prey to the beasts and birds of the desert. If they be right, it should be amended as follows :—

The heads of the leviathan
thou brok'st, and thou didst give
Him for a prey to beasts and birds,
which in the desert live.

The original word, עָם, rendered by our translators *people*, and by Rous *folk*, means properly the *inhabitants of the desert*, whether men or beasts. In the prophetical writings, the same word is three times translated *wild* beasts (see Isaiah xiii. 21, xxxiv. 14; Jer. l. 39).

In Rous, Ps. lxxx. 9,

"Before it thou a room didst make."

Emendation,—

Before it thou didst room prepare.

In Ps. lxxxix. 17, Rous writes "horn *and pow'r.*" Does the translator mean that the *horn* is something distinct from the *power* when he thus couples them? Is not horn rather the symbol of power? If so, they should not thus be *coupled*, as if horn denoted one thing, and power another.

In Ps. ci. 3, Rous writes,—

"I will *endure* no wicked thing."

Prose translation,—

"I will *set* no wicked thing."

"Non *proponam* rem nefariam."—JUNIUS.

"Nec mihi exemplum *statuam* sequendum."—BUCHANAN.

The two Latin translators agree with the *prose* translation in English; but all the three differ from Rous, inasmuch as an active *promoter* of evil differs from a too patient *endurer* of it.

In Ps. cii. 8, long metre, last two lines of the stanza, Rous writes,—

"The madmen are against me sworn,
The men against me that arose."

Proposed emendation,—

And those to ruin me are sworn,
Who mad with rage against me rose.

Rous's expression, the *madmen*, is one liable to be

misunderstood, as if it meant people who were insane, and not those frantic with rage.

In Ps. civ. 6, last two lines of the stanza, Rous writes,—

> "The waters stood above the hills,
> when thou the word but said."

Proposed emendation,—

> The waters, standing o'er the hills,
> a shoreless ocean made.

The second of Rous's two lines, besides having no authority from the original, is not even grammatical English, since "thou said," to be grammatical, should be "thou saidst." But apart from the inaccuracy of the expression, we do not read in the first chapter of Genesis that God *said* to the waters, "Stand above, or cover the hills."

It is at once admitted that line 2 of the above emendation is not in the original; but on examination it will be found to agree well with the preceding and subsequent context.

In the 30th verse of this 104th Psalm, the translator seems not happy in giving the precise meaning. He thus writes:—

> 30 "Thy quick'ning spirit thou send'st forth,
> then they created be;
> And then the earth's decayed face
> renewed is by thee."

The objection to this translation is, that the reader is led to think that the very same beings, which in the preceding verse are said to die and return to dust, are created again, which is not the fact. Another race endowed with the same properties are formed, but those who died in the autumn do not again live in the spring, if we except such cases as the caterpillar. This may perhaps appear hypercriticism and excessive particularity. Perhaps it is. At the same time, the facts of the case referred to in ver. 30 would seem somewhat more exactly brought out by the following emendation:—

> Thou send'st thy quick'ning spirit forth,
>   whence rise another race;
> And thus by thee renewèd is
>   the earth's decayèd face.

In Psalm cxix. 136, Rous, without apparent necessity, turns *present* tenses of the verb into past, thus:—

> 136 " Rivers of waters from mine eyes
>   *did run* down, when I *saw*
> How wicked men run on in sin,
>   and do not keep thy law."

Proposed emendation,—

> The tears in rivers from mine eyes
>   run down, while sad I see
> The wicked trampling on thy law
>   without all fear of thee.

In Psalm cxx. 4, Rous fails to convey the proper meaning. The stanza, of which ver. 4 is a part, runs thus in Rous:—

> 3 " What shall be giv'n thee? or what shall
>   be done to thee, false tongue?
> 4 Ev'n burning coals of juniper,
>   sharp arrows of the strong."

Proposed emendation,—

> What shall be giv'n to thee, false tongue?
> or what to thee be done?
> Fierce, lasting fires, and arrows sharp
> sent from the Mighty One.

Rous's translation of this passage fails to convey the important idea that God, the Mighty One, is the punisher of the false tongue. Rous's word, *strong*, will not, to the great majority of readers, convey this idea. Now, all the commentators whom I consulted agree in thinking that by the term *mighty*, God is intended. By Bishop Patrick, the original word is translated by the word Almighty, clearly showing what was his notion of its import.

If Bishop Patrick's translation be thought good, the fourth line of the above emendation may run thus:—

> From the Almighty One.

In Ps. cxxvi. 1, Rous's word, *dream'd*, should be *dream*; that is, a *past* tense should be a present.

In Ps. cxxxiii. 1, Rous omits the word rendered by the word *pleasant*. As the notion of deriving *pleasure* from unity is a *motive* too important to be lost sight of, the stanza of Rous may be amended thus:—

> Behold how pleasant, and how good,
> and how becoming well,
> Together such as brethren are
> in unity to dwell!

In Ps. cxxxix. 8, Rous unfortunately, and in very bad taste, applies to heaven the word *lo*, which our translators apply to hell.

Would this misplacement of the *lo* by Rous be rectified by either of the following ways?—by *omitting* it, and putting "Lord" in its place, thus:—

PREFATORY REMARKS.

> Ascend I heav'n, thou, Lord, art there ;
> there, if in hell I lie.

Or thus :—

> Lie I in hell, lo, thou art there ;
> there, soar I to the sky.

The only other failure in Rous's translations to which I would at present refer is in Ps. cxliii. 4, in Rous thus :—

> 4 "My sp'rit is therefore overwhelm'd
> in me perplexedly ;
> Within me is my very heart
> *amazed wondrously.*"

Prose translation, last clause, is,—

> "My heart within me is desolate"

Proposed emendation,—

> Whence overwhelm'd my spirit is
> with sore perplexity ;
> Within me does my very heart
> in desolation lie.

To Rous's stanza there are two objections, one, that it has no rhyme ; another, and a more material one, is, that it seems not to give the sense of the *last clause,* as the idea of *desolateness* is left out, and that of *amazement* substituted. Possibly the fault may be in me misapprehending Rous's idea of *amazement.* One thing is quite clear, that the emendation is more *literal* than Rous's translation of the last clause, and to his last line alone the objection is made.

Respecting our version, viewed as a translation, there is one other remark to be made, namely, that in some instances the translation is too much *expanded,* as in Ps. xlviii. 6. In other places it is too *condensed ;* as in Ps. lxvii., short metre, which very unaccountably has a stanza *less* than the common metre of the same Psalm. This is rectified in the proposed emendations.

In a considerable number of verses in several of the Psalms, what in Rous is condensed into *two* lines, has in the emendations been expanded into four; see, for examples, Psalms xvi. xix. lxv. lxxxviii. etc.

These remarks on the supposed defects of Rous's version of the Psalms, considered as a specimen of *versification,* of *style,* and of *translation,* are not made for the purpose of depreciating the labours of the translator; but for the purpose of showing the possibility of materially *improving* a version in some respects good. If above 270 lines faulty in measure can be rectified; if seventy stanzas without rhyme can in this respect be set right; if the many faults of style, either existing from the date of composition, or caused by the lapse of time, can be remedied; and if the instances of faulty translation can be amended, the labour will not be in vain. The Book of Psalms is one of great importance; and as our metrical version of it is in weekly, nay, daily use by many millions in the Christian world, it is evidently proper that it should be made as free from faults of every kind as possible. Whether these objects have been successfully accomplished in the following proposed emendations, it belongs to others to determine. If the writer has even succeeded in pointing out what is wrong in our version, it is the first step towards a remedy; for though the proposed emendations should

PREFATORY REMARKS.

be deemed a failure, if the faults referred to be admitted to exist, it may lead others who are better qualified for the task to the successful accomplishment of it.

In all of the Psalms *some* changes have been made. In a considerable number, the proposed changes are neither numerous nor of great importance.

The most *considerable* changes will be found in the following Psalms:—

7	16	28	38	55	69	87	96	106	135
9	17	29	42	58	73	88	97	107	136
10	18	31	44	60	74	89	99	113	140
11	19	32	48	65	78	94	104	118	142
13	21	35	50	68	81	95	105	119	150

After making all the proposed emendations, the writer of these remarks wrote out a complete copy of our version of the Psalms, incorporating, as he proceeded, all the proposed changes. In this copy of the Psalms he is not aware that there is any line wrong in measure, any sentence which is ungrammatical.

In making these changes he is not conscious of having injured or darkened the meaning of any passage or any sentence in the Psalms, and he has attempted to correct Rous's supposed mistranslations referred to in the preceding pages. If in these literary attempts he has fallen into mistakes of any kind, as he very possibly may, he will take it kindly that these be pointed out.

EMENDATIONS.

PSALM I.

1 OH for the blessedness of him [1]
    who walketh not astray
In counsel of ungodly men,
    nor stands in sinners' way ;
Who sits not in the scorner's chair, [2]
2   But places his delight
On God's pure law, and meditates [3]
    on his law day and night.

3 He's like a tree, which near a stream [4]
    refreshing juice receives,
Whose boughs are crown'd with timely fruit,
    and with unfading leaves ;
And all he doth shall prosper well. [5]
4   The wicked are not so ;
But they are like unto the chaff,
    which wind drives to and fro.

5 In judgment therefore shall not stand
    such as ungodly are ;
Nor in th' assembly of the just
    shall wicked men appear.
6 Because the way of godly men
    is to Jehovah known ;
Whereas the way of wicked men [6]
    shall quite be overthrown.

PSALM II.

1 WHY rage the heathen? and vain things
 why do the people mind?
2 Kings of the earth prepare themselves,[1]
 and rulers are combined
 Against Jehovah, and his King
 Anointed; these their words:
3 Asunder let us break their bands,
 and cast from us their cords.[2]

4 He who in heaven sits shall laugh,[3]
 the Lord shall scorn them all.
5 Then shall he speak to them in wrath,
 in rage he vex them shall.
6 Yet him in spite of ev'ry foe[4]
 I have my King ordain'd;
 His throne on Sion's holy hill
 shall firmly be maintain'd.

7 The sure decree I will declare;
 the Lord hath said to me,
 Thou art mine only Son; this day
 I have begotten thee.
8 Me ask, and for inheritance[5]
 I'll make the heathen thine:
 And for possession I to thee
 will give earth's utmost line.

9 Thou shalt, as with a weighty rod
 of iron, break them all;
 Them, as a potter's vessel, thou[6]
 shalt dash to pieces small.
10 Now, therefore, kings, be wise; be taught,
 ye judges of the earth:
11 Serve God in fear, and see that ye
 join trembling with your mirth.

12 Kiss ye the Son, lest by his wrath[7]
 ye perish in the way,
 If once his wrath begin to burn:
 blest all who on him stay.

PSALM III.

1 O LORD, how are my foes increased?
    against me many rise.
2 And many say that for my soul[1]
    in God no succour lies.
3 Yet thou my shield and glory art,
    th' uplifter of my head.
4 I cried, and, from his holy hill,
    the Lord me answer made.

5 I laid me down and slept, I waked,
    for God sustainèd me.
6 I will not fear though thousands ten
    set round against me be.
7 Arise, O Lord; me save, my God;[2]
    for thou hast struck my foe;
The teeth of the ungodly thou
    hast broken by thy blow.

8 Salvation from all ill belongs[3]
    unto the Lord alone:
O let thy blessing ever, Lord,
    thy people be upon.

PSALM IV.

1 GIVE ear unto me when I call,
    God of my righteousness;
Have mercy, hear my prayer; thou hast
    enlarged me in distress.
2 How long will ye, O sons of men,[1]
    my glory turn to shame?
How long love vanity, and try
    by lies to hurt my name?

3 But know, that for himself the Lord
    the godly man doth choose:
The Lord, when I implore his help,[2]
    to hear will not refuse.
4 Fear, and sin not: talk with your heart
    on bed, and silent be.

5 Present the gifts of righteousness,³
   and in the Lord trust ye.
6 O who will show us any good?
   is that which many say:
Lord, let thy count'nance shine on us[1]
   with its most cheering ray.
7 Upon my heart, bestow'd by thee,
   more gladness I have found
Than they enjoy'd, when corn and wine
   did most with them abound.
8 I both will lay me down in peace,
   and rest securely take;
Because thou only me to dwell
   in safety, Lord, dost make.

PSALM V.

1 GIVE ear unto my words, O Lord,
   my mournful musings weigh.[1]
2 Hear my loud cry, my King, my God;[2]
   for I to thee will pray.
3 Lord, thou shalt me at dayspring hear;[3]
   I'll at the dawn direct
My prayer to thee; and, looking up,
   an answer will expect.
4 For thou art not a God who doth[4]
   in wickedness delight;
Neither shall evil dwell with thee,
5   Nor fools stand in thy sight.
All evil-doers, Lord, thou hat'st;
6   Cutt'st off who liars be:
The bloody and deceitful man
   abhorrèd is by thee.
7 But I into thy house will come
   in thine abundant grace;
And I will worship in thy fear
   toward thy holy place.

PSALM VI.

8 Because of slandering enemies,
    Lord, in thy righteousness
Do thou me lead, do thou thy way
    make straight before my face.

9 For lies alone are in their mouth,
    their heart loves only wrong;[5]
Their throat devours like open graves,
    they flatter with their tongue.

10 O God, destroy them; let them be
    by their own counsel quell'd:
Them for their many sins cast out,
    for they 'gainst thee rebell'd.

11 But glad be all who trust in thee,[6]
    in shouts their voices raise;
For them thou sav'st, let all who love
    thy name thee ever praise.

12 For, Lord, unto the righteous man
    thou wilt thy blessing send:
With favour thou wilt every saint,[7]
    as with a shield, defend.

PSALM VI.   L.M.

1 REBUKE me not in anger, Lord;[1]
    Nor in displeasure hot chastise.[2]
2 My bones are vex'd, and I am weak;
    To heal me, Lord, in pity rise.
3 Sore vex'd, Lord, also is my soul;
    How long shall I thine absence mourn?[3]
4 O save me, for thy mercies' sake;
    For my deliv'rance, Lord, return.
5 For those who sleep in death's domain
    Of thee shall no remembrance have;
And who shall thee extol with praise
    Amid the silence of the grave?
6 I weary with my groaning am,[4]
    Throughout the night my sleepless bed

I caused have to swim ; and I[5]
  My couch with tears have watered.

7 From cruel foes, and wasting grief,[6]
  The look of age bedims mine eyes
8 Depart, ye wicked workers all ;
  For God has heard my weeping cries.
9 My supplication God has heard,
  My prayer received most graciously.[7]
10 Sore vex'd and shamed be all my foes,
  Confounded and turn'd back be they.

PSALM VI. C.M.

1 O LORD, in indignation great,[1]
    do thou rebuke me not ;
  Nor on me lay thy chast'ning hand,
    in thy displeasure hot.
2 Since I am weak, O Lord, on me[2]
    have mercy, and me spare :
  Heal me, O Lord, because thou know'st
    my bones much vexed are.

3 Sore vexed is my soul : but, Lord,
    How long stay wilt thou make ?
4 Return, Lord, free my soul ; and save
    me, for thy mercies' sake.
5 Because of thee in death there shall
    no more remembrance be :
  Of those now lying in the grave,[3]
    who shall give thanks to thee ?

6 I weary with my groaning am,
    and all the night my bed[4]
  Was wet with weeping ; with my tears
    my couch I watered.
7 By reason of my vexing grief
    mine eye consumed is ;
  It waxes old, because of all
    who are mine enemies.

PSALM VII.

8 But now, depart from me, all ye
   who work iniquity :
Because Jehovah heard my voice,
   he heard my mourning cry.
9 Unto my supplication's voice⁵
   the Lord did hearing give ;
When I to him my prayer address,
   the Lord will it receive.
10 Ashamed and troubled sore be all
   who en'mies are to me ;
Let them return, and suddenly
   ashamèd let them be.

PSALM VII.

1 O LORD my God, in thee do I
   my confidence repose :
Deliver me from all who are
   my persecuting foes ;
2 Lest th' enemy in wrath my soul¹
   should, like a lion, tear,
In pieces rending it, while there
   is no deliverer.
3 O Lord, my God, if true it be
   that I committed this ;
If true, as said, that in my hands
   iniquity there is :
4 If I rewarded ill to him
   who never served me so ;
Nay, if I saved not him who was²
   without a cause my foe ;
5 Me let the foe pursue and take,
   and, with avenging thrust,
O let him lay at once my life
   and honour in the dust.
6 Rise, Lord, in anger raise thyself,
   since raging are my foes ;

C 2

PSALM VII.

    Wake, to the appointed judgment come ;
      mine innocence disclose.

7 So thine assembled people shall
    still waiting thee attend ;
  O therefore, for their sakes, thy throne[3]
    of judgment re-ascend.
8 Jehovah shall the people judge ;[4]
    my judge, Jehovah, be.
  After my righteousness, and mine
    integrity in me.

9 O let the wicked's malice end ;
    but stablish steadfastly
  The righteous : for the righteous God
    the hearts and reins doth try.
10 In God, who does the upright save,
    is my defence and stay.
11 God just men judges ; God is wroth
    with ill men every day.

12 If he return not from his sin,
    then God his sword will whet ;[5]
  His bow he has already bent,
    and has it ready set :
13 He also has for him prepared
    the instruments of death ;
  Against the persecutors he
    his shafts ordainèd hath.

14 Behold, he with iniquity
    doth travail, as in birth ;
  A plot of mischief he conceived,[6]
    and falsehood has brought forth.
15 He made a pit, and dug it deep,
    another there to take ;
  But he is fall'n into the ditch,
    which he himself did make.

16 His deeds of mischief on himself
   shall be returnèd home;
His vi'lent dealing also down
   on his own head shall come.[7]
17 According to his righteousness
   the Lord I'll magnify;
And will sing praise unto the name
   of God who is most high.

PSALM VIII.

1 HOW excellent in all the earth,
   Lord, our Lord, is thy name!
Who hast thy glory far advanced
   above the starry frame.
2 From infants' and from sucklings' mouth
   thou, Lord, didst strength ordain,[1]
For sake of foes, that so thou mightst
   th' avenging foe restrain.

3 When to the heav'ns, thy glorious work,[2]
   I raise my wond'ring eye,
Unto the moon, ordain'd by thee,
   and star-bespangled sky;
4 Then say I, What is man, that he
   remember'd is by thee?
Or what the son of man, that thou
   so kind to him shouldst be?

5 For thou but little lower hast[3]
   him than the angels made;
With glory and with dignity
   thou crownèd hast his head.
6 Thou mad'st him ruler of thy works,[4]
   all under him didst lay;
7 Sheep, oxen, all of every field,
   and every beast of prey;

8 All fowl and fish, which skim the air,
   or pass through ocean's ways;

9 How great, O Lord, our Lord, thy name!
  through all the earth's thy praise.

PSALM IX.

1 LORD, thee I'll praise with all my heart,
   thy wonders all proclaim.
2 In thee, most High, I'll greatly joy,
   and sing unto thy name.
3 When back my foes were turn'd, they fell,
   and perish'd at thy sight:
4 For thou maintain'dst my right and cause;
   on throne sat'st judging right.

5 The heathen thou rebukèd hast,
   the wicked overthrown;
  Thou hast put out their names, that they
   may never more be known.
6 O en'my! thy destructions have [1]
   now reach'd a lasting end;
  Thy cities razed, nor ev'n their names
   shall down through time descend.

7 But God's eternal, and he doth [2]
   for judgment set his throne;
8 He'll judge the world in righteousness,
   he'll justice give each one.
9 God also will a refuge be [3]
   for those who are oppress'd;
  A refuge will he be in times
   of trouble to distress'd.

10 And they who know thy name, in thee
    their confidence will place:
   For thou hast not forsaken those
    who truly seek thy face.
11 O sing ye praises to the Lord
    who dwells in Sion hill;
   And through all nations of the world [4]
    his deeds record ye still.

PSALM X.

12 When he inquireth after blood,
    he then remembers them:
The humble he will ne'er forget [5]
    who call upon his name.
13 Lord, pity me; behold the grief
    which I from foes sustain;
Thou, Lord, who from the gates of death
    dost raise me up again:

14 That I, in Sion's daughters' gates,[6]
    may all thy praise advance;
And that I always may rejoice
    in thy deliverance.
15 The heathen are sunk in the pit
    which they themselves prepared;
And in the net which they have hid
    their own feet are insnared.

16 By judgments which he executes[7]
    Jehovah is made known:
Insnared the wicked is by deeds,
    which he himself has done.
17 The wicked shall be doom'd to hell,[8]
    as their assign'd abode;
And all the nations who forget
    to seek the mighty God.

18 For those who needy are shall not[9]
    forgotten always be;
And what the humble poor expect,
    their eyes at length shall see.
19 Arise, Lord, let not man prevail;
    judge heathen in thy sight:
20 That they may know themselves but men,
    the nations, Lord, affright.

PSALM X.

1 O WHEREFORE is it, Lord, that thou[1]
    dost stand from us afar?

And wherefore hidest thou thyself
   when times so troublous are?
2 The wicked in his cruel pride
   doth persecute the poor:
In snares, which they themselves have form'd,[2]
   let them be taken sure.

3 The wicked of his heart's desire
   doth talk with boasting great;
Extols with praise the covetous,[3]
   whom yet the Lord doth hate.
4 The wicked, through his pride of face,[4]
   on God forbears to call;
And in the counsels of his heart
   the Lord is not at all.

5 His ways for ever grievous are;[5]
   thy judgments from his sight
Removèd are: at all his foes
   he puffeth with despite.
6 Within his heart he thus hath said,
   I shall not movèd be;
And no adversity at all
   shall ever come to me.

7 His mouth is fill'd abundantly[6]
   with cursing, guile, and wrong;
And vanity and mischief are
   beneath his lying tongue.
8 He lurking sits in villages;
   he slays the innocent:
Against the poor who pass him by
   his cruel eyes are bent.

9 He, lion-like, lurks in his den,[7]
   intent the poor to take;
And him, when drawn into his net,
   his prey doth quickly make.
10 Himself he humbleth very low,
   he croucheth down withal.

PSALM X.

    That so a multitude of poor
      may by his strong ones fall.

11 Thus says he in his heart, God keeps
      this not in memory ;
    He hides his countenance, and he
      this deed shall never see.
12 O Lord, do thou arise ; O God,
      lift up thy hand on high :
    Let not the humble of the land
      by thee forgotten be.
13 Why does the wicked man presume [8]
      Jehovah to despise ?
    Because that God will be his judge
      he in his heart denies.
14 Thou hast it seen ; their mischief thou [9]
      and malice wilt repay :
    The poor commits himself to thee,
      who art the orphan's stay.

15 The arm break of the wicked man,
      and of the evil one ;
    Search out his deeds of wickedness,
      until thou findest none.
16 Jehovah is, and shall be king
      unto eternity ;
    The heathen people from his land
      are perish'd utterly.

17 The prayer of those who humble are, [10]
      thou, Lord, didst deign to hear ;
    Thou wilt prepare their heart, and thou
      to hear wilt bend thine ear ;
18 To judge the fatherless, and those
      who are oppressèd sore ;
    That man, who is but sprung from dust, [11]
      may them oppress no more.

PSALM XI.

1 SINCE in the Lord I put my trust,¹
    why thus address me? fly
Impending ills, as speeds a bird
    unto your mountain high.
2 For, lo, the wicked bend their bow,
    their shafts on bowstring fit,
That those who upright are in heart
    they privily may hit.
3 If the foundations be destroy'd,
    what can the righteous do?
4 God's holy temple is in heaven,
    his throne of judgment too:
His eyes behold, his eyelids try
5   men's sons. The just he proves:
But his soul hates the wicked man,
    and him who vi'lence loves.

6 Snares, fire and brimstone, furious storms,
    on sinners he shall rain:
This, as the portion of their cup,
    shall unto them pertain.
7 Because the Lord who righteous is,
    delights in righteousness;
With his approving look he will
    the upright deign to bless.

PSALM XII.

1 HELP, Lord, because the godly man¹
    fades rapidly away;
And from among the sons of men
    the faithful fast decay.
2 Unto his neighbour every one
    speaks words of vanity:
They speak with a deceitful heart;
    with lips of flattery.

3 God shall cut off all flatt'ring lips,
    proud tongues blaspheming thus,

PSALM XII.

4 We'll with our tongues prevail, our lips
    are ours : who's lord o'er us ?
5 For poor oppress'd, and for the sighs
    of needy, rise will I,
Says God, and him in safety set
    from such as him defy.

6 Jehovah's words are words most pure ;
    they are like silver tried,[2]
Which in the furnace seven times
    has been well purified.
7 Lord, thou shalt them preserve and keep
    for ever from this race.
8 On all sides walk the wicked, when
    vile men are high in place.

PSALM XIII.

1 HOW long wilt thou forget me, Lord ?[1]
    to never ending days ?
How long shall I in sorrow mourn
    the hidings of thy face ?
2 How long perplex'd must be my soul ?
    and daily sad my heart ?
How long shall threat'ning powerful foes
    increase my inward smart !

3 O Lord, my God, my case regard,[2]
    unto my prayer attend :
Mine eyes enlighten, lest I should
    to death's long sleep descend :
4 Lest enemies insulting say,[3]
    Against him we've prevail'd ;
And those who trouble me rejoice
    to see me grieved and fail'd.

5 But I have all my confidence[4]
    upon thy mercy set ;
My heart within me shall rejoice
    in thy salvation great.

6 Unto the Lord in grateful songs [5]
  let praise presented be;
For he abundantly hath shown
  his bounty unto me.

PSALM XIV.

1 THAT there is not a God, the fool
    doth in his heart conclude:
They are corrupt, their works are vile;
  not one of them does good.
2 Upon men's sons the Lord from heav'n
    did cast his eyes abroad,
To see if any understood,
  or did seek after God.
3 They altogether filthy are,
    they all aside are gone;
Not one there is who doeth good,
  no, not so much as one.[1]
4 Are workers of iniquity[2]
    so void of knowledge grown,
That they my people eat as bread,
  and God refuse to own?

5 There fear'd they much; for God is with
    the whole race of the just.
6 You mock the poor for purposing[3]
    to make the Lord his trust.
7 Let Israel's help from Sion come:
    when back the Lord shall bring
His captives, Jacob shall rejoice,
  and Israël shall sing.

PSALM XV.

1 WHO in thy tabernacle, Lord,
    shall lastingly abide?
And who in Sion's holy hill
  as dweller shall reside?

2 The man who walketh uprightly,[1]
 and worketh righteousness,
And what he thinketh in his heart,
 that do his words express.

3 Who neither slanders with his tongue,
 nor to his friend does hurt ;
Nor yet against his neighbour will
 take up a bad report.

4 By whom the wicked are despised ;
 but those the Lord who fear
He honours ; and performs his oath
 though to his hurt he swear.

5 No money he to usury puts,
 nor take reward will he
Against the guiltless. Who does thus
 shall never movèd be.

PSALM XVI.

1 DO thou, O God, me safe preserve[1]
 from persecuting foes ;
For I in thee, a faithful God,
 my confidence repose.

2 My soul, thou to Jehovah saidst,
 Thou art a God to me ;
My goodness, stinted, small at best,
 extendeth not to thee ;

3 But to the saints on earth, whose worth
 supplies my chief delight.

4 God will with sorrows manifold[2]
 idolaters requite ;
Of mingling in their bloody rites
 I shun the guilt and shame ;
Nor will I of their idol gods
 pronounce the very name.

5 The Lord, my rich inheritance,[3]
 me feeds with bounteous hand ;

He fills my cup, and guards my lot
　　　　from every hostile band.
6　Unto me happily the lines⁴
　　　　in pleasant places fell;
　　　Yea, what inheritance I got
　　　　in beauty does excel.

7　I will Jehovah praise, who does
　　　　by counsel me conduct;
　　　And in the seasons of the night
　　　　my reins do me instruct.
8　Before me still the Lord I set:
　　　　since it is so that he⁵
　　　Doth ever stand at my right hand,
　　　　I shall not movèd be.

9　Hence fill'd with gladness is my heart,
　　　　and joy shall be exprest
　　　Ev'n by my glory; and my flesh
　　　　in confidence shall rest.
10　Because my soul in grave to dwell
　　　　shall not be left by thee;
　　　Nor wilt thou let thy Holy One⁶
　　　　the least corruption see.

11　Thou wilt me show the path of life,
　　　　of joys there is full store
　　　Before thy face; at thy right hand
　　　　are pleasures evermore.

PSALM XVII.

1　JEHOVAH, listen to the right,¹
　　　　attend unto my cry;
　　　O hear my prayer unfeign'd and far
　　　　from all hypocrisy.
2　And from before thy presence forth
　　　　my sentence do thou send:
　　　My case behold with equal eyes,²
　　　　and me from wrong defend.

PSALM XVII.

3 Thou didst me prove and visit, Lord;[3]
    thou didst by night me try;
  Yet nought shall find, since to my lips[4]
    I shall the rein apply.
4 Men's works are a deceitful guide;[5]
    my way thy precepts show;
  A way which kept me from the paths
    in which destroyers go.
5 Uphold my goings, Lord, me keep[6]
    within thy paths divine,
  That so my footsteps may not slide
    from ways which, Lord, are thine.
6 I callèd have on thee, O God,
    because thou wilt me hear;
  That thou mayst hearken to my speech,
    incline to me thine ear.
7 Thy wondrous loving-kindness show,[7]
    thou who, by thy right hand,
  Sav'st them who trust in thee from those
    who up against them stand.
8 As th' apple of the eye me keep;
    thy wings my shelter be
9 From wicked, cruel, deadly foes[8]
    in wrath surrounding me.
10 In their own fat they are enclosed;
    their mouth speaks loftily.
11 Our steps they've compass'd; to the ground
    down bowing set their eye.
12 He like a rav'nous lion is
    intent upon his prey,
  Or lion young, which lurking does
    in secret places stay.
13 Arise, mine en'my disappoint,
    and cast him down, O Lord;
  Preserve me from the wicked man,
    the man who is thy sword.[9]

14 From men, who are thy hand, O Lord,
   from worldly men me save,
Who only in this present life
   their fleeting portion have.¹⁰

Whose belly with thy treasure hid
   thou fill'st : they children have
In plenty ; their remaining goods ¹¹
   they to their children leave.
15 But as for me, I, Lord, thy face
   in righteousness will see ;
And with thy likeness, when I wake,
   I satisfied shall be.

PSALM XVIII.

1 I'LL thee, Jehovah, love, my strength.
2   My fortress is the Lord,
   My rock, and he who does to me¹
      deliverance afford :
   My God, my strength, whom I will trust
      a buckler unto me,
   The power from which my safety comes,
      my lofty tower is he.

3 Unto the Lord, who worthy is
     of praises, I will cry ;
  And then I shall preservèd be,
     safe from mine enemy.
4 Floods of ill men affrighted me,
     death's pangs about me went ;
5 Hell's sorrows me encompassèd :
     death's snares did me prevent.
6 Distress'd, I call'd upon the Lord,
     cry to my God did I ;
  He from his temple heard my voice,
     to his ears came my cry.
7 Then th' earth, as terror-struck, did shake,
     trembling upon it seized ;

PSALM XVIII.

The hills' foundations were convulsed,
   because he was displeased.

8 Up from his nostrils came a smoke,
   and from his mouth forth came [2]
Devouring fire ; by it were coals
   converted into flame.
9 He also bow'd the heavens high,[3]
   and from his throne came down ;
Beneath his feet was darkness spread
   in all its midnight frown.

10 He rode in his angelic car,
   and quick as thought did fly ;[4]
Upon the rapid tempest's wings
   his flight was from on high.
11 He darkness made his secret place :
   around him, for his tent,
Dark waters were, and thickest clouds
   of th' airy firmament.

12 When flash'd the brightness of that light
   which darted from the sky,
His thick clouds pass'd away, hailstones
   and coals of fire did fly.
13 The Lord, too, in the heav'ns sent forth
   the thunder's deaf'ning noise ;
By hailstones and by coals of fire
   the Highest raised his voice.

14 Yea, he his arrows sent abroad,
   and them he scatterèd ;
His lightnings also he shot out,
   and them discomfited.
15 The waters' channels then were seen,
   the world's foundations vast
At thy rebuke discover'd were,[5]
   and at thy powerful blast.

16 Jehovah from above sent down,
   and took me from below;
   From many waters he me drew,⁶
   which would me overflow.
17 He me preserved from my strong foe,
   and those who did me hate;
   Because he saw that they for me
   too strong were, and too great.
18 On every side they me beset⁷
   in trouble's dismal day;
   But then Jehovah was to me
   an all-sufficient stay.
19 He to a place of ample room⁸
   from all my straits me brought,
   Because in me he took delight
   he my deliv'rance wrought.
20 According to my righteousness
   he did me recompense,
   Rewarded me according to
   my hands' pure innocence.
21 For I God's ways kept, from my God
   did not turn wickedly.
22 Before me were his judgments, I
   his laws put not from me.
23 Before him upright was my heart,⁹
   its inmost thoughts sincere;
   And I from mine iniquity
   did keep myself with care.
24 After my righteousness the Lord
   hath recompensèd me,
   After the cleanness of my hands
   appearing in his eye.
25 Thou upright to the upright art,¹⁰
   art gracious to the good.
26 Pure to the pure; but froward men
   shall be by thee withstood.

PSALM XVIII.

27 For thou wilt the afflicted save
    who low in sorrow lie ;[11]
  But wilt bring down the countenance
    of them whose looks are high.

28 The Lord will light my candle so,
    that it will shine full bright :
  The Lord my God will also turn
    my darkness into light.

29 By thee through troops of men I break,
    and them discomfit all ;
  And by th' assistance of my God,
    I scale the highest wall.[12]

30 All perfect is the way of God,[13]
    Jehovah's word is tried ;
  He is a buckler to all those
    who still in him confide.

31 Who but the Lord is God? but God,
    who is a rock and stay ?

32 God girdeth me with all my strength,[14]
    and perfect makes my way.

33 He made my feet swift as the hinds,[15]
    set me on places high.

34 Me war he taught ; hence by mine arms
    bows snapt in pieces lie.

35 The shield of thy protecting help[16]
    thou didst on me bestow ;
  Thy right hand me upheld, and great
    thy kindness made me grow.

36 From narrow and from slipp'ry ways[17]
    thou hast deliver'd me ;
  I now walk safely, and my feet
    are kept from sliding free.

37 My routed foes I did pursue,
    and did them overtake ;
  Nor did I turn again till I
    an end of them did make.

PSALM XVIII.

38 I wounded them, nor could they rise;
    who at my feet did fall.
39 Thou girdedst me with strength for war;
    my foes thou brought'st down all:
40 And thou hast giv'n to me the necks [18]
    of all my cruel foes;
  That I might them destroy, who did
    from hatred me oppose.
41 They cried aloud, but there was none [19]
    who would or could them save;
  They cried unto the Lord, but he
    to them no answer gave.
42 Then small as dust, the sport of winds, [20]
    I did mine en'mies beat;
  And out I cast them, as the dirt
    which lies upon the street.

43 Thou mad'st me free from people's strife,
    the heathen's head to be:
  A people whom I have not known
    shall service do to me.
44 At hearing they shall me obey,
    to me they shall submit.
45 Strangers for fear shall fade away,
    who in close places sit.
46 Jehovah lives, bless'd be my Rock;
    salvation's God I'll praise;
47 God me avenges, and above [21]
    the people me doth raise.
48 He saves me from mine enemies;
    yea, thou hast lifted me
  Above my foes; and from the man
    of vi'lence set me free.

49 I therefore will to thee give thanks [22]
    through every heathen tribe;
  And to thy name, O Lord, in songs,
    due praises will ascribe.

50 He great deliv'rance gives his king:
    he mercy doth extend
To David, his anointed one,
    and his seed without end.

PSALM XIX.

1 THE heavens, created by his power,[1]
    God's glory great proclaim:
The doings of his hand shine forth
    throughout the starry frame.
2 The day to each succeeding day
    employs instructive speech;
And night to night in constant round
    does useful knowledge teach.
3 Although they use no tongue, nor words,
    nor utter vocal sound,
4 Their line and language fill the world,
    and reach earth's farthest bound.
    In them he set the sun a tent;
5   Who, as a bridegroom bright,
Forth issuing from his chamber, comes
    amid a blaze of light.[2]

Up rising in the eastern sky,
    he skims the fields of space,
Rejoicing, as a strong man does,
    to run his destined race.[3]
6 To heav'n's end, where his course began,
    he speeds his round again;
And nothing from his powerful heat
    can unimpress'd remain.

7 God's law is perfect, and converts
    the soul in sin which lies:[4]
Jehovah's testimony's sure,
    And makes the simple wise.
8 The statutes of the Lord are right,
    and do rejoice the heart:

The Lord's command is pure, and does
light to the eyes impart.

9 Unspotted is the fear of God,⁵
and ever doth endure :
Jehovah's judgments all are truth
and righteousness most pure.
10 They more than gold, yea, much fine gold,
to be desirèd are :
Than honey, honey from the comb
which droppeth, sweeter far.
11 By them too is thy servant warn'd
against all sin to guard ;⁶
And those who them observe with care,
shall reap a great reward.
12 Who can his errors understand ?
O cleanse thou me within
13 From secret faults. Thy servant keep
from all presumptuous sin :

And do not suffer them to have
dominion over me :
Then, upright I and innocent,⁷
from many a sin shall be.
14 The words proceeding from my mouth,
the thoughts sent from my heart,
Accept, O Lord, since thou my strength
and my Redeemer art.

PSALM XX.

1 JEHOVAH hear thee in the day
when trouble he doth send :
And let the name of Jacob's God
thee from all ill defend.
2 From out his sanctuary's height¹
may he thy helper be :
From Sion, his own holy hill,
may he give strength to thee.

PSALM XXI.

3 May he remember all thy gifts,
    accept thy sacrifice :
4 Grant thee the wishes of thy heart,[2]
    and speed thy counsel wise.
5 In thy salvation we'll rejoice ;
    in our God's name we will
Display our banners : all thy prayers[3]
    O may the Lord fulfil.

6 Now know I God his king doth save :
    he from his holy heav'n
Will hear him, with the saving strength
    by his own right hand giv'n.
7 Some trust in chariots, and some[4]
    in steeds to battle train'd :
But we in God the Lord, by whom
    our cause will be maintain'd.

8 Our foes defeated, and brought down[5]
    lie prostrate on the sand ;
While we, who were before borne down,
    are raised, and upright stand.
9 O Lord, our Saviour, may we still
    in thy salvation share ;
And may the King incline his ear,
    when we present our prayer.

PSALM XXI.

1 THE king in thy great strength, O Lord,
    shall very joyful be :
In thy salvation great rejoice[1]
    how veh'mently shall he !
2 Thou him with what his heart desired[2]
    hast in thy beauty bless'd ;
And thou hast not withheld from him
    whate'er was his request.

3 Nay, more than he desired thou gav'st[3]
    in goodness manifold :

Since thou hast set upon his head
a crown of purest gold.
4 When he desirèd life of thee,
thou life to him didst give;
A length of days so great, that he
for evermore should live.

5 In the salvation wrought by thee
his glory is made great;
Both honour high and majesty
thou hast upon him set.
6 For thou indeed for evermore [4]
most blessèd him hast made;
And with thy countenance thou hast
made him supremely glad.

7 Since firmly in Jehovah's help [5]
the king doth still confide;
And by the grace of the most High
he shall unmoved abide.
8 Thy hand shall find out every one
who is thine enemy;
Thy right hand shall find out those men
who hatred bear to thee.

9 They'll burn as in a fiery ov'n,
when kindled is thine ire;
God shall them swallow in his wrath,
devour them shall the fire.
10 By thee throughout the earth their fruit [6]
shall be denied a place;
And from among the sons of men
their seed thou wilt erase.

11 For they destruction did devise
against thee, and thy cause;
But to effect their wicked plot
their power unequal was.
12 Thou therefore shalt make them turn back, [7]
when arrows thou shalt place

Upon thy strings, in readiness
   to fly against their face.
13 In thine almighty strength, O Lord,³
   be thou exalted high;
So we thy wondrous power with praise
   will celebrate with joy.

PSALM XXII.

1 MY God, my God, why hast thou me
   forsaken? why so far
Art thou from helping me, and from
   my words which roaring are?
2 All day, my God, to thee I cry,
   yet am not heard by thee;
And in the season of the night,
   I cannot silent be.
3 But thou art holy, thou who dost
   still dwell 'midst Israel's praise.
4 Our fathers hoped in thee, they hoped,
   and thou didst them release.
5 When unto thee they sent their cry,
   to them deliv'rance came:
When they put confidence in thee,
   they were not put to shame.
6 But I'm regarded as a worm,
   and as no man am prized:
Reproach of men I am, and by
   the people am despised.
7 All seeing me, laugh me to scorn;[1]
   shoot out the lip do they;
They nod and shake their heads at me,
   and thus insulting say,[2]
8 This man did trust in God, that he
   would free him by his might:
Let him deliver him, since he[3]
   had in him such delight.

9 But thou art he who from the womb [4]
    didst me in safety take;
  When I was on my mother's breasts
    thou me to hope didst make.
10 Cast wholly on thy care I was,
    from infancy till now;
  And even from my very birth [5]
    my God and guide art thou.
11 O be not far, for trouble's near,
    and none to help me found.
12 Bulls many compass me, strong bulls
    of Bashan me surround.
13 Their mouths they open'd wide on me,
    upon me gape did they,
  As gapes a lion ravening
    and roaring for his prey.
14 Like water I'm pour'd out, my bones
    all out of joint do part:
  Within me, as the melting wax,
    so melted is my heart.
15 Dried up, as potsherd, is my strength;
    my tongue is cleaving fast [6]
  Unto my jaws; unto the dust
    of death thou brought me hast.
16 For cruel dogs have compass'd me:
    the wicked, who did meet
  In their assembly, me enclosed;
    they pierced my hands and feet.
17 I all my bones may tell; on me
    they rudely look and stare.
18 They lots upon my vesture cast,
    and clothes among them share.
19 But be not far, O Lord, my strength;
    give speedy help to me.
20 From sword my soul, from power of dogs,
    my darling set thou free.

PSALM XXII.

21 Me from the roaring lion's mouth,
  O set in safety free :⁷
For from the horns of unicorns
  thou gav'st an ear to me.
22 I will show forth thy name unto
  those who my brethren are ;
Amid the congregation great⁸
  thy praise I will declare.
23 Ye who Jehovah fear, him praise ;⁹
  him glorify all ye
The seed of Jacob ; fear him all
  who Israel's children be.
24 For he despised not nor abhorr'd
  th' afflicted's misery ;
Nor from him hid his face, but heard
  when he to him did cry.
25 Within the congregation great
  my praise shall be of thee ;
My vows before those fearing him¹⁰
  shall be perform'd by me.
26 The meek shall eat, and shall be fill'd ;
  to God they'll praises give,¹¹
Who faithfully seek after him :
  your heart shall ever live.
27 All ends of th' earth remember shall,¹²
  and turn unto the Lord ;
And he by every nation shall
  in worship be adored.
28 Because the kingdom is the Lord's,¹³
  and ever will be his ;
And he among the nations all
  the Sovereign Ruler is.
29 The rich shall eat, and worship shall :¹⁴
  all who to dust descend
Shall bow to him ; none of them can
  his soul from death defend.

30 To him shall service do, a seed [15]
 who by Jehovah shall
Be deem'd a chosen ransom'd race
 in generations all.

31 They coming, shall declare abroad [16]
 his truth and righteousness
Unto a people yet unborn,
 in that he has done this.

PSALM XXIII.

1 THE Lord's my shepherd, I'll not want.
2 He makes me down to lie
In pastures green: he leadeth me
 the noiseless waters by.
3 My soul, when wand'ring, he restores;[1]
 and me to walk doth make
Within the paths of righteousness,
 ev'n for his own name's sake.
4 Yea, though I walk in death's dark vale,
 yet I will fear no ill:[2]
For thou art with me; and thy rod
 and staff me comfort still.
5 With plenty thou my table spread'st
 in presence of my foes;
My head thou dost with oil anoint.
 and my cup overflows.
6 Goodness and mercy all my life
 shall surely follow me:
And in God's house for evermore
 my dwelling-place shall be.

PSALM XXIV.

1 THE earth, with all which it contains,[1]
 belongs unto the Lord;
The world and all the countless tribes
 with which the world is stored.

PSALM XXIV.

2 For he upon the spreading seas [2]
    its firm foundations laid ;
And he to be its strong support
    the flood of waters made.

3 Who is the man who shall ascend
    into the hill of God ?
And who within his holy place
    shall have a firm abode ?

4 Whose hands are clean, whose heart is pure,
    and who to vanity
Hath neither lifted up his soul,
    nor sworn deceitfully.

5 This man the Lord, who rules the world,
    will with his favour bless ;
The God of his salvation will
    him bless with righteousness.

6 Of those who after him inquire,
    this is the happy race ;
Who seek with all their heart's desire,
    O Jacob's God, thy face. [3]

7 Lift up, ye gates, your heads on high ;
    ye doors which ne'er decay, [4]
Be lifted up, that so the King
    of glory enter may.

8 But who of glory is the King ?
    the mighty Lord is this ;
Jehovah, who both great in might
    and strong in battle is.

9 Lift up, ye gates, your heads ; ye doors,
    doors which shall ne'er decay,
Be lifted up, that so the King
    of glory enter may.

10 But who is he who is the King
    of glory ? who is this ?
The Lord of hosts, and none but he,
    the King of glory is.

PSALM XXV.

S. M.

1 TO thee I lift my soul:
2 O Lord, I trust in thee:
 Me let not, O my God, be shamed,[1]
  nor foes rejoice o'er me.
3 Let none who wait on thee[2]
  be put to shame at all;
 Let those who without cause transgress,
  into reproaches fall.

4 Show me thy ways, O Lord;
  thy paths, O teach thou me:
 And do thou lead me in thy truth,
  therein my teacher be:
5 For thou art God who dost
  to me salvation send,
 And I on thee do all the day
  with patient hope attend.

6 Thy tender mercies, Lord,[3]
  I pray thee keep in mind,
 And loving-kindness; O be still,
  as thou wast always, kind.
7 My sins and faults of youth
  do thou, O Lord, forget:
 O in thy mercy think on me,[4]
  and in thy goodness great.

8 God good and upright is:
  his way he'll sinners show.
9 The meek he will in judgment guide,
  and make his path to know.
10 The whole paths of the Lord
  are truth and mercy sure,
 To those who keep his covenant[5]
  and testimonies pure.

11 Now, for thine own name's sake,
  O Lord, I thee entreat

To pardon mine iniquity :
  for it is very great.
12 Whoe'er Jehovah fears,[6]
  and will his laws obey,
He him most graciously will teach
  to choose and keep his way.

13 His soul shall dwell at ease ;
  and his posterity
Shall flourish still, and of the earth
  inheritors shall be.
14 With those who fear him is
  the secret of the Lord ;
The knowledge of his covenant
  he will to them afford.

15 Mine eyes upon the Lord
  continually are set ;
For he it is who shall bring forth
  my feet out of the net.
16 Turn unto me thy face ;
  and to me mercy show ;
Because I am most desolate,[7]
  and am brought very low.

17 My heart's griefs are increased :
  me from distress relieve.
18 Look on my trouble and my pain,
  and all my sins forgive.
19 Consider thou my foes,
  because they many are ;
And cruel is the hatred which
  these foes against me bear.

20 O do thou keep my soul,
  do thou deliver me :
And let me never be ashamed,
  for trusting, Lord, in thee.

21 Let uprightness and truth
    keep me, who thee attend.
22 Redemption, Lord, to Israel
    from all his troubles send.

PSALM XXV. C.M.

1 TO thee I lift my soul, O Lord :
2   My God, I trust in thee :
  Let me not be ashamed ; nor let
    my foes rejoice o'er me.
3 Yea, let thou none ashamèd be
    who still on thee attend :
  Ashamèd let them be, O Lord,
    who without cause offend.

4 Thy ways, Lord, show ; teach me thy paths :
5   Lead me in truth, teach me :
  For thou art of my safety God ;[1]
    I wait all day on thee.
6 Thy mercies, which most tender are,
    O Lord, keep thou in mind,
  And loving-kindness ; O be still,
    as thou wast ever, kind.

7 Let not the errors of my youth,
    nor since, remember'd be :
  In mercy, for thy goodness' sake,
    O Lord, remember me.
8 Jehovah gracious is and good,[2]
    he upright is also :
  He therefore sinners will instruct
    in ways where they should go.

9 He will in judgment guide the meek [3]
    who him with care obey ;
  He will the meek and humble teach
    the knowledge of his way.
10 The whole paths of Jehovah are
    both truth and mercy sure,

PSALM XXV.

To those who keep his covenant,
and testimonies pure.

11 Now, for thine own name's sake, O Lord,
I humbly thee entreat
To pardon mine iniquity;
for it is very great.
12 What man fears God? he him shall teach
the way which he shall choose.
13 His soul shall dwell at ease; his seed
the earth, as heirs, shall use.

14 The secret of the Lord is with
such as do fear his name;
And he his holy covenant
will manifest to them.
15 Unto the Lord my waiting eyes
continually are set;
For he it is who shall bring forth
my feet out of the net.

16 O turn thee unto me, O God,
me show thy mercy great;¹
Because I sore afflicted am,
and truly desolate.
17 Enlarged the troubles of my heart
me from distress relieve.
18 Look on my sufferings and pain,
and all my sins forgive.

19 Consider thou mine enemies,
for great their numbers are;
And cruel is the hatred which⁵
these foes against me bear.
20 O do thou keep my soul; O God,
do thou deliver me:
Let me not be ashamed; because
I put my trust in thee.

21 O let integrity and truth
    keep me, who thee attend.
22 Redemption, Lord, to Israel
    from all his troubles send.

PSALM XXVI.

1 SINCE, Lord, I've walked in uprightness,[1]
    let me by thee be tried;
I've trusted also in the Lord;
    I therefore shall not slide.
2 Examine me, and do me prove;
    try heart and reins, O God:
3 For thy love is before mine eyes,
    thy truth's way was my road.[2]

4 With persons vain I have not sat,
    nor with dissemblers gone:
5 The wicked's company I hate;
    to sit with such I shun.
6 My hands in innocence, O Lord,
    I'll wash and purify;
So to thy holy altar go,
    and compass it will I:

7 That I, with voice of thanksgiving,
    may publicly declare,
And tell of all thy works, O Lord,
    which very wondrous are.
8 The habitation of thy house,
    Lord, I have lovèd well;
I greatly in that place delight
    where doth thine honour dwell.

9 Me do not class with wicked men,[3]
    nor such as blood would spill:
10 Who mischief plot, and whose right hand
    corrupting bribes do fill.
11 But as for me, I still will walk
    in mine integrity:

Be my Redeemer, and, O Lord,
  be merciful to me.

12 My foot upon an even place
  doth stand with steadfastness:
Within the congregations great¹
  I will Jehovah bless.

PSALM XXVII.

1 THE Lord my light and safety is,¹
  who me shall make dismay'd?
My life's strength is the Lord, of whom
  then shall I be afraid?
2 What time mine enemies and foes,²
  most wicked persons all,
Me to devour against me rose,
  they stumbled and did fall.

3 Against me though an host encamp,³
  yet fearless were my heart:
Though war against me rise, this would
  strong confidence impart.
4 One thing I of the Lord desired,
  and will seek to obtain,
That all days of my life I may
  within God's house remain;

That I the beauty of the Lord⁴
  may there delighted see,
And that I in his temple may
  a blest inquirer be.
5 For he in his pavilion shall
  me hide in evil days;
In secret of his tent me hide,
  and on a rock me raise.

6 And, even at this very time,
  my head shall lifted be

Above all those who are my foes,
 and who encompass me :⁵
I therefore to his dwelling-place
 will sacrifices bring
Of thanksgiving ; I'll sing, yea, I
 to God will praises sing.

7 O Lord, give ear unto my voice,
 what time I cry to thee ;
Upon me also mercy have,
 and kindly answer me.
8 When thou didst say, Seek ye my face,
 then unto thee reply
Thus did my heart, Above all things
 thy face, Lord, seek will I.

9 Hide not thy countenance from me :
 nor put away from thee
Thy servant in thine anger : thou
 hast been a help to me.
O God, who my salvation art,⁶
 me leave not, nor forsake :
10 Though me my parents both should leave,
 the Lord will me up take.

11 O Lord, instruct me in thy way,
 to me a leader be
In a plain path, because of those
 who hatred bear to me.
12 Me give not to mine en'mies' will ;
 for witnesses who lie
Against me risen are, and such
 as breathe out cruelty.

13 I would have fainted had I not⁷
 expected still to see
Jehovah's goodness in the land
 of those who living be.

14 Wait on the Lord, and be thou strong,
    and he shall strength afford
Unto thy heart; again, I say,
    wait thou upon the Lord.

PSALM XXVIII.

1 TO thee, O Lord, my rock, I'll cry;[1]
    an answer soon vouchsafe;
Lest I, unheard, become like those
    descending to the grave.
2 Hear thou my supplicating voice,
    what time to thee I cry;
When to thy holy oracle
    I lift my hands on high.
3 With bad men class me not, nor such[2]
    as work iniquity;
Who to their friends speak peace, while in
    their hearts doth mischief lie.
4 Reward them for their wicked deeds,[3]
    accomplish'd, or but tried:
According to their guilt do thou
    their punishment decide.
5 God will not build, but pull them down,[4]
    who would not understand
Jehovah's works, nor would regard
    the doing of his hand.
6 For ever blessed be the Lord,[5]
    who kindly deign'd to hear
My supplicating voice, and to
    my prayer has lent an ear.
7 The Lord's my strength and shield; my heart
    upon him did rely;
And I am helped: hence my heart
    is filled with vivid joy,[6]
And with my song I will him praise.
8   Their strength is God alone:

He also is the saving strength
of his anointed one.
9 O thine own people do thou save,
bless thine inheritance ;
Them also do thou feed, and them
for evermore advance.

PSALM XXIX.

1 O ALL ye mighty of the earth,[1]
give glory to the Lord ;
Unto Jehovah boundless power
ascribe with one accord.
2 The glory due unto the Lord
in songs of praise proclaim ;
In beauteous robes of holiness[2]
adore Jehovah's name.
3 The Lord's voice on the waters is ;
the God of glory great
In thunder speaks ; on many floods
Jehovah has his seat.
4 The Lord's voice is of wondrous power ;
is power's impressive sign ;
Jehovah's voice is also full
of majesty divine.
5 The voice of the Eternal doth
asunder cedars tear ;
Jehovah's voice the cedars breaks
which Lebanon doth bear.
6 He makes them like a calf to skip ;[3]
skip lightly too as they,
Ev'n Lebanon and Sirion
like unicorns at play.
7 God's voice divides the flames of fire ;
8   It makes the desert shake :
The Lord's voice makes the wilderness
of Kadesh all to quake.

9 God's voice doth make the hinds to calve,
 it makes the forest bare :
 While in his temple every one
 his glory doth declare.

10 Jehovah sits, as on a throne,[4]
 upon the waters great ;
 The Lord, an everlasting king,
 in glory hath his seat.

11 To give his people needed strength
 the Lord will never cease ;
 Jehovah will his people bless
 with never-ending peace.

PSALM XXX.

1 I'LL thee, O Lord, extol, for thou
 hast lifted me on high,
 And over me thou to rejoice
 mad'st not mine enemy.

2 O thou who art the Lord my God,
 I in distress to thee,
 In loud cries lifted up my voice,
 and thou hast healèd me.

3 O Lord, thou hast my soul brought up,
 from borders of the grave ;
 That I to pit should not go down,
 thou didst alive me save.

4 O ye who are his holy ones,
 sing praise unto the Lord ;
 And give unto him thanks when ye
 his holiness record.

5 For but a moment lasts his wrath ;
 life in his favour lies :
 Though weeping for a night endure,[1]
 at morn doth joy arise.

6 In my prosperity I said,
 that nothing shall me move,

PSALM XXXI.

7 O Lord thou hast my mountain made
   to stand firm by thy love :

But soon as thou, O gracious God,[2]
   didst hide thy face from me,
My prosperous state was quickly changed
   into calamity.

8 I therefore made my earnest cry [3]
   ascend unto the Lord ;
Into Jehovah's listening ear
   my supplication pour'd.

9 What profit is there in my blood,
   when ended are my days ?
Shall silent dust declare thy truth,
   or celebrate thy praise ?

10 Hear, Lord, have mercy ; send me help :[4]
11   Thou mad'st me, Lord, when sad,
To leap for joy ; from sackcloth loosed,
   I'm made by thee right glad ;

12 That sing thy praise my glory may,
   and never silent be.
O Lord my God, for evermore
   I will give thanks to thee.

PSALM XXXI.

1 IN thee, O Lord, I put my trust,
   shamed let me never be ;
According to thy righteousness
   do thou deliver me.

2 Bow down thine ear to me, with speed [1]
   to me deliv'rance send :
To save me my strong rock be thou,
   from danger me defend.

3 Because thou art my rock, and thee
   I for my fortress take ;
Be thou my leader and my guide,[2]
   ev'n for thine own name's sake.

PSALM XXXI.

4 And since thou art my source of strength,³
   me pull out of the net,
Which they for my entanglement
   so privily have set.

5 Into thy hands I do commit
   my spirit; thou art he,⁴
O thou, JEHOVAH, God of truth,
   who hast redeemèd me.

6 All those who lying vanities
   regard, I have abhorr'd:
But as for me, my confidence
   is fixèd on the Lord.

7 I'll in thy mercy gladly joy:
   for thou my miseries
Consider'd hast; thou hast my soul
   known in adversities:

8 And thou hast not enclosèd me
   within the en'my's hand;
But mad'st my feet, before confined,
   in ample room to stand.

9 O Lord, upon me mercy have,
   for trouble is on me:
Mine eye, my belly, and my soul,
   with grief consumèd be.

10 For spent with sorrow is my life,
   my years with sighs and groans:
My sin, while it impairs my strength,
   consumes my very bones.

11 I was to all my foes a scorn,⁵
   unto my friends a fear;
And specially reproach'd by those
   who were my neighbours near:
On seeing me they from me fled.⁶

12   I am as much forgot,
As men are out of mind when dead:
   I'm like a broken pot.

13 For slanders I from many heard;
    fear compass'd me while they
   Against me consultations held
    to take my life away.
14 But I, O Lord, my confidence⁷
    did place alone in thee;
   I strongly said, Thou art my God,
    a sure defence to me.
15 My times are wholly in thy hand:
    deliver me from those
   Whose hands would hurt me, and who are
    my persecuting foes.
16 Thy countenance to shine do thou
    upon thy servant make:
   To me from foes salvation send,⁸
    for thy great mercies' sake.
17 Since I have call'd on thee, O Lord,⁹
    me from reproaches save:
   Shamed let the wicked be, let them
    be silent in the grave.
18 To silence put the lying lips,¹⁰
    which things most grievous say,
   And charges false, in pride and scorn,
    upon the righteous lay.
19 How great the good which thou for them¹¹
    who fear thee keep'st in store,
   And wrought'st for those who trust in thee
    the sons of men before.
20 In secret of thy presence thou
    shalt hide them from man's pride:
   From strife of tongues thou safely shalt,
    as in a tent, them hide.
21 For ever blessèd be the Lord,¹²
    to me so wondrous kind,
   When I within a city wall'd
    had nearly been confined.

PSALM XXXII.

22 For from thy sight cut off I am,
    I in my haste had said;
  My voice yet heardst thou, when to thee
    with cries my prayer I made.

23 O love the Lord, all ye his saints;[13]
    because Jehovah guards
  The faithful, and he plenteously
    the deeds of pride rewards.

24 All ye whose hope and confidence[14]
    upon the Lord depend,
  Be still courageous, and he strength
    unto your heart shall send.

PSALM XXXII.

1 O TRULY blessèd is the man[1]
    on whom bestow'd has been
  The pardon of his trespasses,
    the cov'ring of his sin.

2 Bless'd he whom God will never charge
    with his iniquity:
  Whose spirit from its former stains,
    and from all guile, is free.

3 So long as I refrain'd my speech,[2]
    and silent was my tongue,
  My very bones wax'd old, because[3]
    I roarèd all day long.

4 For both by day and night on me,
    thy hand did heavy lie,
  So that my moisture turned is
    to summer's drought thereby.

5 I therefore have acknowledgèd[4]
    my sin, O Lord, to thee;
  And all concealment have removed
    from mine iniquity.
  I will confess unto the Lord
    my trespasses, said I;

And thou didst freely of my sin
  forgive th' iniquity.

6 For this shall every godly one
  his prayer address to thee;[5]
At such a time he thee shall seek,
  as found thou mayest be.
Surely, when flooding waters great
  up swell unto the brim,
They shall not overwhelm his soul,
  nor once come near to him.

7 Thou art my hiding-place, thou shalt
  from trouble keep me free:
With songs for my deliverance
  thou shalt encompass me.
8 I will instruct thee, and thee teach,
  the way where thou shalt go;
And, with my guiding eye, I will
  to thee direction show.

9 Be not ye like the horse or mule,[6]
  which do not understand;
Whose mouth, lest they come near to thee,
  a bridle must command.
10 Of sorrows an abundance shall[7]
  on wicked men be pour'd;
But mercy shall encompass him
  whose trust is in the Lord.

11 Be glad, ye righteous, in the Lord,
  in him do ye rejoice:
All ye who upright are in heart,
  lift up for joy your voice.

PSALM XXXIII.

1 REJOICE, ye righteous, in the Lord,
  it comely is and right,

For upright men, with thankful voice,¹
to praise the Lord of might.
2 The Lord praise with the harp, to him
sing with the psaltery;
Upon a ten-string'd instrument
make ye sweet melody.
3 A new song to him sing, and play
with loud noise skilfully;
4 For right the Lord's word, all his works²
are done in verity.
5 He loveth righteousness; he loves
with equity to rule;
And of the goodness of the Lord
the spacious earth is full.
6 The heavens by Jehovah's word
did their beginning take;
And by the breathing of his mouth
he all their hosts did make.
7 The waters of the seas he brings
together as an heap;
And lays, as in storehouses, up³
the treasures of the deep.
8 Let all who dwell upon the earth,
with rev'rence fear the Lord;
Let all the world's inhabitants
him dread with one accord.
9 For he but spoke the word, and done
it was without delay;
Establishèd it firmly stood,
whatever he did say.
10 The Lord to nought the counsel brings,⁴
which heathen nations take;
The people's deep devices he
of no effect doth make.
11 The counsel of Jehovah shall⁵
remain for ever sure;

PSALM XXXIV.

The secret purpose of his heart
shall evermore endure.

12 The nation blessèd is, whose God
JEHOVAH is, and those
A blessèd people are whom for
his heritage he chose.
13 The Lord from heav'n looks down and sees [6]
all sons of men full well :
14 He from his dwelling-place beholds
all on the earth who dwell.
15 He forms alike and sees their hearts, [7]
his eye marks all their deeds ;
No safety to a king from hosts,
to man from strength proceeds.
17 An horse for preservation is [8]
a most deceitful thing ;
Nor by the greatness of his strength
Can he delivr'ance bring.
18 Behold, on those who fear his name, [9]
Jehovah sets his eye ;
On those who on his mercy do
With confidence rely.
19 To rescue them from death ; in dearth [10]
the means of life to yield.
Our soul upon Jehovah waits,
our helper and our shield.
21 Since in his holy name we trust,
our heart shall joyful be.
22 Lord, let thy mercy be on us,
as we do hope in thee.

PSALM XXXIV.

1 I'LL God at all times bless ; his praise [1]
my mouth shall still express.
2 My soul shall boast in God : the meek
shall hear with joyfulness.

PSALM XXXIV.

3 Let us together bless the Lord,[2]
  exalt his name with me.
4 I sought the Lord, he heard, and me
  from all my fears did free.
5 To him they look'd, and lighten'd were:
  nor had they cause for shame.
6 This poor man cried, God heard, from all
  his ills deliv'rance came.
7 The angel of the Lord encamps,
  encompassing all those[3]
  In whose hearts reigns the fear of God,
  and saves them from all foes.
8 O taste and see that God is good:
  all trusting him are bless'd.
9 Fear God, his saints: none fearing him
  shall be with want oppress'd.
10 The lions young may hungry be,
  and they may lack their food:
  But those who truly seek the Lord
  shall not want any good.
11 O children, hither do ye come,
  and unto me give ear;
  I shall you teach to understand
  how ye the Lord should fear.
12 What man is he who life desires,
  to see good would live long?
13 Thy lips refrain from words of guile,
  from evil keep thy tongue.
14 Shun evil, and do good, seek peace,
  pursue it earnestly.
15 Jehovah's eyes are on the just;
  he listens to their cry.
16 Jehovah's face is set against
  those who do wickedly,
  That he may quite out from the earth
  cut off their memory.

17 The righteous to Jehovah cry,
and he to them gives ear;
And they out of their troubles all
by him deliver'd are.
18 To those of broken spirit, God [4]
is still a present friend;
To those who are of contrite heart
he doth salvation send.

19 The troubles which afflict the just
in number many be;
But yet at length out of them all
Jehovah sets him free. [5]
20 He carefully preserves his bones,
no harm shall them befall;
No, not so much as one of them
can broken be at all.

21 Ill shall the wicked slay; laid waste
the haters of the just.
22 The Lord redeems his servants' souls;
saves all who in him trust.

PSALM XXXV.

1 PLEAD, Lord, with those who plead; and fight [1]
with those who fight with me.
2 Take thou of shield and buckler hold,
stand up my help to be.
3 Draw likewise out the spear, and do
against them stop the way,
Who me pursue: unto my soul,
I'm thy salvation, say.

4 Confounded and ashamed be they
who for my soul have sought:
Turn'd back be those who plot my hurt,
and to confusion brought.
5 Quite scatter'd let them be like chaff
which flies before the wind;

PSALM XXXV.

And let the angel of the Lord
 pursue them hard behind.

6 With darkness cover'd be their way,
 and slipp'ry let it prove;
And let the angel of the Lord
 pursue them from above.
7 For they without a cause for me [2]
 hid in a pit their net;
To take my life they dug the pit,
 and snares in secret set.

8 Let ruin seize him unawares; [3]
 and let his net withal
Himself entrap; into the same
 destruction let him fall.
9 My soul shall joy in God; and glad
 in his salvation be:
10 And all my bones shall joyful say,
 Who is, O Lord, like thee,

Who dost set free the poor from him
 who is for him too strong;
The poor and needy from the man
 who spoils and does him wrong?
11 False witnesses rose; to my charge
 what I knew not they laid. [4]
12 They, to the spoiling of my soul,
 me ill for good repaid.

13 But as for me, when they were sick,
 I sad in sackcloth mourn'd:
My humbled soul did fast, my prayer
 into my bosom turn'd.
14 I did behave as if he were [5]
 my brother or my friend;
As one who for his mother mourns,
 I down in grief did bend.

15 But in my trouble they rejoiced,
   they in assemblies met;
Yea, men the basest of the vile,
   themselves against me set:
They me, without my knowledge, tore:
   at rest they would not be.
16 With mocking hypocrites, at feasts
   they gnash'd their teeth at me.
17 How long, Lord, look'st thou patient on?[6]
   me press'd with en'mies strong
From ruin save; my life so dear,
   O save from lions young.
18 I'll thanks to thee, Jehovah, give,
   within the assembly great;
And where much people gather'd are,
   thy praises forth will set.
19 Let not o'er me my causeless foes
   rejoice nor look so high;
Nor let my causeless haters wink[7]
   with proud and scornful eye.
20 For peace they do not speak at all;
   but crafty plots prepare
Against all those who in the land
   most inoffensive are.
21 With gaping mouths, they 'gainst me said,
   Ha, ha! our eye doth see.
22 Lord, thou hast seen, hold not thy peace;
   Lord, be not far from me.
23 Bestir thyself, O Lord my God,
   unto my judgment wake,[8]
Decide my righteous cause, and me
   from foes' oppression take.
24 O Lord my God, do thou me judge
   after thy righteousness;
And let them not their joy o'er me
   triumphantly express:

PSALM XXXVI.

25 Nor let them say within their hearts,
    Ah, we would have it thus;
Nor suffer them to say, that he
    is swallow'd up by us.

26 Confounded and ashamed be all
    who at my hurt are glad;
Let haters who against me boast
    with shame and scorn be clad.

27 Let those who love my righteous cause
    be glad, shout, and not cease
To say, The Lord be magnified,
    who loves his servant's peace.

28 Thy righteousness shall also be
    declarèd by my tongue;
And gladly will my mouth proclaim ⁋
    thy praises all day long.

PSALM XXXVI.

1 THE wicked deeds of him who walks [1]
    in sin's forbidden road,
Declares that he before his eyes
    has not the fear of God.

2 Himself he vainly flattereth [2]
    with self-deceiving eye,
Until be found the hatefulness
    of his iniquity.

3 Deceit's the language of his lips, [3]
    his words iniquity:
He to be wise, and to do good,
    has left off utterly.

4 Of mischief, lying on his bed,
    he forms a secret plot:
He sets himself in ways not good,
    he ill abhorreth not. [4]

5 Thy mercy, Lord, 's above the heavens; [5]
    thy truth is to the clouds:

6 Thy justice like the mountains great;
   thy judgments deep as floods:
 Lord, thou preservest man and beast.
7   How precious is thy grace!
 In shadow, therefore, of thy wings [6]
   men's sons their trust shall place.
8 They with the fatness of thy house
   shall be well satisfied;
 From rivers of thy pleasures thou
   wilt drink to them provide.
9 Because the fountain pure of life [7]
   remains alone with thee;
 And in that purest light of thine
   they clearly light shall see.
10 To those who know thee, still do thou [8]
   thy loving-kindness show;
 On those who upright are in heart
   thy righteousness bestow.
11 Let not my haughty enemies
   me trample with their feet;
 Nor let, O Lord, the wicked's hand
   remove me from my seat.
12 There fallen, ruined are they
   who work iniquities;
 Cast down they are, and never shall
   be able more to rise. [9]

PSALM XXXVII.

1 DO not for evil-doers fret
     thyself unquietly;
 Nor cherish envy towards those
   who work iniquity.
2 For, even like the fading grass, [1]
   soon be cut down shall they;
 And, like the green but tender herb,
   they wither shall away.

3 Set thou thy trust upon the Lord,
    and be thou doing good ;
  So thou inhabit shalt the land,
    and verily have food.
4 Delight thyself in God ; he'll give
    thy heart's desire to thee.
5 Trust God, commit to him thy way,
    it bring to pass shall he.
6 And, like the shining light, he shall
    thy righteousness display ;
  And he shall bring thy judgment forth
    like noon-tide of the day.
7 Rest in the Lord, and patiently
    wait for him : do not fret
  For him who, prosp'ring in his way,
    success in sin doth get.
8 From anger do thou cease, and wrath
    see thou forsake also :
  Fret not thyself in any wise,
    that evil thou shouldst do.
9 For those who evil-doers are,[2]
    cut off by God, shall fall :
  But those who wait upon the Lord
    the earth inherit shall.
10 For when a little time has pass'd,
    the wicked shall not be ;
  His place thou shalt consider well,
    but it thou shalt not see.
11 But by inheritance the earth
    the meek ones shall possess :
  They also shall delight themselves
    in an abundant peace.
12 The wicked plots against the just,
    and whets at him his teeth :
13 The Lord shall laugh at him, because
    his day he coming seeth.

14 The wicked have unsheath'd the sword,³
    and bent their bow, to slay
  The needy and the poor, to kill
    the men of upright way.

15 But yet their sword, 'gainst others drawn,
    shall enter their own heart:
  Their bended bows shall broken be,
    and into pieces part.

16 The little which a just man has⁴
    is more and better far
  Than is the much abounding wealth
    of those who wicked are.

17 For sinners' arms shall broken be;
    but God the just sustains.

18 God just men's days doth know, and still
    their heritage remains.

19 They shall not be ashamed when they
    the times of evil see;
  And in the days of famine they,
    still satisfied shall be.

20 But wicked men, Jehovah's foes,
    as fat of lambs, decay;
  They shall consume, yea, into smoke
    they shall consume away.

21 The wicked borrows, but the debt⁵
    he faithless does not pay;
  Whereas the righteous mercy shows,
    and gives his own away.

22 For those on whom God's blessing rests
    the earth inherit shall;
  And those who cursèd are of him
    shall be destroyèd all.

23 A good man's footsteps by the Lord
    are orderèd aright;
  And in the way in which he walks
    he greatly doth delight.

PSALM XXXVII.

24 Although he fall, he's not undone,[6]
    but up again shall stand;
  For him Jehovah still upholds
    with his almighty hand.
25 I have been young, and now am old,
    yet have I never seen
  The righteous left, nor that his seed
    for bread have beggars been.
26 He's ever merciful, and lends:[7]
    his seed is therefore bless'd.
27 Shun evil, and do good, and dwell
    in everlasting rest.
28 For God loves judgment, and his saints
    leaves not in any case;
  They're kept for ever: but cut off
    shall be the sinner's race.
29 The righteous shall possess the land,
    and ever in it dwell:
30 The righteous man doth wisdom speak:
    his tongue of judgment tell.
31 In's heart the law is of his God,
    his steps slide not away.
32 The wicked man doth watch the just,
    and seeketh him to slay.
33 Jehovah will not him forsake,
    nor leave him in his hands:
  The righteous he will not condemn,[8]
    when he in judgment stands.
34 Wait on the Lord, and keep his way,
    and thee exalt shall he
  Th' earth to inherit; when cut off
    the wicked, thou shalt see.
35 I saw the wicked great in power,
    spread like a green bay-tree:
36 He pass'd, lo, was not; him I sought,
    but found he could not be.

37 Mark thou the perfect, and behold
 the man of uprightness ;
For surely of the upright man
 the latter end is peace.

38 But down into destruction deep[9]
 transgressors shall descend ;
To be cut off, both root and branch,
 shall be the sinner's end.

39 But the salvation of the just
 proceedeth from the Lord ;
Who in the time of their distress
 will strength to them afford.

40 God them deliver shall and help ;[10]
 he them shall free and save
From wicked men ; because in him
 their confidence they have.

PSALM XXXVIII.

1 O LORD, in indignation great,[1]
 do thou rebuke me not ;
Nor lay on me thy chast'ning hand,
 in thy displeasure hot.

2 For fast in me thine arrows stick,
 thy hand doth press me sore :

3 No health now in my flesh remains
 nor soundness any more.

Because thine anger lies on me,
 I've thus afflicted been ;
Nor can my bones find any rest,—
 sad produce of my sin.[2]

4 My sins gone up above my head
 have caused me thus to mourn ;
They press me as a grievous load,
 too heavy to be borne.[3]

5 My ulcers are corrupt, and smell ;[4]
 my folly makes it so.

PSALM XXXVIII.

6 I troubled am, and much bow'd down ;
    all day I mourning go.
7 For a disease which loathsome is
    so fills my loins with pain,
  That in my weak and weary flesh
    no soundness doth remain.

8 So feeble and infirm am I,
    and broken am so sore,
  That, through disquiet of my heart,
    I have been made to roar.
9 O Lord, the whole of my desire
    is still before thine eye ;
  The secret groanings of my heart[5]
    not hidden are from thee.

10 My heart doth pant incessantly,
    my strength doth quite decay ;
  As for mine eyes, their wonted light
    is from me gone away.
11 My lovers and my friends remain[6]
    far distant from my sore ;
  And distant stand the men who were
    my kinsmen kind before.

12 Nay, those who seek my life lay snares ;
    and those who would me wrong
  Things mischievous express, and frauds[7]
    imagine all day long.
13 But, like the deaf, I did not hear,[8]
    I noticed nought amiss ;
  And silent was I as the dumb,
    whose mouth ne'er open'd is :

14 Mute was I as the deaf, whose mouth
    gives no reproofs at all.
15 For, Lord, thou art my hope ; my God,
    thou'lt hear me when I call.
16 O hear me, said I, lest they should[9]
    rejoice o'er me with pride ;

And o'er me magnify themselves,
  whene'er my foot doth slide.
17 For ready I'm to halt, my grief
  is still before mine eye:
18 For I'll declare my sin, and grieve
  for mine iniquity.
19 But lively are mine enemies,
  and strong are they beside;
  And those who hate me wrongfully
  are greatly multiplied.
20 And those who render ill for good,[10]
  as en'mies me withstood;
  Opposing me, because they saw
  me follow what is good.
21 Forsake me not, O Lord; my God,
  far from me never be.
22 O Lord, who my salvation art,
  haste to give help to me.

PSALM XXXIX.

1 I'LL look well, said I, to my ways,
  lest with my tongue I sin:
  Before the wicked I my mouth
  will keep with bridle in.
2 In silence I was like the dumb,[1]
  myself I did restrain
  From speaking good; but thus the more
  increasèd was my pain.
3 Within me heated was my heart;
  and, while I musing was,
  The fire did burn; then from my tongue
  these words I did let pass:
4 Make me, O Lord, to know mine end,[2]
  and measure of my days,
  I thus will know how frail I am,
  how fast my frame decays.

PSALM XL.

5 Lo, thou my days mad'st but a span;
   mine age is in thine eye
As nothing: sure each man at best
   is wholly vanity.
6 Sure each man walks in empty show;
   they vex themselves in vain:
They heap up wealth, and do not know
   to whom it shall pertain.

7 And now, O Lord, what wait I for?
   my hope is fix'd on thee.
8 Me free from all my trespasses,
   the fool's scorn make not me.
9 A word I spoke not, like the dumb,
   because the deed was thine.[3]
10 Remove thy stroke; I by thy blow
   in wasting weakness pine.
11 When man, corrected for his sin,[4]
   thou mak'st in sickness lie,
Thou wast'st his beauty as a moth:
   sure each man's vanity.
12 O hear my cry, Lord, at my tears
   and prayers not silent be:
I sojourn as my fathers all,
   and stranger am with thee.
13 O me in mercy do thou spare,[5]
   that I may strength regain,
Before far hence I do depart,
   and here no more remain.

PSALM XL.

1 WITH patience and with constancy,
   I waited for the Lord,
And he at length inclined his ear,
   my cry and prayer he heard.
2 He took me from a fearful pit,
   and from the miry clay,

    And on a rock he set my feet,
      establishing my way.

3 He put a new song in my mouth,
    our God to magnify:
  Many shall see it, and shall fear,
    and on the Lord rely.
4 O blessèd is the man who does[1]
    in God the Lord confide;
  Respecting not the proud, nor those
    who turn to lies aside.

5 O Lord my God, full many are
    thy works of wonder done;
  Thy thoughts of mercy toward us[2]
    above all thoughts are gone:
  In order none can reckon them
    to thee: if them declare,
  And speak of them I would, they more
    than can be number'd are.

6 No sacrifice nor offering
    didst thou at all require;
  Mine ears thou bor'dst: sin-off'ring thou[3]
    and burnt didst not require:
7 Then these my words, Behold, I come,[4]
    a servant, Lord, to thee;
  Within the volume of the book
    it written is of me:

8 To do thy will is my delight,
    O thou my God who art;
  Yea, all the precepts of thy law
    I have within my heart.
9 Within the congregation great
    I righteousness did preach:
  Lo, thou dost know, O Lord, that I
    refrainèd not my speech.

10 I never did thy righteousness[5]
    conceal within my heart,
  I thy salvation have made known,
    thy faithfulness declared :
  Thy kindness, which most loving is,
    concealèd have not I,
  Nor from the congregation great
    have hid thy verity.
11 Thy tender mercies do not thou,[6]
    O Lord, from me restrain ;
  O let thy loving-kindnesses,
    and truth, me still maintain.
12 For countless evils compass me,
    and mine iniquities
  Such hold upon me taken have,
    I cannot lift mine eyes :

  They more than hairs are on my head,
    hence is my heart dismay'd.
13 Be pleasèd, Lord, to rescue me ;
    Lord, hasten to mine aid.
14 Confounded and ashamed be all
    who seek my soul to kill ;
  Yea, backward let them driven be,
    and shamed, who wish me ill.
15 To punish these their shameful deeds,[7]
    all desolate let be
  The men who in derision say,
    Aha, aha ! to me.
16 In thee be glad, and joyful all,
    who seeking thee abide ;
  Who thy salvation love, say still,
    The Lord be magnified.
17 I'm poor and needy, yet the Lord
    the care of me doth take :
  My helper thou, and saviour art,[8]
    my God, no tarrying make.

PSALM XLI.

1 BLESS'D he who in compassion does
    the poor man's case regard;
  For him in trouble with relief
    Jehovah will reward.[1]
2 God will him keep, and save alive;
    he bless'd on earth shall live;
  And to his enemies' desire
    thou wilt him not up give.
3 God will give strength when he on bed
    of languishing doth mourn;
  And in his sickness sore, O Lord,
    thou all his bed wilt turn.
4 I said, O Lord, do thou extend
    thy mercy unto me;
  O do thou heal my soul; because[2]
    I have offended thee.
5 Those men who are mine enemies,
    of me do evil say,
  When shall he die, that so his name
    may perish quite away?
6 To see me if he comes, he speaks
    vain words: meanwhile his heart[3]
  Is plotting mischief, which he spreads,
    when forth he does depart.
7 My haters jointly whispering,
    against me hurt devise.
8 Thus say they, He is sore diseased;[4]
    he lies, no more to rise.
9 Yea, ev'n mine own familiar friend,
    on whom I did rely,
  Who ate my bread, has now his heel
    against me lifted high.
10 But, Lord, be merciful to me,
    and up again me raise,
  That I my haters may requite
    according to their ways.

11 By this I know that certainly
    I favour'd am by thee;
Because my hateful enemy
    rejoices not o'er me.⁵

12 But as for me, thou me uphold'st
    in mine integrity;
And me before thy countenance
    thou sett'st continually.

13 The Lord, the God of Israel,
    be bless'd for ever then,
From age to age eternally.
    Amen, yea, and amen.

PSALM XLII.

1 AS pants the hunted hart for streams,¹
    when sore with thirst distress'd;
So pants my soul for God, to be
    with dews divine refresh'd.

2 I thirst for God, the living God,
    source of my chief delight.
When shall I to his courts repair,
    to worship in his sight?

3 From this cut off, my tears are meat
    both in the night and day;
While constantly, Where now thy God?
    my foes insulting say.

4 Pour'd out in tears my very soul,
    when I recall to mind
The days when I to worship God
    with tribes assembling join'd.

With them into God's house I went,
    with voice of joy and praise;
I mingled with the multitude,
    who kept the holy days.

5 O why art thou cast down, my soul?
    why in me so dismay'd?

Trust God, for I shall praise him yet,
   his count'nance is mine aid.

6 My soul's cast down in me, my God;
   thee therefore mind I will
From Jordan's land, the Hermonites,
   and ev'n from Mizar Hill.
7 While loudly pour thy water-spouts,[2]
   deep unto deep doth call;
Thy breaking waves pass over me,
   thy threat'ning billows all.
8 His loving-kindness yet the Lord
   command will in the day,
His song's with me by night; to God,
   by whom I live, I'll pray:
9 To God who is my rock, I'll say,
   Why me forgett'st thou so?
Why, for my foes' oppression great,[3]
   thus mourning do I go?
10 It pierces, like a sword, my bones,[4]
   when me my foes upbraid;
Ev'n when by them, Where is thy God?
   'tis daily to me said.
11 O why art thou cast down, my soul?
   why, thus with grief oppress'd,
Art thou disquieted in me?
   in God still hope and rest:

For praises yet I'll sing to him,
   who graciously to me
The health is of my countenance,
   yea, mine own God is he.

PSALM XLIII.

1 ME judge, O God, and plead my cause
   against a godless race;
Me from th' unjust and guileful man
   do thou in safety place.[1]

PSALM XLIV.

2 Since thou the God art of my strength,[2]
    why cast me thus away?
Why go I for oppressing foes
    thus mourning all the day?

3 O send thy light forth and thy truth;
    let them be guides to me,
And bring me to thy holy hill,
    on which thy dwellings be.

4 Then will I to God's altar go,
    to God my greatest joy;[3]
Yea, God, my God, thy name to praise
    my harp I will employ.

5 O why art thou cast down, my soul?[4]
    why crush'd with vexing care?
Why so disquieted in me?
    or why approach despair?
Still hope in God; for him to praise
    good cause I yet shall have:
He of my count'nance is the health,
    my God, who will me save.

PSALM XLIV.

1 O GOD, we with our ears have heard,
    our fathers have us told,
What works thou in their days hadst done,
    in times which were of old.

2 Thy hand which drove the heathen out,[1]
    there planted Israel's race;
Thou, Lord, the nations didst afflict,
    and cast them from their place.

3 Our fathers' sword got not the land,[2]
    nor did their arm them save;
Thy favour, right hand, countenance,
    to them possession gave.

4 Thou art my King: for Jacob, Lord,
    deliv'rances command.

5 Through thee we shall push down our foes,
   who up against us stand;
  We, through thy name, shall tread down those
   who ris'n against us have.
6 For in my bow I shall not trust,
   nor shall my sword me save.
7 But from our foes thou hast us saved,
   our haters put to shame.
8 In God we glory all the day,
   and ever praise thy name.

9 But now thou hast rejected us,
   hast shame upon us pour'd;
  And when our armies go to war,
   they go without thee, Lord.[3]
10 Thou mak'st us terror-struck from foes,[4]
   disgraceful flight to take;
  And those who hatred bear to us,
   our goods their plunder make.

11 Like sheep for meat thou gavest us;
   'mong heathen cast we be.
12 Thou didst for nought thy people sell;
   their price enrich'd not thee.
13 Thou mak'st us a reproach to those[5]
   who are our neighbours near;
  Derision and a scorn to them
   who all around us are.
14 A by-word also thou dost us
   among the heathen make;
  The people, in contempt and pride,
   at us their heads do shake.
15 Confused for ever is my mind[6]
   from deeply felt disgrace;
  Nor can I more for very shame
   endure to show my face.
16 For constantly we're shock'd with words[7]
   of scorn and blasphemy;

Words utter'd by our vengeful foe
   in cruel enmity.
17 Though we have borne all this, yet we[8]
   deserted not thy cause ;
Nor were we in thy covenant false
   by trampling on thy laws.
18 Our heart ne'er wander'd from thy way,[9]
   our steps no wand'ring made ;
19 Though us thou brok'st in dragons' place,
   and cover'dst with death's shade.
20 If we God's name forgot, or stretch'd
   to a strange god our hands,
21 Shall not God search this out ? for he
   heart's secrets understands.
22 Yea, for thy sake we 're kill'd all day,
   esteem'd as slaughter-sheep.[10]
23 Rise, Lord, cast us not ever off ;
   awake, why dost thou sleep ?
24 O wherefore hidest thou thy face ?
   forgett'st our cause distress'd,
25 And our oppression ? For our soul
   is to the dust down press'd :

Our body also to the earth[11]
   fast cleaving, prostrate lies.
26 Redeem us for thy mercies' sake,
   and for our help arise.

PSALM XLV.   C.M.

1 GOOD matter fills my heart ; the King's
   the subject of my song ;[1]
Swift, as a ready writer's pen,
   is my reciting tongue.
2 Thou fairer art than sons of men :
   into thy lips is store
Of grace infused ; God therefore thee
   hath bless'd for evermore.

3 O thou who art the Mighty One,
   thy sword gird on thy thigh;
  Cloth'd with thy glory excellent,²
   and with thy majesty.
4 For meekness, truth, and righteousness,
   in state ride prosp'rously;
  And thy right hand shall thee instruct
   in things which fearful be.
5 Thine arrows sharply pierce the heart
   of th' en'mies of the King;
  And under thy subduing power³
   the people down shall bring.
6 For ever and for ever is,
   O God, thy throne of might;
  The sceptre of thy kingdom is
   a sceptre which is right.
7 Thou lovest good, and hatest ill;
   hence God, thy God, most high,⁴
  Above thy fellows hath with th' oil
   of joy anointed thee.
8 Of aloes, myrrh, and cassia,
   a smell thy garments had;
  Robes from the iv'ry wardrobes brought,⁵
   by which they made thee glad.
9 Among thy noble female train,
   kings' daughters too were seen;
  Upon thy right hand, robed in gold
   of Ophir, stood the queen.⁶
10 O daughter, hearken and regard,
    and do thine ear incline;
   Forget henceforth thy father's house,
    and people who are thine.
11 So to the King thy beauty shall⁷
    impart intense delight;
   Because he is thy Lord, for thee
    to worship him is right.

12 Tyre's princely daughter shall be there,
    presenting off'rings great :
From other lands the rich and great
    thy favour shall entreat.
13 Behold, the daughter of the King
    all glorious is within ;
With rich embroideries of gold
    her garments wrought have been.
14 She shall be brought unto the King
    in robes with needle wrought ;
Her fellow-virgins following
    shall unto thee be brought.
15 They shall be brought with gladness great,
    and joy on every side,
Into the palace of the King,
    and there they shall abide.
16 Instead of fathers held so dear,
    thy children thou mayst take,
And in all places of the earth
    them noble princes make.
17 Thy name remember'd I will make
    through ages all to be :
The people therefore evermore
    shall praises give to thee.

PSALM XLV.   S. M.

1 MY thoughts revolving are
        good matter for a song :
And in composing speak of things
    which to the King belong :
In honour of the King
    my ready tongue recites,
As rapidly as moves the pen
    of him who swiftly writes.

2 Thou 'rt fairest of all men ;
    grace in thy lips doth flow :

PSALM XLV.

His blessings therefore evermore
  God does on thee bestow.
3 Thy sword gird on thy thigh,
  thou who art great in might :
Appear in dreadful majesty,
  and in thy glory bright.

4 For meekness, truth, and right,
  ride prosp'rously in state ;
And thy right hand shall teach to thee
  things terrible and great.
5 Thy shafts shall pierce their hearts [1]
  who to the King are foes,
And them into subjection bring
  who did his power oppose.

6 Thy royal seat, O God,
  for ever shall remain :
The sceptre of thy kingdom doth
  all righteousness maintain.
7 Thou lov'st right, and hat'st wrong ;
  hence God, thy God, most high, [2]
Above thy fellows has with th' oil
  of joy anointed thee.

8 Of myrrh and spices sweet
  a smell thy garments had ;
Robes from the iv'ry wardrobes brought,
  by which they made thee glad.
9 And in thy glorious train
  kings' daughters waiting stand ;
And thy fair queen, in Ophir's gold, [3]
  doth stand at thy right hand.

10 O daughter, take good heed,
  incline, and lend thine ear ;
Forget henceforth thy kindred all,
  and father's house most dear.
11 Thy beauty to the King
  shall yield intense delight :

And since he is thy Lord, for thee
  to worship him is right.

12 The daughter there of Tyre
    with costly gift shall be,
  And all the wealthy of the land
    shall make their suit to thee.
13 The daughter of the King
    all glorious is within;
  And with embroideries of gold
    her garments wrought have been.

14 She'll brought be to the King
    in robes with needle wrought;
  And her attendant virgin train⁴
    shall unto thee be brought.
15 With gladness brought they'll be,
    and joy on every side,⁵
  Into the palace of the King,
    and there they shall abide.

16 And in thy fathers' stead,
    thy children thou mayst take,
  And in all places of the earth
    them noble princes make.
17 I will show forth thy name
    to generations all:
  The people therefore evermore
    to thee give praises shall.

PSALM XLVI.

1 GOD is our refuge and our strength,
    in straits a present aid;
2 Though therefore ev'n the earth remove,¹
    we will not be afraid:
  Though mountains into seas be cast,
3   Although the waters roar,
  Sore troubled be, though swelling seas
    shake mountains on their shore;

4 A river is, whose streams make glad
   the city of our God ;
The holy place, in which the Lord
   most high hath his abode.
5 God in the midst of her doth dwell ;
   her nothing shall remove :[2]
The Lord to her a helper will,
   and that right early, prove.
6 The nations of the heathen raged,[3]
   the kingdoms movèd were :
The Lord but utterèd his voice,
   the earth did melt for fear.
7 The Lord of hosts upon our side
   doth constantly remain :
Yea, Jacob's God our refuge is,[4]
   us safely to maintain.
8 Come, and behold what wondrous works
   have by the Lord been wrought ;
Behold, what desolations great[5]
   he on the earth has brought.
9 Unto the ends of all the earth
   wars into peace he turns ;
The bow he breaks, the spear he cuts,
   in fire the chariot burns.
10 Be still, and know that I am God ;
   among the heathen I
Will be exalted ; I on earth
   will be exalted high.
11 Our God, who is the Lord of hosts,
   is still upon our side ;
Yea, Jacob's God our refuge will
   for evermore abide.

PSALM XLVII.

1 ALL people, clap your hands ; to God
   with voice of triumph shout :

2 For terrible the Lord most high,
    great King the earth throughout.
3 The heathen people under us
    he surely shall subdue;
  And he will make the nations round[1]
    beneath our feet to bow.

4 He'll choose for us a heritage,[2]
    where we in peace may dwell;
  A lot, for excellence like that
    of his loved Israël.
5 God is gone up with shouts, the Lord
    with trumpets sounding high.
6 Sing praise to God, sing praise, sing praise,
    praise to our King sing ye.

7 For God is King of all the earth;
    with knowledge praise express.
8 God rules the nations: God sits on
    his throne of holiness.
9 The princes of the people are
    assembled willingly;
  The people here of Abraham's God,
    we congregated see.

  Because the shields that guard the earth
    belong to God alone;
  And he, exalted very high,
    in glory hath his throne.

PSALM XLVIII.

1 GREAT is the Lord, and greatly he
    is to be praisèd still.
  Within the city of our God,
    upon his holy hill.
2 Mount Sion stands most beautiful,
    the joy of all the land;
  The city of the mighty King
    on her south[1] side doth stand.

3 Within her palaces the Lord
    is for a refuge known.
4 For kings who were assembled there
    have by together gone.
5 Soon as the city they beheld,
    they, awe-struck, would not stay;
  But, sorely troubled at the sight,
    they sped them thence away,

6 Fear—pain—they felt, as woman feels,[2]
    when she a child doth bear;
7 Despair—as Tarshish crews, whose ships
    with east wind broken are.
8 As we have from our fathers learn'd[3]
    the wonders done of old;
  So, in the city of the Lord,
    our eyes did this behold;
  In our God's city, which his hand
    for ever stablish will.
9 We of thy loving-kindness thought,
    Lord, in thy temple still.
10 According to thy name, O Lord,
    all lands thy praise express;
  And thy right hand, O mighty Lord,
    is full of righteousness.
11 Because thy judgments are made known,
    let Sion hill rejoice.[4]
  Let Judah's daughters joyful all
    send forth a cheerful voice.
12 Walk Sion and the city round;[5]
    her lofty turrets tell:
13 Consider ye her palaces,
    observe her bulwarks well;
  That ye may tell posterity.
14   For this God will abide
  Our God for evermore; he will
    ev'n unto death us guide.

PSALM XLIX.

1 HEAR this, all people ; lend an ear,[1]
  all in the world who dwell ;
2 Both low and high, both rich and poor.
3   My mouth shall wisdom tell :
My heart shall knowledge meditate.
4   I will incline mine ear
To parables, and on the harp
  my sayings dark declare.

5 Amid the days when vice prevails,[2]
  why fill'd with vexing fear ?
When wicked guileful men for me
  with snares are ever near.
6 Of those who do in riches great
  their confidence repose,
And proudly boast because their wealth
  in stream abundant flows :

7 None by his wealth his brother can
  redeem by any way ;
Nor from his gain to God for him
  sufficient ransom pay
8 (Their soul's redemption precious is,
  And it can never be),
9 That still he should for ever live,
  and not corruption see.

10 Because he sees that wise men die,
  and brutish fools also
Do perish ; and their wealth the dead
  must let to others go.
11 Their inward thought is, that their house
  and dwelling-places shall
For ever stand ; hence they their lands
  by their own names do call.
12 But yet in honour shall not man
  abide continually ;
. But, passing hence, may be compared
  unto the beasts which die.

13 The very height of folly is
    their wisdom and their way ;
  Yet their posterity approve
    what they do fondly say.

14 Like sheep they in the grave are laid,
    and death shall them devour ;
  And in the morning upright men
    shall over them have power :
  Their beauty from their dwelling shall
    consume within the grave.
15 But from the grave God will me free,
    for he shall me receive.

16 Be not at all afraid when one
    thou dost enrichèd see,
  Nor when the honours of his house
    augmented greatly be :[3]
17 For he shall carry nothing hence,
    when death his days doth end ;
  Nor shall his glory after him
    into the grave descend.

18 Though he his soul did fondly bless
    while he on earth did live
  (And when thou to thyself dost well,
    men will thee praises give) ;
19 He'll yet go to his fathers' race,[4]
    to dwell with lasting night.
  Nor shall they any more behold
    the cheering beams of light.

20 Thus man, though high in honour placed,
    if yet he be unwise,
  As, like a fool, he senseless lives,
    so like a beast he dies.

PSALM L.   S. M.

1 THE Lord Almighty spoke,
    and sent his summons forth,

PSALM L.

From rising to the setting sun,
   throughout the spacious earth.[1]
2 Jehovah, Sovereign Judge,
   from Sion hill his throne,
Where beauty in perfection shines,
   in all his glory shone.[2]

3 Our God shall surely come,
   and silent be no more :[3]
Around him thund'ring tempests rage,
   and wasting fires before.
4 Unto the heavens above[4]
   he from on high shall call,
And to the earth below, that he
   may judge his people all.

5 Together let my saints
   to me assembled be,
Those who by sacrifice have made
   a covenant with me.
6 And then the heavens shall
   his righteousness declare :
Because the Lord himself is he
   by whom men judgèd are.

7 My people Israel hear,
   speak will I from on high,
Against thee I will testify ;
   God, ev'n thy God, am I.
8 I for thy sacrifice
   no blame will on thee lay,
Nor for burnt-off'rings which to me
   thou offer'dst every day.

9 I'll take no calf nor goats
   from house or fold of thine :
10 For beasts of forests, cattle all
   on thousand hills, are mine.
11 The fowls on mountains high
   are all to me well known :

The many wild beasts of the field,
  I reckon all mine own.
12 Were I in want of food,⁵
  I would not tell it thee ;
Since th' earth and all its fulness do
  belong by right to me.
13 Will I eat flesh of bulls ?
  or goats' blood drink will I ?
14 Thanks offer thou to God, and pay
  thy vows to the Most High.
15 And call upon me when
  in trouble thou shalt be ;
I will deliver thee, and thou
  my name shalt glorify.
16 But to the wicked man
  God says, My laws and truth
Shouldst thou declare ? how dar'st thou take
  my cov'nant in thy mouth ?
17 Since thou instruction hat'st,
  which should thy ways direct,
And since my words behind thy back
  thou casting dost reject.
18 When thou a thief didst see,⁶
  with him thou didst consent ;
And with the vile adulterer
  thy straying footsteps went.
19 Thou giv'st thy mouth to ill,
  deceitful is thy tongue ;
20 Thou sitt'st, and 'gainst thy brother speak'st,
  thy mother's son dost wrong.
21 Because I silence kept,
  while thou these things hast wrought ;
That I was altogether like
  thyself, has been thy thought :
But thee I will reprove,
  and set before thine eyes,

PSALM L.

  In order rank'd, thy wicked deeds,
   and thine iniquities.
22 Now, ye who God forget,[7]
   consider this with care;
  Lest I, when none deliver can,
   should you in pieces tear.

23 Me glorifies the man[8]
   who offers thanks and praise;
  I'll God's salvation show to him
   who orders right his ways.

PSALM L.   C. M.

1 THE mighty God, Jehovah, spoke,[1]
   and sent his summons forth;
  From rising to the setting sun,
   throughout the spacious earth.
2 Jehovah, Sovereign Judge of all,[2]
   from Sion hill his throne,
  Where beauty in perfection shines,
   in all his glory shone.
3 Our God himself at length shall come,[3]
   and silent be no more:
  Around him are the raging storms,
   devouring fires before.
4 He to the heavèns from above,
   and to the earth below,
  Shall call, that he his judgments may
   unto his people show.
5 From everywhere before me let
   my saints assembled be;
  Those who by sacrifice have made
   a covenant with me.
6 And then the heavèns shall declare
   his righteousness abroad:
  Because the Lord himself doth come;
   none else is judge but God.

7 Hear, O my people, and I'll speak;
  O Israel by name,
  Against thee I will testify;
  God, ev'n thy God, I am.
8 I for thy sacrifices few
  reprove thee never will,
  Nor for burnt-off'rings to have been
  before me offer'd still.
9 I'll take no bullock nor he-goats
  from house or fold of thine:
10 For beasts of forests, cattle all
  on thousand hills, are mine.
11 Well known to me are all the fowls⁴
  which lofty mountains yield;
  And mine by claim of right are all
  the wild beasts of the field.
12 I would not, if in want of food,⁵
  to thee for need complain;
  Since th' earth and all its fulness do
  to me by right pertain.
13 That I to eat the flesh of bulls
  take pleasure, dost thou think?
  Or that I need, to quench my thirst,
  the blood of goats to drink?
14 To me, thy God, with grateful heart,
  thanksgiving offer thou:
  Perform to the Most High thy word,
  and fully pay thy vow:
15 And in the day of trouble great
  see that thou call on me;
  I will deliver thee, and thou
  my name shalt glorify.
16 But God unto the wicked says,
  Why shouldst thou mention make
  Of my commands? how dar'st thou in
  thy mouth my cov'nant take?

17 Since thou all good instruction hat'st,⁶
    nor ever hast it heard;
    And since thou cast'st behind thy back,
    and slight'st my every word.

18 When thou a thief didst see, then straight
    thou join'dst with him in sin,
    And with the vile adulterers
    thou hast partaker been.
19 To evil thou dost give thy mouth,
    deceitful is thy tongue.
20 Thou sitt'st, and 'gainst thy brother speak'st,
    thy mother's son dost wrong.

21 These things thou wickedly hast done,
    and I have silent been:
    Thou thought'st me to be like thyself,
    a favourer of sin:
    But I will sharply thee reprove,
    and I will order right
    Thy sins and thine iniquities
    before thy very sight.

22 Consider this, and be afraid,
    ye who forget the Lord,
    Lest I in pieces tear you all,
    when none can help afford.
23 Me truly glorifies the man,⁷
    who offers gifts of praise;
    I'll God's salvation show to him
    who orders right his ways.

PSALM LI.

1 AFTER thy loving-kindness, Lord,
    have mercy upon me:
    For thy compassions great, blot out
    all mine iniquity.
2 Me cleanse from sin, and throughly wash
    from mine iniquity:

3 For my transgressions I confess ;
   my sin I ever see.
4 'Gainst thee, thee only, have I sinn'd,
   in thy sight done this ill ;
  That when thou speak'st thou mayst be just,
   and clear in judging still.
5 Behold, I in iniquity
   was form'd the womb within :
  My mother also me conceived
   in guiltiness and sin.
6 Behold, thou in the inward parts
   with truth delighted art ;
  And wisdom thou shalt make me know
   within the hidden part.
7 Do thou with hyssop sprinkle me,
   I shall be cleansèd so ;
  Yea, wash thou me, and then I shall
   be whiter than the snow.
8 Of gladness and of joyfulness
   make me to hear the voice ;
  That so these very bones which thou
   hast broken may rejoice.
9 All mine iniquities blot out,
   thy face hide from my sin.
10 Create a clean heart, Lord, renew
   a right sp'rit me within.
11 Me cast not from thy sight, nor take
   thy Holy Sp'rit away.
12 Restore me thy salvation's joy ;
   with thy free Sp'rit me stay.
13 Then will I teach thy ways unto
   those who transgressors be ;
  And those who walk in ways of sin[1]
   be turn'd from them to thee.
14 O God, of my salvation God,[2]
   me from the guilt of blood

set free; then of thy righteousness
my tongue shall sing aloud.
15 Let now my closèd lips, O Lord,³
re-open'd be by thee;
Then shall thy praises far abroad
be publishèd by me.
16 For thou desir'st not sacrifice,
else I would give it thee;
Nor wilt thou with burnt-offering
at all delighted be.
17 A broken spirit is to God
a pleasing sacrifice:
A broken and a contrite heart,
Lord, thou wilt not despise.
18 In thy good pleasure, Lord, do good
to Sion, thine own hill:
The walls of thy Jerusalem
build up of thy good-will.
19 Then thee shall righteous off'rings please,
burnt-offerings, which they
With whole burnt-off'rings, and with calves,
shall on thine altar lay.

PSALM LII.

1 WHY boastest thou, O mighty man,
of mischief and of ill?
The goodness of Almighty God
endureth ever still.
2 Thy tongue does slanders mischievous¹
devise with subtilety;
It cuts as does a razor sharp,
working deceitfully.
3 Ill more than good, and more than truth
thou lovest to speak wrong:
4 Thou lovest all-devouring words,
O thou deceitful tongue.

5 God thee for ever shall destroy,[2]
    remove thee, pluck thee out
Quite from thy house, and from the land
    of life he shall thee root.

6 The righteous shall behold, and fear,
    and laugh at him they shall:
7 Lo, this the man who never did[3]
    make God his strength at all:
But still on his abundant wealth
    with confidence relied;
Deriving strength from wicked plots,
    which he had form'd and tried.

8 But I within the house of God
    am like an olive green:
God's mercy still shall be my trust,
    as it has always been.
9 To thee I'll give eternal praise,
    because thou hast done this:
I'll wait upon thy name; for good
    before thy saints it is.

PSALM LIII.

1 THAT there is not a God, the fool
    doth in his heart conclude:
Corrupt they are, their doings vile;[1]
    not one of them does good.
2 Jehovah on the sons of men
    from heaven cast his eyes,
To see if there were any one[2]
    who sought God, and was wise.

3 They altogether filthy are,
    they all are backward gone;
Not one there is who doeth good,
    no, not so much as one.
4 Are workers of iniquity[3]
    so void of knowledge grown,

PSALM LIV.

   That they my people eat as bread,
     and God refuse to own?

5 There stood they, overwhelm'd with fear,[4]
    discouraged and dismay'd,
  Although there was no cause at all
    why they should be afraid:
  For God his bones who thee besieged
    hath scatter'd all abroad;
  Thou hast confounded them, for they
    despisèd are by God.

6 Let Israel's help from Sion come:
    when back the Lord shall bring
  His captives, Jacob shall rejoice,
    and Israël shall sing.

PSALM LIV.

1 ME save, O God, by thy great name,[1]
    and judge me by thy strength:
2 Hear thou my prayer, O God; give ear
    unto my words at length.
3 For those who strangers are to me
    do up against me rise;
  Oppressors seek my life, and God
    set not before their eyes.

4 My helper is the Lord my God,
    lo, therefore I am bold:
  He takes the part of every one
    who does my soul uphold.
5 He ill and mischief to my foes[2]
    will certainly repay:
  O for thy truth's sake cut them off,
    and sweep them clean away.
6 I'll offer largely, Lord, to thee
    my gifts of thankfulness;[3]
  Thy name, O Lord, for it is good,
    I will with praises bless.

7 For he to me deliv'rance gave
    from all adversities;
  And its desire mine eye hath seen⁴
    upon mine enemies.

PSALM LV.

1 LORD, hear my prayer, nor hide thyself¹
    from my entreating voice:
2 Attend and hear me; in my plaint
    I mourn and make a noise.
3 Because of th' en'my's voice, and for
    bad men's oppression great;
  They cast on me iniquity,
    and they in wrath me hate.
4 Sore pain'd within me is my heart;
    death's terrors on me fall.
5 On me comes trembling, horror has
    o'erwhelmèd me withal.
6 O that I, like a dove, had wings,
    said I; then would I flee
  Far hence, that I might find a place
    where I at rest might be.
7 Lo, then far off I wander would,
    and in the desert stay;
8 From windy storm and tempest I
    would speed my flight away.
9 Destruction on them bring, O Lord,
    their tongues do thou divide;
  For in the city violence
    and strife I have espied.
10 Both day and night upon the walls
    they pass the city round:
  In midst of it does mischief reign
    and sorrows there abound.
11 Abundant wickedness there is
    within the city found;

PSALM LV.

Deceit and guile do every day
in all her streets abound.

12 No foe he was who me reproach'd,—
a foe I could endure ;
Nor boasting hater, then I would²
have made myself secure.
13 But thou, man, who mine equal, guide,
and mine acquaintance wast :
14 We join'd sweet counsels, to God's house
in company we pass'd.
15 Let death upon them seize, and down
let them go quick to hell;
For wickedness doth much abound
among them where they dwell.
16 I'll call on God, God me will save ;
17   To him address my prayer³
At evening, morning, and at noon ;
and he my voice shall hear.

18 He has deliverèd my soul,
that it in peace might be,
From battle which against me raged ;
for many were with me.
19 Th' eternal God will them afflict,
and he my prayer will hear :⁴
Because they never changes have,
the Lord they do not fear.

20 To ruin those at peace with him
his hands with guilt he stain'd ;
The covenant which he had made,
by breaking he profaned.
21 Than butter smoother were his words,⁵
while in his heart was war ;
His speeches softer were than oil,
and yet drawn swords they are.

22 Cast thou thy burden on the Lord,
and he shall thee sustain ;

Yea, he will cause the righteous man
    unmovèd to remain.
23 But thou, O Lord my God, those men
    in justice shalt o'erthrow,
And in destruction's dungeon dark
    at last shalt lay them low:

The bloody and deceitful man
    shall not live half his days:
But upon thee with confidence
    I will depend always.

PSALM LVI.

1   BE merciful to me, O God;
        for man would me devour;¹
    While he against me daily fights
        by his oppressive power.
2   Me daily swallow up would they
        who look on me with spite;
    Since, O Most High, not few the foes
        who do against me fight.
3   When I'm afraid I'll trust in thee;
4   In God I'll praise his word;
    I will not fear what flesh can do,
        my trust is in the Lord.
5   They daily wrest my words; their thoughts
        are all to do me ill.
6   They meet, they lurk, they mark my steps,
        they wait my soul to kill.
7   Wilt thou to men of wicked deeds
        prolong'd indulgence show?
    In indignation down, O God,
        do thou these people throw.
8   Thou know'st my many wand'rings all,
        my dangers, and my fears;²
    Thou hast a book for my complaints:
        a bottle for my tears.

PSALM LVII.

9 My foes shall, when I cry, turn back;
    God is, I know, for me.
10 In God his word I'll praise; his word
    in God shall praisèd be.
11 I trust in God; I will not fear
    what man can do to me.
12 Thy vows upon me are, O God:
    I'll render praise to thee.
13 Wilt thou not, who from death me sav'dst,
    my feet from falls keep free,
  To walk before God in the light
    of those who living be?

PSALM LVII.

1 BE merciful to me, O God;¹
    be merciful to me;
  Because my soul her confidence
    reposes, Lord, in thee.
  My place of refuge I will make
    thy shelt'ring wings alone,
  Until these sad calamities
    be altogether gone.
2 My cry I will cause to ascend
    unto the Lord most high;
  To God, who doth all things for me
    perform most perfectly.
3 From heav'n he shall send down, and me
    from his reproach defend
  Who would devour me: God his truth
    and mercy forth shall send.
4 Among fierce lions is my soul,
    I firebrands live among,
  Men's sons, whose teeth are spears and darts,
    a sharp sword is their tongue.
5 Be thou exalted very high
    above the heav'ns, O God;

And let thy glory be proclaim'd
   o'er all the earth abroad.
6 My soul's bow'd down; for they a net
   have spread, my steps to snare:
Into the pit, which they have dug²
   for me, they fallen are.
7 My heart is fix'd, my heart is fix'd,
   O God; I'll sing and praise.
8 My glory wake; wake psalt'ry, harp;
   myself I'll early raise.
9 I'll praise thee 'mong the people, Lord;
   'mong nations sing will I:
10 For great to heav'n thy mercy is,
   thy truth is to the sky.
11 Exalted far above the heav'ns
   thy name, Jehovah, be;³
Thy glory let be far advanced
   above the earth and sea.

PSALM LVIII.

1 DO you, O council of our land,¹
   speak righteousness indeed?
O ye the sons of men, from you
   do judgments just proceed?
2 You practise evil in your hearts,
   then sin in open day,
Since o'er the land in balance false,²
   you deeds and causes weigh.
3 From good the wicked are estranged,
   ev'n from the very womb;
With lying lips they stray as soon
   as to the world they come.
4 Like serpent's poison, mischievous
   their poison doth appear;
They hear not, as the adder deaf,
   which closely stops her ear;

PSALM LIX.

5 That so she may not hear the voice
    of one who charm her would,
No, not though he most skilful were,[3]
    and charm most wisely could.
6 Their teeth within their mouth, O God,
    break thou in pieces small;
Break out, O Lord, the powerful teeth[4]
    of these young lions all.

7 Let them like waters melt away,
    which downward always flow:[5]
In pieces be his arrows cut,
    when he shall bend his bow.
8 Just like a snail which melts away,
    let each of them be gone;
As woman's crude, untimely birth,
    which never sees the sun.

9 God shall them sweep away before
    your pots the thorns can find,
Both quickly, and in fury great,
    as with a stormy wind.
10 The righteous, when he vengeance sees,
    shall be delighted then;[6]
The righteous one shall wash his feet
    in blood of wicked men.

11 So men shall say, The righteous man
    reward shall never miss:
God verily o'er all the earth
    a judge impartial is.

PSALM LIX.

1 ME rescue, O my God, from those
    who are mine enemies;
And be thou my defence from them
    who up against me rise.
2 From such as work iniquity[1]
    do thou deliver me;

And give me safety from the men
of bloody cruelty.
3 For, lo, they for my soul lay wait:
the men of power combine [2]
Against me, Lord; not for my fault,
nor any sin of mine.
4 To catch me innocent they run,
themselves they ready make;
Awake to aid me with thy help;
and do thou notice take.
5 Wake then, O Lord, thou God of hosts,
thou God of Israël,
To visit heathen all: spare none
who wickedly rebel.
6 At evening-tide my foes return, [3]
return with threat'ning sound,
Like growlings of an angry dog,
and walk the city round.
7 Their mouth pours out their inward rage, [4]
within their lips are swords:
For thus they say, Who, where is he,
who now can hear our words?
8 But thou, O Lord, shalt laugh at them,
and all the heathen mock.
9 While he's in power I'll wait on thee;
for God is my high rock.
10 My God, who every mercy gives, [5]
shall me betimes prevent;
Upon mine en'mies God shall let
me see my heart's content.
11 Them slay not, lest thy saints forget; [6]
but scatter them abroad
By thy strong power; and bring them down,
O thou our guardian God.
12 On them, for all their sinful words, [7]
thine anger shall abide;

PSALM LX.

And they shall for their oaths and lies
   be taken in their pride.
13 Consume, consume them in thy wrath,
   that they may no more be :
And that in Jacob God bears rule
   to th' earth's ends let them see.

14 And let them with the night return,
   return with threat'ning sound,
Like growlings of a dog in rage,
   and walk the city round.
15 And let them wander up and down,
   in search of food to eat ;
And let them grudge when they shall not
   be satisfied with meat.

16 But of thy power I 'll sing aloud :
   at morn thy mercy praise :
For thou to me a refuge wast,
   my tower, in troublous days.
17 O God, thou art my strength, I will
   sing praises unto thee,
For God is my defence, a God
   of mercy unto me.

PSALM LX.

1 O LORD, thou hast rejected us,
   hast scatter'd us abroad ;[1]
Displeasèd thou hast justly been ;
   return to us, O God.
2 The land to tremble thou hast made ;[2]
   didst breaches in it make :
Do thou its many breaches heal,
   for still we see it shake.

3 Thou things, which heavy are and hard,
   hast on thy people sent ;
We have been caused by thee to drink
   wine of astonishment.

4 A banner has by thee been given
   to those thy name who fear;
That in defence of truth by them
   it may display'd appear.
5 That thy loved people may be free'd
   from those who them enslave,[3]
Give ear unto me when I cry,
   with thy right hand me save.
6 God in his holiness hath said;
   I joy; his words ne'er fail;[4]
I Shechem will divide; my line
   will measure Succoth's vale.

7 I Gilead claim as mine by right;
   Manasseh mine shall be;
While Ephraim is my tower of strength [5]
   laws Judah gives for me;
8 I'll Moab make my slave; my shoe[6]
   I'll over Edom throw;
And over Palestina's land
   I will in triumph go.

9 O who will kindly bring me to[7]
   the city fortified?
O who to Idumea's land
   will deign to be my guide?
10 O God, who hadst rejected us,[8]
   this thing wilt thou not do?
Ev'n thou, O God, who didst not forth
   with former armies go?
11 Help us from trouble; for the help
   is vain which man supplies.
12 Through God we'll valiant be; he shall
   tread down our enemies.

PSALM LXI.

1 O GOD, give ear unto my cry;
   unto my prayer attend.

2 From th' utmost corner of the land
  my cry to thee I'll send.
 What time my heart is overwhelm'd
  with sore perplexity,
 Do thou me lead unto the Rock
  which higher is than I.

3 For thou to me in danger wast
  a shelter by thy power;[1]
 And for defence against my foes
  thou hast been a strong tower.
4 Within thy tabernacle I
  for ever will abide;
 And under thy protecting wings
  with confidence me hide.

5 For thou the vows which I did make,
  O God, didst deign to hear:
 Thou hast giv'n me the heritage
  of those thy name who fear.
6 A life prolong'd for many days
  thou to the king shalt give;
 As many generations are
  the years which he shall live.

7 To dwell for ever with the Lord[2]
  shall be his great reward;
 O let thy mercy and thy truth
  him from all evil guard.
8 Thus I unto thy holy name
  will praise for ever sing;
 That I my vows may daily pay,
  and promised victims bring.[3]

PSALM LXII.

1 MY soul with firm unshaken trust[1]
  depends on God indeed;
 Since my salvation and my strength
  from him alone proceed.

2 He only my salvation is,
    and my strong rock is he:
  He only is my sure defence;
    much moved I shall not be.

3 How long will ye against a man
    plot mischief? ye shall all
  Be slain; ye as a tott'ring fence
    shall be, and bowing wall.

4 Their sole design's to cast him down
    from his excellency:
  They joy in lies; with mouth they bless,
    but they curse inwardly.

5 Upon the Lord alone, my soul,
    do thou with patience wait;
  On him thine expectation rests
    in every pressing strait.

6 He only my salvation is,
    and my strong rock is he;
  He only is my sure defence:
    I shall not movèd be.

7 In God my glory placèd is,
    and my salvation sure;
  In God the rock is of my strength,
    my refuge most secure.

8 Ye people, place your confidence
    in him continually;
  Before him pour ye out your heart:
    God is our refuge high.

9 Mean men are surely vanity,
    and great men are a lie;
  Together weigh'd they lighter are
    than merest vanity.

10 In deeds oppressive place no trust,
    in robb'ry be not vain;
  Nor let your hearts be set on wealth,
    when great becomes your gain.

11 The Lord to me hath spoken once,
   nay, this I heard again,
That power does to Almighty God,[2]
   and him alone, pertain.
12 Nor power alone, but mercy too,
   belongs to thee, O Lord;
For thou according to his work
   dost every man reward.

PSALM LXIII.

1 LORD, thee my God I'll early seek:
   my soul does thirst for thee;
My flesh longs in a dry parch'd land,
   in which no waters be:[1]
2 That I thy power again may see,[2]
   and brightness of thy face,
As thee I formerly have seen
   within thy holy place.
3 Since better is thy love than life,
   my lips thee praise shall give.
4 Thus in thy name I'll lift my hands,
   and bless thee while I live.
5 As with the most delicious fare,[3]
   my soul shall fillèd be;
And then my mouth with joyful lips
   shall praises sing to thee:
6 When I do thee upon my bed
   remember with delight,
And when on thee I meditate
   in watches of the night.
7 In shadow of thy wings I'll joy;
   for thou my help hast been.
8 My soul thee follows hard; and me
   thy right hand doth sustain.
9 The men who seek my life shall sink[4]
   down to earth's lowest room.

10 They by the sword are doom'd to fall,
    and foxes' prey become.
11 Yet shall the king in God rejoice,
    and each one glory shall
  Who keeps his oath : but stopp'd shall be [5]
    the mouth of liars all.

PSALM LXIV.

1 WHEN, Lord, I make my prayer to thee,[1]
    my supplication hear ;
  In safety keep me from the foe,
    of whom I stand in fear.
2 Me from their secret counsel hide
    who do live wickedly ;
  From insurrection of the men
    who work iniquity :
3 Who sharpen their malicious tongues,
    until they cut like swords ;
  On whose bent bows are arrows set,
    ev'n sharp and bitter words :
4 That they may at the guiltless man
    in secret aim their dart ;
  They fearless launch the sudden shaft
    to pierce him to the heart.
5 In ill encouraging themselves,
    their snares they closely lay :[2]
  They conference in secret have ;
    Who shall them see ? they say.
6 For wicked plots they search with care,
    nay, search on search they heap :
  Of each of them the inward thought,
    and very heart, is deep.
7 But God will shoot at them a shaft,
    and wound them suddenly :
8 So on themselves their tongue shall fall ;
    all seeing them shall fly.[3]

9 And terror shall possess all men,
    God's works they shall declare;
For they shall wisely notice take
    what these his doings are.

10 In God the righteous shall rejoice,
    and put in him their trust;
And all who upright are in heart
    in God shall humbly boast.⁴

PSALM LXV.

1 IN Sion, Lord, with silent awe,¹
    I'll praise to thee address;
And pay the vows which had been made
    in seasons of distress.
2 To raise a suppliant voice to thee,
    who hearer art of prayer,
All flesh, of every tribe and tongue,
    shall to thy courts repair.
3 Iniquities, I must confess,
    prevail against me do:
But as for our transgressions all,
    them wash away shalt thou.²
4 Bless'd is the man whom thou dost choose,
    and mak'st approach to thee,
That he within thy courts, O Lord,
    may still a dweller be:

We surely shall be satisfied
    with thine abundant grace,
And with the goodness of thy house,
    ev'n of thy holy place.
5 O God, who our salvation art,³
    thou, in thy righteousness,
By fearful works unto our prayers
    thine answer dost express:

All, therefore, to earth's farthest bounds,⁴
    and those who distant be

    Upon the sea, their confidence
      will place, O Lord, in thee.
6 Who, girt with power, establishes [5]
      by his great strength the hills;
7 Who noise of seas, the roar of waves,
      and people's tumult, stills.

8 Those dwelling in the utmost parts
      are at thy signs afraid:
    The coming of the morn and ev'n
      by thee are joyful made.
9 Thou visitest the parchèd earth, [6]
      thou mak'st it rich with showers;
    God's river from the teeming clouds
      its watery treasure pours.

    It scatters riches o'er the land,
      makes store of corn to grow;
    Thou, Lord, hast this provision made,
      thou hast arranged it so.
10 Her rigs thou wat'rest plenteously,
      her furrows down are press'd;
    With showers thou dost her mollify,
      her spring by thee is bless'd.

11 So thou the year most lib'rally
      dost with thy goodness crown;
    And all thy paths abundantly
      on us drop fatness down.
12 They drop on deserts' pathless tracks, [7]
      and on their pastures wide;
    Right pleasantly the little hills
      rejoice on every side.

13 With flocks the pastures cover'd are,
      with corn the valleys clad;
    And now they shout and sing to thee,
      for thou hast made them glad.

PSALM LXVI.

1 O ALL ye lands, to God with joy
    aloft your voices raise.
2 Sing forth the honour of his name,
    and glorious make his praise.
3 Say unto God, How terrible
    in all thy works art thou !
  The greatness of thy power will make
    thy foes to thee to bow.

4 All on the earth shall worship thee,
    they shall thy praise proclaim
  In songs : they cheerfully shall sing[1]
    unto thy holy name.
5 Come, and the wondrous works of God
    with admiration see :
  In's working to the sons of men
    most terrible is he.

6 The sea into dry land he turn'd,
    whence they a passage had ;[2]
  They march'd safe through the flood on foot,
    there we in him were glad.
7 He ruleth ever by his power ;[3]
    on nations is his eye :
  O let not the rebellious dare
    to lift themselves on high.

8 O all ye people, bless our God ;
    proclaim aloud his praise :[4]
9 Who safe preserves our soul in life,
    our feet from sliding stays.
10 For thou didst prove and try us, Lord,
    as finers silver try ;
11 Brought'st us into the net, and mad'st
    loads on our loins to lie.[5]
12 Thou hast caused men ride o'er our heads ;[6]
    and though we had to pass
  Through fire and water, yet thou brought'st
    us to a wealthy place.

13 I'll bring burnt-off'rings to thy house;
   to thee my vows I'll pay,
14 Which my lips utter'd, my mouth spoke,
   when trouble on me lay.

15 Burnt-sacrifices of fat rams
   with incense I will bring;
   Of bullocks and of goats I will
   present an offering.
16 All fearing God, come, hear, I'll tell
   what he did for my soul.
17 I with my mouth unto him cried,
   my tongue did him extol.

18 If in my heart I sin regard,
   the Lord me will not hear:
19 But surely God me heard, and to
   my voice of prayer gave ear.
20 O let the Lord, our gracious God,
   for ever blessèd be,
   Who neither turn'd my prayer from him,
   nor yet his grace from me.

PSALM LXVII. S.M.

1 THY mercy show us, Lord,[1]
   O bless us with thy grace:
   And kindly cause to shine on us
   the brightness of thy face:
2 That so thy wond'rous ways
   may through the earth be known;
   And that among the nations all
   thy saving health be shown.

3 Let people praise thee, Lord;
   let people all thee praise.
4 O let the nations all be glad,
   in songs their voices raise:
   Thou'lt justly people judge,
   on earth rule nations all.

PSALM LXVIII.

5 Let people praise thee, Lord ; let them
    thee praise, both great and small.
6 The earth shall yield her fruit,
    our God shall blessing send.
7 God us shall bless ; him men shall fear
    to th' earth's remotest end.

PSALM LXVII. C.M.

1 LORD, unto us be merciful,
    do thou us also bless ;
  And graciously cause shine on us
    the brightness of thy face :
2 That so thy way upon the earth
    to all men may be known ;
  And also among nations all
    thy saving health be shown.
3 O let the people praise thee, Lord ;
    let people all thee praise.
4 O let the nations all be glad,
    and sing for joy always :
  For rightly thou wilt people judge,
    and nations rule on earth.
5 Let people praise thee, Lord ; let all
    thy saints thee praise with mirth.
6 Then shall the earth yield her increase ;
    God, our God, bless us shall.
7 God shall us bless ; and of the earth
    the ends shall fear him all.

PSALM LXVIII.

1 LET God arise, and scatterèd
    let all his en'mies be ;
  Let those who hatred bear to him,[1]
    before his presence flee.
2 As smoke is driv'n, so drive thou them ;
    as fire melts wax away,

Before God's face let wicked men
   so perish and decay.

3 But glad let all the righteous be :[2]
   let them before God's sight
  Be very joyful; yea, let them
   rejoice with all their might.
4 To God sing, to his name sing praise;
   extol him with your voice,
  Who rides on heav'n by his name JAH,
   before his face rejoice.

5 Because the Lord a father is
   unto the fatherless;
  God is the widow's judge, within
   his place of holiness.
6 In fam'lies God the lonely sets;[3]
   the pris'ners frees from bands;
  But those men who rebellious are
   inhabit parchèd lands.

7 O God, what time thou wentest forth
   before thy people's face;
  When through the pathless wilderness[4]
   thy glorious marching was;
8 Then at God's presence shook the earth,
   then drops from heaven fell;
  This Sinai shook before the Lord,
   the God of Israël.

9 O God, thou to thine heritage
   didst send a plenteous rain,
  By which thou, when it weary was,[5]
   didst it refresh again.
10 Thy congregation then did make
   their habitation there:
  Of thine own goodness, for the poor,
   thou didst, O God, prepare.

PSALM LXVIII.

11 The Lord himself did give the word,
    which widely soon was spread;
Since great the company of them
    this word who publishèd.
12 The kings of numerous hosts were forced
    to speed their flight away;[6]
And women, who remain'd at home,
    distributed the prey.
13 Though ye have lien among the pots,
    like doves ye shall appear,
Whose wings with silver, and with gold
    whose feathers cover'd are.
14 When there th' Almighty scatter'd kings,
    like Salmon's snow 't was white.
15 God's hill is like to Bashan hill,
    like Bashan hill for height.
16 Why do ye leap, ye mountains high?
    this is the hill where God
Desires to dwell; yea, God in it
    will still make his abode.
17 God's chariots twenty thousand are,
    thousands of angels strong;
In 's holy place God is, as in
    mount Sinai, them among.
18 Thou hast, O Lord, most glorious,
    ascended up on high;
In triumph hast victorious led[7]
    captive captivity:
Thou hast receivèd gifts for men,
    for such as did rebel;
Yea, ev'n for them, that God the Lord
    in midst of them might dwell.
19 Bless'd be the Lord who daily us
    with benefits doth load;
And who is in abundant grace
    of our salvation God.

20 Salvation's God alone is he,
    who is our God most strong;
  And unto God the Lord from death
    the passages belong.

21 But surely God shall wound the head
    of them who are his foes;
  The hairy scalp of him who still
    on in his trespass goes.

22 God said, My people I will bring
    again from Bashan hill;
  Them from the sea's alarming depths
    up bring again I will;

23 That in the blood of slaughter'd foes
    thy foot may be imbrued,
  Mayst see thy dogs lick up the blood
    of en'mies all subdued.

24 Thy goings they have seen, O God;
    thy steps of majesty;
  Thy steps, my God, my mighty King,
    within the sanctuary.

25 First vocal, instrumental bands [8]
    pass'd last along the way;
  Between them ranged the virgin train,
    who did on timbrels play.

26 Within the congregations great [9]
    bless God with one accord:
  All ye from Israel's fountain sprung,
    extol the mighty Lord.

27 With their prince, little Benjamin,
    princes and council there
  Of Judah were, there Zabulon's
    and Napht'li's princes were.

28 Thy God supplies thy strength; make strong
    what thou wrought'st for us, Lord.

29 For thy house at Jerusalem
    kings shall thee gifts afford.

PSALM LXIX.

30 The spearmen's host, the multitude
  of bulls, which fiercely look,
Those calves, which people forth have sent,
  O Lord our God, rebuke.
Till every one submissively
  shall silver pieces bring :[10]
The people who delight in war
  disperse, O God, our King.

31 Then princes of distinguish'd power
  shall come from Egypt lands ;
And Ethiopia to God
  shall soon stretch out her hands.

32 To God, ye kingdoms of the earth,
  sing praise with one accord ;
Lift up your voice in cheerful songs[11]
  of praise unto the Lord.

33 To him who rules the heav'ns of heav'ns,
  which he of old did found ;
Lo, he sends out his voice, a voice
  which does in might abound.

34 Ascribe ye strength unto our God ;
  for his excellency
Is over Israël, his strength
  is in the clouds on high.

35 Thou'rt from thy temple dreadful, Lord ;
  Israel's own God is he,
Who gives his people strength and power:
  O let God blessèd be.

PSALM LXIX.

1 ME save, O God, because the floods
  do so environ me,
That ev'n unto my very soul
  come in the waters be.

2 I'm downward sinking in deep mire,[1]
  where standing there is none :

I'm come into the waters deep
  where floods have o'er me gone.

3 I weary with my crying am,
   my throat is also dried;
  Mine eyes do fail, while for my God
   I waiting still abide.
4 The cruel men who towards me
   a causeless hatred bear,
  Than ev'n the hairs upon my head
   in numbers greater are:

  Those who would me destroy, and who
   my foes are wrongfully,
  Are mighty: so what I took not,
   to render forced was I.
5 Lord, thou my folly know'st, my sins
   not hidden are from thee.
6 Let none, who waits on thee be shamed,
   Lord God of hosts, for me.

  O Lord, thou God of Israël,
   let none, who waits on thee,[2]
  On my account, at any time
   put to confusion be.
7 Because for thee I've borne reproach,
   my face is hid with shame.
8 To brethren strange, to mother's sons
   an alien I became.

9 For me has eaten up the zeal,
   which to thy house I bear;
  And the reproaches cast on thee,
   upon me fallen are.
10 My tears and fasts, t' afflict my soul,
    were turnèd to my shame.
11 When sackcloth I did wear, to them
    a proverb I became.

PSALM LXIX.

12 On me is slander cast by those
    who in the gate do sit ;³
  And drunkards made of me their song
    their theme of scornful wit.
13 But, in an acceptable time,
    my prayer is, Lord, to thee :
  In truth of thy salvation, Lord,
    and mercy great, hear me.
14 Deliver me out of the mire,
    from sinking do me keep :
  Free me from those who do me hate,
    and from the waters deep.
15 Let not prevail on me the flood,
    whose water overflows ;
  Nor deep devour me, nor the pit
    her mouth upon me close.
16 Hear me, O Lord, because thy love
    and kindness is most good ;
  O turn to me, according to
    thy mercies' multitude.
17 Nor from thy servant hide thy face :
    I'm troubled, soon attend.
18 Draw near my soul, and it redeem ;
    me from my foes defend.
19 Well known to thee is my reproach,
    my shame, and my disgrace :
  Those who as en'mies me oppose,
    are all before thy face.
20 My heart is broken with reproach ;⁴
    sore grieved, I look'd for one
  To pity me, but none I found ;
    I comforters found none.
21 They also bitter gall did give
    to me instead of meat :
  They gave me vinegar to drink,
    ev'n when my thirst was great.⁵

22 Before them let their table prove
    a snare ; and do thou make
Their very welfare to become
    a trap themselves to take.

23 So darken'd let their eyes become,
    that sight may them forsake ;
And let their loins be made by thee
    continually to shake.

24 Thine indignation, and thy wrath,
    be down upon them pour'd ;[6]
And let thy furious anger take
    fast hold of them, O Lord.

25 Consign'd to desolation be
    their dwellings every one ;[7]
And in their tabernacles all
    inhabitants be none.

26 For persecutors they're of him,
    whom thou didst smite before ;
They talk unto the grief of those
    whom thou hast wounded sore.

27 Unto their former wickedness
    add thou iniquity ;
And never of thy righteousness
    let them partakers be.

28 These men from out the book of life
    be pleased thou to erase ;[8]
Nor let their names among the just
    and righteous find a place.

29 But now I am in poverty,
    and sorrowful am I :
By thy salvation, O my God,
    let me be set on high.

30 The name of God I with a song
    most cheerfully will praise ;
And I, in giving thanks to him,
    his name will highly raise.

PSALM LXX.

31 This to the Lord a sacrifice
    more pleasing far will prove
Than bullock, ox, or any beast
    possessing horn and hoof.
32 When this the humble shall behold,⁹
    it joy to them shall give :
O all ye who Jehovah seek,
    your heart shall ever live.

33 For God the poor hears, and will not
    his prisoners contemn.
34 Let heav'n, and earth, and seas, him praise,
    and all which move in them.
35 For God will Judah's cities build,
    and he will Sion save,
That they may dwell therein, and it
    in sure possession have.

36 His servants' offspring there shall dwell,
    his praises there proclaim ;¹⁰
And there shall be the dwelling-place
    of those who love his name.

PSALM LXX.   S. M.

1 LORD, hasten me to save ;¹
    with speed, Lord, succour me.
2 Let those who my destruction seek
    shamed and confounded be :
Turn'd back and shamed be they
    who in my hurt delight.
3 Turn'd back be those who say, Ha, ha !²
    their insults to requite.

4 In thee let all be glad,
    and joy who seek for thee :
Let those who thy salvation love
    say still, God praisèd be.
5 But needy I and poor ;³
    come, Lord, O make no stay :

My helper and deliv'rer thou ;
O Lord, make no delay.

PSALM LXX. C. M.

1 MAKE haste, O God, me to preserve ;
  with speed, Lord, succour me.
2 Let those who my destruction seek
  shamed and confounded be :
  Turn'd back and greatly shamed be they
  who in my hurt delight.
3 Turn'd back be those who say, Ha, ha !
  their insults to requite.

4 O Lord, in thee let all be glad,
  and joy who wait on thee :
  Let them who thy salvation love
  say still, God praisèd be.
5 But I am poor and destitute ;
  come, Lord, no longer stay ;
  My helper and deliv'rer thou ;
  O Lord, make no delay.

PSALM LXXI.

1 O LORD, my hope and confidence
  is placed alone in thee ;
  O never let thy servant then
  put to confusion be.[1]
2 Deliver me, in righteousness,
  and me from danger free :
  Incline thine ear unto my prayer,
  and safety grant to me.

3 Thou art my house of strength, to which[2]
  I ever may resort :
  To save me thou didst give command,
  thou art my rock and fort.
4 Me free, my God, from wicked hands,
  hands cruel and unjust :

5 For thou, O Lord God, art my hope,
    from youth thou art my trust.

6 Thou from my birth hast been my stay,[3]
    my guide from infant days;
  Thou took'st me from my mother's womb;
    I'll thee for ever praise.
7 To many I a wonder am;
    but thou'rt my refuge strong.
8 Fill'd let my mouth be with thy praise
    and honour all day long.

9 O do not cast me off, when me[4]
    old age doth overtake;
  And when my strength diminish'd is,
    me do not then forsake.
10 For those who are mine enemies[5]
    me odious strive to make;
  And those who for my soul lay wait
    together counsel take.

11 They said, God leaves him; him pursue
    and take: none will him save.
12 Be not far from me, O my God,
    thy speedy help I crave.
13 Confound, consume them, who unto
    my soul are enemies:
  Reproach and shame let cover those
    who do my hurt devise.

14 But I with expectation firm
    will hope continually;
  And yet with praises more and more
    I thee will magnify.
15 Thy justice and salvation great[6]
    my mouth abroad shall show,
  Throughout the day; for great their sum,
    too great for me to know.

16 With constancy I will go on
    in strength of God the Lord ;
Thy righteousness, ev'n thine alone,
    I purpose to record.
17 O God, from ev'n the days of youth,
    by thee I have been taught ;
And hitherto I have declared
    what wonders thou hast wrought.[g]
18 And now, O God, forsake me not,
    old and grey-headed grown :
Until I shall to all to come
    thy power have fully shown.
19 Thy righteousness, Jehovah, is
    exalted very high,
Who hast so great things done : O God,
    who is like unto thee ?
20 Thou, Lord, who great adversities,
    and sore, to me didst show,
Shalt quicken, and bring me again
    from depths of earth below.
21 My greatness and my power thou wilt
    increasing far extend :
On every side against all grief
    thou wilt me comfort send.
22 Thee for thy truth I'll also praise,
    my God, with psaltery :
Thou Holy One of Israël,
    I'll sing with harp to thee.
23 My lips shall much rejoice in thee,
    when I thy praises sound ;
My soul, which thou redeemèd hast,
    with joy shall much abound.
24 Thy justice shall throughout the day
    be by my tongue proclaim'd ;
For those who seek to do me wrong[h]
    confounded are and shamed.

PSALM LXXII.

1 O GOD, thy judgments give the king,
    his son thy righteousness.
2 He shall thy people and thy poor
    with upright judgment bless.[1]
3 The lofty mountains shall bring forth
    unto the people peace ;
 Peace also shall the little hills[2]
    produce by righteousness.
4 The people's poor he'll justly judge,
    the needy's children save ;
 And he shall break in pieces those[3]
    who them oppressèd have.
5 They shall thee fear, while sun and moon
    remain, through ages all ;[4]
6 Like rain on mown grass he shall drop,
    or showers on earth which fall.
7 The just shall flourish in his days,
    and prosper in his reign :
 He shall, while does the moon endure,[5]
    abundant peace maintain.
8 The limits of his kingdom shall
    from sea to sea extend :
 They from the river shall reach forth
    unto earth's utmost end.
9 The dwellers in the wilderness[6]
    bow down before him must ;
 And those who are his enemies
    shall lick the very dust.
10 The kings of Tarshish, and the isles,
    to him shall presents bring ;
 To him shall offer costly gifts
    Sheba's and Seba's king.
11 Yea, all the kings upon the earth
    before him down shall fall ;
 And all the nations of the world
    do service to him shall.

12 For he the needy shall preserve,
   when he to him shall call;
  The poor also, and him who has [7]
   no help of man at all.

13 The poor man and the indigent [8]
   he shall in mercy spare;
  The needy shall in safety live
   through his protecting care.

14 From violence, and from deceit,
   he shall their soul set free;
  And in his eyes most precious deem'd, [9]
   and dear their blood shall be.

15 Yea, he shall live, and giv'n to him
   shall be of Sheba's gold:
  For him they 'll always pray, and he
   shall daily be extoll'd.

16 Of corn a handful in the earth
   on tops of mountains sown,
  Shall prosp'rous grow, and beauteous wave, [10]
   like trees on Lebanon.

  The city shall be flourishing,
   her citizens abound
  In number shall, like to the grass
   which grows upon the ground.

17 His name for ever shall endure;
   last like the sun it shall:
  Men shall be bless'd in him, and bless'd
   all nations shall him call.

18 Now blessèd be the Lord our God,
   the God of Israël,
  For he alone doth wondrous works,
   in glory which excel.

19 And blessèd be his glorious name
   to all eternity:
  The whole earth let his glory fill.
   Amen, so let it be.

PSALM LXXIII.

1 GOD truly is to Israel good,
    to each pure-hearted one.
2 But as for me, my steps near slipp'd,
    my feet were almost gone.
3 For envious I was, and grudged[1]
    the foolish ones to see,
Who, though they walk in wicked ways,
    enjoy prosperity.
4 For still their strength continues firm;[2]
    their death of bands is free.
5 Not toil'd they are like other men,
    nor plagued, as others be.
6 Hence they with overbearing pride,
    as with a chain are bound;[3]
With violence they cover'd are,
    as with a garment round.
7 Their eyes stand out with fat; they have
    more than their hearts could wish.
8 Corrupt they are; their talk of wrong
    both lewd and lofty is.
9 They set their mouths against the heav'ns
    most blasphemous their talk;[4]
And through the earth their sland'ring tongue
    without restraint doth walk.
10 His people, therefore, oftentimes
    look back, and turn about;
Since waters of a cup so full
    to them are pourèd out.
11 And thus they say, How can it be
    that God these things doth know?
Or, Can there in the Highest be
    knowledge of things below?
12 Behold, these, though ungodly men,
    yet prosper at their will
In worldly things; with large increase
    they grow in riches still.[5]

13 To no effect I cleansed my heart
   from each polluting stain:
   I wash'd my hands in innocence,
   but verily in vain.⁶

14 Because throughout the tedious day⁷
   I've suffer'd chast'nings great;
   And daily, as the morning came,
   new stripes have been my fate.⁸

15 If in this way, so rash and wrong,
   to speak I should intend,
   The whole race of thy children I
   would certainly offend.

16 When this I thought to know, it was
   a thing too hard for me;

17 Till to God's dwelling-place I went,⁹
   then I their end did see.

18 Assuredly thou didst them set
   upon a slipp'ry place;¹⁰
   And down into destruction's depth
   didst cast this wicked race.

19 How in a moment suddenly
   to ruin are they doom'd!
   By overwhelming terrors they
   are utterly consumed.¹¹

20 As visions of the night seem vain¹²
   when men from sleep arise;
   So thou, O Lord, when thou awak'st,
   their image wilt despise.

21 Thus grieved my heart, and stung my reins,
   my thoughts with doubts oppress'd;

22 I seem'd before thy sight a beast,
   of reason not possess'd.¹³

23 I notwithstanding am, O Lord,
   continually with thee;
   And by thine all-supporting hand
   thou still upholdest me.

PSALM LXXIV.

24 Thou, with thy counsel, while I live,
    wilt be my faithful guide;
  And to thy glory afterward
    receive me to abide.
25 Whom have I in the heav'n above
    but thee, O Lord, alone?
  And in the earth whom I desire
    beside thee there is none.
26 My flesh and heart do faint and fail;[11]
    but God, who ne'er decays,
  Will still my strength and portion be
    to everlasting days.
27 For, lo, those who are far from thee
    for ever perish shall;
  Them who a whoring from thee go
    thou hast destroyèd all.
28 But surely it is good for me
    that I draw near to God:
  In God I trust, that all thy works
    I may declare abroad.

PSALM LXXIV.

1 O GOD, why hast thou cast us off?
    is it for evermore?
  Against thy chosen flock why does
    thine anger smoke so sore?
2 O call thy congregation, Lord,[1]
    to thy remembrance kind;
  It was by purchase thine of old;
    O keep it still in mind.

  The rod of thine inheritance,
    which thou redeemèd hast,
  This Sion hill, thy dwelling-place,
    in ages which are past.
3 Come, see these desolations long,
    O come, with friendly haste;

See all the ruins of thy house,
   which foes have made a waste.

4 Where met thy congregation once,
   there foes profanely roar :
  In triumph set their standards up
   thy very face before.
5 In times of old was famed the man,
   who did utensils wield,
  To cut and square the trees with which
   thy dwelling-place was ceil'd.

6 But now, in sacrilegious hands,
   the axe and hammer sound.
  To break and spoil the carvèd work,
   which long thy temple crown'd.
7 Thy sanctuary foes pollute,
   its sacred courts they burn ;[2]
  And, casting down its walls, thy house
   to desolation turn.

8 Thus said they in their hearts, Let us
   lay waste on every hand :
  They burnt up all the synagogues
   of God within the land.
9 No cheering signs we now behold ;
   no prophet thou dost send ;[3]
  None have we to inform us when
   these woful days shall end.

10 How long, Lord, shall our enemies
    reproachfully exclaim ?
   Shall adversaries always stain
    with blasphemy thy name ?
11 Thy right hand of almighty power,
    why dost thou still restrain ?
   O from thy bosom stretch it out,
    thy people's cause maintain.[4]

12 For God is certainly my King,
    ev'n from the times of old ;
The God who works throughout the earth [5]
    salvation manifold.
13 By thine unbounded power, O Lord,
    thou didst divide the sea ;
Within the deep the dragons' heads,
    all broken were by thee.[6]
14 The heads of the leviathan [7]
    thou brok'st, and thou didst give
Him for a prey to beasts and birds,
    which in the desert live.
15 Thou clav'st the fountain and the flood,
    which did with streams abound :
Thou driedst the mighty rivers up
    unto the very ground.
16 Thine only is the day, O Lord,
    thine also is the night ;
And thou alone prepared hast
    the sun and shining light.
17 By thee the borders of the earth
    were settled everywhere :
The summer and the winter both
    by thee appointed were.
18 That enemies have thee reproach'd,
    remember thou, O Lord ; [8]
That fools with their blaspheming tongues
    on thee contempt have pour'd.
19 Thy mourning dove from wicked crowds
    do thou in safety set ; [9]
Thy multitudes of poor do not
    for ever, Lord, forget.
20 Unto thy cov'nant have respect ;
    for earth's dark places be
Quite fill'd with those who vi'lence love,
    and horrid cruelty.

21 O let not those who are oppress'd
　　return unheard with shame: [10]
　Let those who poor and needy are
　　give praise unto thy name.

22 Arise, O God, and vindicate
　　the cause which is thine own:
　Remember how thou art reproach'd,
　　Lord, by the foolish one.

23 Forget not thou the threat'ning voice [11]
　　of them who are thy foes,
　Opposing thee with boastful tongue,
　　which still in boldness grows.

PSALM LXXV.

1 TO thee, O God, we render thanks,
　　we render thanks to thee;
　Because thy wondrous works declare
　　thy great name near to be.

2 When o'er this congregation I [1]
　　shall sovereign power obtain,
　I purpose that with uprightness
　　I'll justice cause to reign.

3 Throughout the limits of the land
　　prevail disorders great;
　But I will powerfully support
　　the pillars of the state. [2]

4 To fools I said, with warning voice,
　　Do not act foolishly;
　And to the men of wickedness,
　　Lift not your horn on high.

5 Lift not your horn on high, nor speak
6 　with stubborn neck. But know,
　That greatness not from east nor west,
　　nor any point, doth flow.

7 But God is judge; he puts down one,
　　and sets another up.

8 For in the hand of God most high
 of red wine is a cup :

 'Tis full of mixture, he pours forth,
  and makes the wicked all
 Wring fully out its bitter dregs :
  yea, and they drink them shall.
9 These judgments I will ever show,[3]
  I Jacob's God will praise.
10 All horns of bad men I'll cut off ;[4]
  but good men's horns will raise.

PSALM LXXVI.

1 IN Judah's land God is well known,
  his name's in Israel great :
2 In Salem is his dwelling-place,[1]
  on Sion hill his seat.
3 There arrows of the bow he broke,[2]
  the shield, the sword, the war.
4 More glorious thou than hills of prey,
  more excellent art far.

5 The men of fearless heart are spoil'd,[3]
  they slept their sleep outright ;
 And powerless were the hands of those
  who were the men of might.
6 When thy rebuke, O Jacob's God,
  had forth against them past,
 Their horses and their chariots too
  were into dead sleep cast.[4]

7 Thou, Lord, even thou, art he who should
  be fear'd ; and who is he
 Who may stand up before thy sight,
  if once thou angry be ?
8 From heav'n thou judgment mad'st be heard ;[5]
  the earth was still with fear,
9 When God for judgment rose, to save
  all meek on earth who were.

10 Surely the very wrath of man
    unto thy praise redounds :
  And thou to his remaining wrath [6]
    wilt set restraining bounds.
11 Vow to the Lord your God, and pay :
    all ye who near him be,
  Present your off'rings unto him ;
    for to be fear'd is he.
12 The spirit proud of princes he [7]
    will crush with whelming fears;
  And to the monarchs of the earth
    he terrible appears.

PSALM LXXVII.

1 I WITH my voice pour'd out to God [1]
    my supplicating cry ;
  I cried with voice of prayer to God,
    who did his ear apply.
2 I in my trouble sought the Lord,
    by night my sore did run,
  And ceasèd not ; my grievèd soul
    did consolation shun.
3 Though God I to remembrance call'd,
    my trouble still remain'd ;
  Nor was my burden'd spirit eased [2]
    by utt'ring my complaint.
4 Mine eyes debarr'd from rest and sleep,
    thou makest still to wake ;
  So great my trouble is, that I
    unable am to speak.
5 The days of old I call'd to mind, [3]
    and oft did meditate
  Upon thy deeds of mercy done
    in years of ancient date.
6 I call'd by night my songs to mind, [4]
    communèd with my heart ;

My spirit carefully inquired
　　how I might ease my smart.

7 For ever will the Lord cast off,
　　and gracious be no more?
8 For ever does his promise fail?
　　spent all his mercy's store?
9 Is 't true that to be good and kind⁵
　　the Lord forgotten hath?
And that his tender mercies he
　　hath shut up in his wrath?

10 Then did I say, That surely this
　　is mine infirmity:
I 'll mind the years of the right hand
　　of him who is Most High.
11 I will recall to mind the works⁶
　　performèd by the Lord:
The wonders done of old by thee
　　I surely will record.

12 I also will of all thy works
　　my meditation make;
And of thy doings to discourse
　　great pleasure I will take.
13 O God, thy way most holy is
　　within thy loved abode;
And what god can be once compared
　　in greatness to our God?

14 Thou art a wonder-working God
　　by thine almighty hand:
Thy mighty power thou hast made known
　　to men of every land.⁷
15 To thine own people with thine arm
　　thou didst redemption bring;
To Jacob's sons, and to the tribes
　　who do from Joseph spring.⁸

16 The waters, Lord, perceivèd thee,
    thee well the waters saw;
And they aside in terror fled;[9]
    the depths were struck with awe.
17 The clouds pour'd out their watery stores,
    sound loudly did the sky;
And swiftly with destructive power
    thy shafts abroad did fly.
18 Thy thunder's voice along the heav'ns
    a mighty noise did make;
The lightnings lighten did the world,
    th' earth tremble did and shake.
19 Thy way is in the sea, and in
    the waters great thy path;
Unseen thy footsteps are, O Lord;
    none knowledge thereof hath.
20 Thy people thou didst onward lead,
    as led a flock of sheep;
By Moses' hand and Aaron's thou
    didst them conduct and keep.

PSALM LXXVIII.

1 ATTEND, my people, to the laws[1]
    which now from me proceed;
Unto the words which I shall speak
    give ye attentive heed.
2 My mouth shall speak a parable,
    and sayings dark of old;
3 Words which we heard and knew, and which
    our fathers have us told.
4 Nor will we from their offspring dear
    these weighty truths conceal;
To generations yet unborn[2]
    these things declare we will.
Jehovah's praises we'll declare,
    and his almighty strength,

PSALM LXXVIII.

The wondrous works which he has done,
   we will show forth at length.

5 His testimony and his law
   he did in Israel place,
And charged our fathers them to show
   to their succeeding race;
6 That generations yet to come
   might them completely know;
And sons unborn, who should arise,
   might to their sons them show:

7 That they might set their hope in God,
   nor let from mem'ry fall
The wondrous doings of their God,
   but keep his precepts all:
8 And might not, like their fathers, be
   a stiff rebellious race;
A race not right in heart; whose mind
   with God unsteadfast was.[3]

9 Like Ephraim's sons, who, though equipp'd[4]
   with bows and other arms,
Did yet in day of battle flee
   from wounds and war's alarms.
10 They broke God's cov'nant, and refused[5]
   in his commands to go;
11 Forgot his works and wonders great,
   which he to them did show.

12 The wonders which his hand perform'd,[6]
   their ancestors beheld,
Within the bounds of Egypt's land,
   in Zoan's fertile field.
13 His arm asunder clave the sea,
   he led them through the deep;
And made the waters up to stand,
   on either side a heap.

14 With cloud by day, with light of fire
 by night, he did them guide.
15 Clave rocks in wilderness, and drink,
 as from great depths, supplied.
16 He from the rocks brought streams, like floods
 made gushing waters run.
17 Yet they, in desert sinning more,
 provoked the highest One.
18 For God they tempted in their heart,
 and, speaking with mistrust.
 They greedily did food require
 to gratify their lust.
19 Against the Lord himself they spoke,
 Whence now, said they, our fare?
 A table in this wilderness
 can God for us prepare?[7]
20 He smote, we grant, the rock, and thence[8]
 gush'd streams and waters great;
 But can he give his people bread;
 or send them flesh to eat?
21 Jehovah heard, and waxèd wroth;
 thus kindled was a flame
 'Gainst Jacob, and 'gainst Israël
 up indignation came.
22 For they believed not God, nor trust
 in his salvation had;
23 Though clouds above he did command,
 and heav'n's doors open made,
24 And manna rain'd on them, and gave
 them corn of heav'n to eat.
25 Man angels' food did eat; to them
 he to the full sent meat.
26 And in the heaven Jehovah did
 his power unbounded show,
 By causing two conspiring winds[9]
 from east and south to blow.

PSALM LXXVIII.

27 Whence flesh as thick as dust he rain'd [10]
    on them in ample store;
    And fowls in number as the sand
    which lies along the shore.
28 At his command, amid their camp,
    these showers of flesh down fell,
    All round the far-extending tents [11]
    where Israel's thousands dwell.
29 So they did eat, and from these stores [12]
    most plenteously were fill'd;
    For he in anger gave to them
    what they themselves had will'd.
30 Still undiminish'd was the strength
    of their perverse desire;
    But while within their mouths the food [13]
    which they did so require,
31 God's wrath upon them came, and slew
    the goodliest of them all; [14]
    So that the flower of Israël,
    o'erthrown by death, did fall.
32 For all this they were not reform'd,
    nay, sinnèd still the more;
    And though he had great wonders wrought,
    were faithless as before. [15]
33 He therefore did their fleeting days
    in vanity consume; [16]
    And by his wrath their years were spent
    in trouble, as their doom.
34 But when he slew them then they did
    to seek him show desire;
    Were penitent, and after God
    right early did inquire.
35 And that the Lord had been their Rock
    they did remember then;
    And that the high Almighty God
    had their Redeemer been.

36 Yet with their mouth they flatter'd him,
and spoke but feignedly ;[17]
And did unto the God of truth
with tongues of falsehood lie.
37 Because, though good their words, their hearts
with him were not sincere ;
Unsteadfast and perfidious they [8]
still in his cov'nant were.
38 But, full of pity, he forgave
their sin, nor did them slay ;
Nor stirr'd up all his wrath, but oft
his anger turn'd away.
39 For he remember'd they 're but flesh,
to life so fleeting born ;
A wind which passeth soon away,
and never shall return.
40 How often did they him provoke [19]
within the wilderness !
And him within the desert grieved
with their rebellious ways !
41 Yea, turning back, they tempted God,
and limits set upon
The doings and the boundless power
of Israel's Holy One.
42 They did not call to mind his hand,
nor yet the day when he
Gave them deliv'rance from the power
of their fierce enemy ;
43 Forgot what signs in Egypt's land
he openly had wrought ;
What miracles in Zoan's field
his hand to pass had brought.
44 How rivers he throughout the land
had turnèd into blood ;
So that nor man nor beast could drink
of standing lake or flood.

45 He brought devouring swarms of flies,
   which did them sore annoy :
   And various kinds of filthy frogs
   he sent them to destroy.

46 He to the caterpillar gave
   the fruits of all their soil ;
   Their labours he deliver'd up
   to locusts for a spoil.

47 Their vines with hail, their sycamores
   he with the frost did blast :

48 He gave to hail their beasts ; their flocks
   hot thunderbolts did waste.

49 He cast on them his furious wrath,
   and indignation strong,
   And trouble sore, by sending forth
   ill angels them among.

50 He to his wrath made way ; their soul
   from death he did not save ;
   But over to the pestilence
   their lives in judgment gave.[20]

51 He smote the first-born everywhere
   through Egypt's guilty land ;
   In all Ham's tents their flower and strength
   lay prostrate by his hand.

52 But his own chosen tribes, like sheep,
   thence to depart he made ;
   And they by him, through deserts wild,
   as guarded flock were led.

53 And he them safely on did lead,
   so that they did not fear ;
   Whereas their en'mies by the sea
   quite overwhelmèd were.

54 To borders of his dwelling-place
   the Lord his people led,
   Unto the mount which his right hand
   for them had purchasèd.

55 The nations who in Canaan dwelt,[21]
    he by his mighty hand
Before his people did expel
    out of their native land;
Which for inheritance to them
    he did by line divide,
And made the tribes of Israël
    within their tents abide.

56 Yet God most high they did provoke,
    and him they tempted still;
Nor to observe his statutes did
    incline their stubborn will;
57 But faithless, like their fathers, chose [22]
    in devious ways to go;
Aside they turn'd, like arrow shot
    from a deceitful bow.

58 For they to anger did provoke
    him with their places high:
And with their graven images
    moved him to jealousy.
59 When God heard this, he waxèd wroth,
    and much loathed Israel then:
60 So Shiloh's tent he left, the tent
    which he had placed with men.

61 And he his strength deliverèd
    into captivity;
He left his glory in the hand
    of his proud enemy.
62 His people also he gave up
    unto the sword's fierce rage:
And sorely was his wrath inflamed
    against his heritage.

63 The fire consumed their choice young men;
    their maids no marriage had;
64 And when their priests fell by the sword,
    their wives no mourning made.

PSALM LXXIX.

65 Jehovah then arose, as one
    who does from sleep awake;
And like a giant who, by wine
    refresh'd, a shout doth make:

66 Upon his en'mies hinder parts
    his stroke resistless came;
And thus upon his foes he put
    an everlasting shame.[23]

67 Yet to his tent, with Joseph placed,[24]
    the Lord return'd no more.
Nor longer would with Ephraim dwell,
    where long he dwelt before:

68 But he made choice of Judah's tribe[25]
    to be the rest above;
And choice he made of Sion hill,
    the place which he did love.

69 He there his sanctuary built
    with lofty turrets crown'd,
And stable as the earth itself,
    which he of old did found.[26]

70 Of David, who his servant was,
    he also choice did make,
And even from the folds of sheep
    was pleasèd him to take:

71 From waiting on the ewes with young,
    he brought him forth to feed
His heritage of Israël,
    his people, Jacob's seed.

72 So after the integrity
    he of his heart them fed;
And by the good skill of his hands
    them wisely governèd.

PSALM LXXIX.

1 O GOD, th' invading heathen have[1]
    thy heritage defaced;

PSALM LXXIX.

   Thy holy temple have defiled,
     Jerusalem laid waste.
2 The bodies of thy servants they
     have given to fowls a prey;
   To rav'nous beasts, thy slaughter'd saints,
     who round unburied lay.

3 About Jerusalem their blood
     like water they have shed;
   And there was none to bear the slain
     to mansions of the dead.[2]
4 We seem to neighbours a reproach,
     fit objects of disgrace;[3]
   By those around us we are mock'd,
     and eyed with scornful gaze.

5 How long, Lord, shall thine anger last?
     to endless years the same?[4]
   And shall thy fervent jealousy
     burn fiercely as a flame?
6 Thy fury on the heathen pour,
     who thee have never known,
   And on the kingdoms who do not
     thy name by worship own.[5]

7 For these are they who Jacob have[6]
     devour'd with cruelty;
   And who his habitations all
     have caused a waste to lie.
8 Remember not our former sins;
     thy tender mercies show;
   O let them come most speedily,[7]
     for we're brought very low.

9 For thy name's glory help us, Lord,
     who hast our saviour been:
   Deliver us; for thy name's sake,
     O cleanse us from our sin.
10 Why say the heathen, Where's their God?
     let him to them be known;

When those who shed thy servants' blood
   are in our sight o'erthrown.
11 O let the pris'ner's sighs ascend
      before thy sight on high;
   And by thy mighty power save those
      who destined are to die.⁸
12 And to our neighbours' bosom cause
      in seven-fold render'd be,
   The vile reproach with which, O Lord,
      they have dishonour'd thee.
13 So we thy people, and thy flock,
      will ever bless thy name;
   And we to generations all
      thy praises will proclaim.

PSALM LXXX.

1 HEAR, Israel's shepherd! who as sheep¹
      dost Joseph's offspring guide;
   Shine forth, O thou who dost between
      the cherubim abide.
2 In Ephraim's, and Benjamin's,
      and in Manasseh's sight,
   Do thou for our salvation come;²
      stir up for us thy might.
3 O Lord our God, restore thou us,³
      afflicted and enslaved,
   And cause thy countenance to shine,
      and so we shall be saved.
4 O Lord of hosts, almighty God,
      how long shall kindled be
   Thy wrath against the prayer address'd
      by thine own flock to thee?
5 To them thou tears of sorrow giv'st,
      instead of bread to eat;
   And tears to them instead of drink
      thou giv'st in measure great.

6 Thou makest us a strife to be
   to neighbours all about;
  Our foes, who laugh among themselves,
   set up a scornful shout.⁴

7 O God of hosts, restore thou us,
   afflicted and enslaved;
  And cause thy countenance to shine,
   and so we shall be saved.

8 A vine from Egypt thou hast brought,
   by thine outstretchèd hand;
  And out thou didst the heathen cast,
   to plant it in their land.

9 Before it thou didst room prepare,⁵
   where it might firmly stand;
  Thou causedst it deep root to take,
   and it did fill the land.

10 Veil'd were the mountains with its shade,
    as with a covering;
   And goodly cedars were the boughs
    which out from it did spring.

11 Upon the west, unto the sea,
    her boughs she did out send;
   Unto the river on the east,
    her branches did extend.

12 Why hast thou then thus broken down
    and ta'en her hedge away?
   So that all passers-by now pluck,
    and make of her a prey.

13 The boar, who from the forest comes,
    does it at pleasure waste;⁶
   By rav'nous beasts it is devour'd,
    and utterly defaced.

14 O God of hosts, we thee beseech,
    return now unto thine;
   Look down from heav'n in love, behold,
    revisit this thy vine;

PSALM LXXX.

15 And vineyard, which thine own right hand
    has planted us among;
  And that same branch, which for thyself
    thou hast made to be strong.
16 Burnt up it is with flaming fire,
    it also is cut down:
  They utterly must perish all
    soon as thy face doth frown.
17 O let thy hand be still upon
    the Man of thy right hand;
  The Son of man, whom for thyself
    thou mad'st in strength to stand.
18 So henceforth we will not go back,
    nor turn from thee at all:
  Be pleased to quicken us, and we
    upon thy name will call.
19 Lord God of hosts, restore thou us,
    afflicted and enslaved;
  And cause thy countenance to shine,
    and so we shall be saved.

PSALM LXXXI.

1 TO God, the source of all our strength,[1]
    lift up in songs your voice;
  Unto the God of Jacob make
    in praise a joyful noise.
2 Take up in vocal praise a psalm,
    the timbrel hither bring;
  Upon the sweetly sounding harp
    and psalt'ry praises sing.
3 At new moon let the priests in charge
    the joyful trumpets blow:
  That all, taught by the warning voice,
    our festal day may know.
4 For this injunction was of old
    on Israel's offspring laid,

A standing, firmly-sanction'd law,
   which Jacob's God had made.

5 To Joseph he this statute gave,
   when he with outstretch'd hand
Through Egypt pass'd, where speech I heard
   I could not understand.
6 His shoulder I from burdens took,
   his hands from pots did free.
7 Thou didst in trouble call on me,[2]
   and I deliver'd thee:

In secret place of thundering
   I did thee answer make;
And at the streams of Meribah
   of thee a proof did take.
8 O thou, my people, give an ear,
   I'll testify to thee;
To thee, O Israel, if thou wilt
   but hearken unto me.

9 There shall not, in the midst of thee,
   be found strange god at all;
Nor unto any god unknown
   shalt thou in worship fall.[3]
10 I am the Lord thy God, who did
   from Egypt land thee guide;
I'll fill thy mouth abundantly,
   do thou it open wide.

11 But yet my people to my voice
   would not attentive be;
And ev'n my chosen Israël[4]
   unmindful was of me.
12 So to the lusts of their own hearts[5]
   I left them for a prey:
And then, in counsels of their own,
   they wander'd far astray.

PSALM LXXXII.

13 O that my people had me heard,
 and chosen had my ways,⁶
14 I would have soon subdued their foes,
 and quell'd their enemies.
15 The haters of the Lord to him
 submission should have feign'd ;
 But they in peace and happiness
 should ever have remain'd.

16 He also should have fed them with
 the finest of the wheat ;
 And stores of honey from the rock,
 I should have made thee eat.

PSALM LXXXII.

1 YE judges, now in council met,¹
 forget not for an hour,
 That God is present, and your Judge,
 however great your power.
2 How long will ye unjustly judge,
 while ye in judgment sit ?
 How long be friends to wicked men,
 and them of crimes acquit ?

3 Defend the fatherless and poor
 from those who them oppress ;
 The needy and afflicted's cause
 decide with uprightness.
4 The needy and the friendless poor
 from all oppressors free ;
 And from the hands of wicked men
 them set at liberty.

5 They know not, nor will understand ;
 they walk in darkness on :
 All the foundations of the land
 are to disorder gone.²
6 I said that ye are gods, and are
 sons of the Highest all :

7 But ye shall die like men, and as
   earth's mortal princes fall.
8 Arise, O God, thou Sov'reign Judge,
   the earth to judgment call :
   For thou shalt, as thine heritage,
   possess the nations all.

PSALM LXXXIII.

1 KEEP not, O God, we thee entreat,
   O keep not silence now :
   Do thou not hold thy peace, O Lord,
   nor longer still be thou.[1]
2 For, lo, thine enemies a noise
   tumultuously have made ;
   And those who hatred bear to thee[2]
   have proudly raised the head.
3 Against thy chosen people they
   most crafty counsel take ;
   And they against thy hidden ones
   close consultations make.[3]
4 Come, said they, and let us cut off[4]
   this nation utterly ;
   That Israel as a people may
   no more remember'd be.
5 For jointly do they plot, in league[5]
   against thee they combine.
6 The tents of Edom, Ishmaelites,
   Moab's, and Hagar's line ;
7 Gebal, and Ammon, Amalek,
   Philistines, men of Tyre ;
8 Th' Assyrians with them join to help
   Lot's children they conspire.
9 Them punish, as thou Midian didst
   Jabin at Kison's strand ;
10 And Sis'ra, who at Endor fell,
   as dung to fat the land.

PSALM LXXXIV.

11 Like Oreb and like Zeeb do thou
    their nobles make to fall;
   Like Zeba and Zalmunna, make
    their chiefs and princes all;
12 Who said, For our possession sure[5]
    God's houses let us take.
13 My God, them as a wheel impell'd,
    as chaff all scatter'd, make.
14 As fire consumes the wood, as flame
    sets mountains dry on fire,
15 Affright and chase them with the storm
    and tempest of thine ire.

16 Their faces fill with shame, O Lord,
    that they may seek thy name.
17 Confounded let them be, and vex'd,
    and perish in their shame:
18 That men may know that thou, to whom
    alone doth appertain
   The name JEHOVAH, dost most high
    o'er all the earth remain.

PSALM LXXXIV.

1 HOW lovely is thy dwelling-place,
    O Lord of hosts, to me!
  How pleasant, and how prized, O Lord,
    thy tabernacles be![1]
2 My thirsty soul longs veh'mently,
    yea faints, thy courts to see:
  My very heart and flesh cry out,
    O living God, for thee.

3 Behold, the very sparrow finds
    an house in which to rest;
  The swallow too, by patient toil,
    provides herself a nest[2]
  Beside thine altars, where she safe
    her young ones forth may bring,

O thou almighty Lord of hosts,
  who art my God and King.

4 Bless'd are the dwellers in thy house,
    they ever give thee praise.
5 And bless'd the man whose strength thou art,
    in whose heart are thy ways:
6 Who, while they pass through Baca's vale,³
    make there refreshing wells;
  The rain also in grateful showers
    the pools with water fills.
7 So they from strength unwearied go
    still forward unto strength,
  Until in Sion they appear
    before the Lord at length.
8 O hear my prayer, Lord God of hosts;
    O Jacob's God, give ear.
9 Look, God, our shield, look on the face
    of thine anointed dear.
10 For in thy courts one day excels
    a thousand; rather in
  My God's house will I keep a door,
    than dwell in tents of sin.
11 For God the Lord's a sun and shield:
    he'll grace and glory give;
  No good will he withhold from those
    who uprightly do live.
12 O thou who art the Lord of hosts,
    the man is truly blest,
  Who with undoubting confidence
    on thee alone doth rest.

PSALM LXXXV.

1 LORD, thou hast favourable been¹
    to thy belovèd land:
  Thou Jacob's captives hast recall'd
    by thine almighty hand.

PSALM LXXXVI.

2 Thou pardonèd thy people hast
    all their iniquities;
Thou all their trespasses and sins
    hast cover'd from thine eyes.

3 Away thy wrath and anger fierce [2]
    thou didst in mercy turn,
4 God of our health us turn, and make,
    thine anger cease to burn.
5 Shall thy displeasure still endure
    against us without end?
Wilt thou to generations all
    thine anger forth extend?
6 To give thy people joy in thee, [3]
    wilt thou not us revive?
7 To us be merciful; to us,
    Lord, thy salvation give.
8 I'll hear what God the Lord will speak:
    he'll to his saints speak peace, [4]
And to his people; but let them
    ne'er turn to foolishness.
9 Near surely his salvation is [5]
    to those who fear our God;
That glory in our land may have
    her permanent abode.
10 Truth met with mercy, righteousness
    and peace kiss'd mutually:
11 Truth springs from th' earth, and righteousness
    looks down from heaven high.
12 Yea, what is good the Lord shall give:
    our land shall yield increase:
13 Justice, to set us in his ways,
    shall go before his face.

PSALM LXXXVI.

1 DO thou, O Lord, bow down thine ear,
    me hear most graciously;

Since I both sore afflicted am,
　　　and placed in poverty.
　2 Because I'm holy, let my soul
　　　by thee preserved be :
　　O thou my God, thy servant save,
　　　who puts his trust in thee.

　3 Since unto thee I daily cry,¹
　　　be merciful to me.
　4 Rejoice thy servant's soul : for, Lord,
　　　I lift my soul to thee.
　5 For thou most gracious art, O Lord,²
　　　and ready to forgive ;
　　And, rich in mercy, thou wilt all
　　　who call on thee relieve.

　6 Hear, Lord, my prayer ; unto the voice
　　　of my request attend :
　7 I'll call in troublous times on thee,
　　　who wilt an answer send.
　8 Among the gods who worshipp'd are,
　　　Lord, there is none like thee ;
　　And like the works which thou hast done,
　　　not any work can be.³

　9 All nations whom thou mad'st shall come
　　　and worship rev'rently
　　Before thy face : and they, O Lord,
　　　thy name shall glorify.
　10 Because thou art exceeding great,
　　　and works by thee are done
　　Which are to be admired : and thou
　　　art God thyself alone.
　11 Me teach thy way, and in thy truth
　　　then walk, O Lord, will I ;
　　Unite my heart, that I thy name
　　　may fear continually.
　12 O Lord my God, with all my heart
　　　I will to thee give praise ;

And I great glory will ascribe
  to everlasting days:
13 Because thy mercy toward me
  in greatness doth excel:
  And thou deliver'd hast my soul
  from out the lowest hell.
14 O God, the proud against me rise,
  and vi'lent men have met,
  Who for my soul have sought: and thee
  have not before them set.
15 But thou, Lord, art a gracious God,
  in whom compassions flow:
  Thy mercy, and thy truth abound,
  thou art to anger slow.
16 O turn to me thy countenance,
  and mercy on me have:
  Thy servant strengthen, and the son
  of thine own handmaid save.
17 Show me a sign for good, that they
  who do me hate may see,
  And be ashamed; because thou, Lord,
  didst help and comfort me.

PSALM LXXXVII

1 ON sacred hills is built his house,
    there worship due him waits:
2 More than in Jacob's dwellings all
    God joys in Sion's gates.
3 Of thee are spoken glorious things,
    thou city of the Lord.
  I Babylon's and Egypt's fame
    will to my friends record:
4 I, too, of Palestine and Tyre
    will candidly declare:
  And I B of Ethiopia own
    that great men born were there.

5 But it of Sion shall be said,[1]
    This man and that man there
Was born ; and he who is Most High
    himself shall stablish her.

6 When register'd the nations are
    by heav'n's omniscient Lord,
Where any man of note was born,
    he'll faithfully record.

7 In Sion's roll shall many be,
    who well could play or sing ;
Long lists of most distinguished names
    all streaming from her spring.

PSALM LXXXVIII.

1 O THOU, who art the Lord my God,[1]
    my saviour in distress,
To thee, both in the night and day,
    I did my cry address.

2 O let my prayer before thee come ;
    unto my cry give ear,

3 For full of troubles is my soul ;
    and death's dark valley near.

4 All knowing me, account me gone,
    fast hast'ning to the grave,
Bereft alike of strength and hope,
    whom nothing now can save.

5 Set free, I seem, among the dead,[2]
    who slain and buried lie,
Whom thou forgett'st, whose very name
    and frail rememb'rance die.

6 Thou hast me laid in lowest pit,
    in deeps and darksome caves.

7 Thy wrath lies hard on me, thou hast
    me press'd with all thy waves.

8 Thou hast put far from me my friends,[3]
    mad'st them me to abhor ;

I'm so shut up, that I despair
  to find deliv'rance more.

9 By reason of affliction great,[4]
  mine eye mourns dolefully :
And daily, Lord, with outstretch'd hands,
  I call by prayer on thee.
10 Wilt thou show wonders to the dead ?
  shall they rise, and thee bless ?
11 Shall in the grave thy love be told ?
  in death thy faithfulness ?

12 Who shall thy righteousness make known ?[5]
  thy wonders who express
To dwellers in the darksome land
  of deep forgetfulness ?
13 But, Lord, to thee I sent my cry[6]
  in anguish and forlorn ;
My prayer again shall rise to thee
  before the dawning morn.

14 O why, Jehovah, dost thou cast
  me off, as in disgrace ?
And why me doom so long to bear
  the hidings of thy face ?
15 I'm sore distress'd, and from my youth
  I ready am to die ;
Thy terrors I have borne, I am
  distracted fearfully.

16 The dreadful fierceness of thy wrath
  quite over me doth go :
Thy terrors great have cut me off,
  they did pursue me so.
17 For me surrounding every day,[7]
  they did like waters roll ;
And, with their congregated force,
  have compassèd my soul.

18 Thou hast put far from me my friends,[5]
    and him who did me love ;
  And those who mine acquaintance were
    to darkness didst remove.

PSALM LXXXIX.

1 GOD'S mercies I will ever sing ;
    and with my mouth I shall
  Thy faithfulness make to be known
    to generations all.
2 For mercy shall be built, said I,
    for ever to endure ;
  Thy faithfulness, fix'd as the heav'ns,
    thou wilt establish sure.
3 With him, whom I for Sovereign chose,
    a covenant I 've made ;[1]
  Unto my servant David, I
    by solemn oath have said,
4 That I thy seed establish shall
    for ever to remain,
  And will to generations all
    thy throne build and maintain.
5 The praises of thy wonders, Lord,
    the heavens shall express ;
  And in the congregation great[2]
    of saints thy faithfulness.
6 For who in heaven with the Lord
    may once himself compare ?
  Who 's like the Lord among the sons
    of those who mighty are ?
7 Great fear in meeting of the saints
    is due unto the Lord ;
  And he by all about him should
    with rev'rence be adored.
8 O God, thou Lord of hosts, what Lord[3]
    has might approaching thine ?

PSALM LXXXIX.

Around thee, as a glorious robe
thy faithfulness doth shine.

9 Ev'n in the raging of the sea
thou over it dost reign;
When rise its waves to threat'ning height,
thou stillest them again.
10 Thou Rahab didst in pieces break,
like one who slaughter'd is;
And with thy mighty arm thou hast
dispersed thine enemies.

11 The heavens are thine, thou for thine own
the earth dost also take;
The world, and all its fulness thou
by thy great power didst make.
12 From thy creating power the north
and south their being had;
Both Tabor mount and Hermon hill
shall in thy name be glad.

13 Thine arm, O Lord, is full of power;
thy hand is great in might;
And thy right hand exceedingly
exalted is in height.
14 Thou justice hast and judgment made
thy throne's firm dwelling-place;
While mercy join'd with perfect truth,
shall go before thy face.

15 How bless'd the people are who hear
the trumpet's joyful sound![4]
Their steps, Lord, by thy cheering smile,
shall be with gladness crown'd.
16 They in thy name shall all the day
rejoice exceedingly;
And they shall in thy righteousness[5]
exalted be on high.

17 Because the glory of their strength
    depends alone on thee;
And by thy favour shall our horn⁶
    of power exalted be.
18 Because Jehovah, our defence,
    to us doth safety bring,
The Holy One of Israël
    is our almighty King.
19 In vision to thy Holy One
    thou saidst, I've help upon
A strong one laid; from Judah's tribe⁷
    I've raised a chosen one;
20 Ev'n David, I have found him out
    a servant unto me;
With consecrating oil my King
    anointed him to be.
21 With him my hand shall stablish'd be;
    mine arm shall make him strong.
22 No enemy shall him deceive,⁸
    nor son of mischief wrong.
23 I will subdue before his face
    all his malicious foes;
A plague I'll be to those who do
    with hatred him oppose.
24 But yet with him my faithfulness
    and mercy still shall be;
And in my name his horn of power
    men shall exalted see.
25 His mighty hand shall reach afar,
    I'll set it in the sea;
And his right hand established
    shall in the rivers be.
26 And he to me shall cry, Thou art
    my Father and my God,
The stable and unchanging Rock
    whence my salvation flow'd.⁹

PSALM LXXXIX.

27 I'll make him my first-born, above
    the kings of every land.
28 My mercy and my covenant
    with him unchanged shall stand.
29 I by my power will make his seed
    for ever to endure,
  And, as the days of heaven, his throne
    shall stable be and sure.
30 But if his children shall forsake
    my laws, and go astray,
  And in my judgments shall not walk,
    but wander from my way:
31 If they my laws break, and do not
    my just commandments keep;[10]
32 I'll visit faults with rods; from sins
    they punishments shall reap.
33 Yet I'll not take from him my love,
    nor make my promise vain;
34 But will my cov'nant, and my word
    most faithfully maintain.[11]

35 Once by my holiness I swore,
    I'll not to David lie;
36 His seed and throne shall, as the sun,
    before me last for aye.
37 Establishèd from age to age,
    it like the moon shall be;
  And like the bow which in the heav'ns[12]
    bears witness faithfully.

38 But him, alas, thou hast cast off,
    nay, him thou didst abhor;[13]
  Against thine own anointed burns
    thine indignation sore.
39 Thy cov'nant with thy servant seems
    unbinding in thine eye;
  Thou hast profaned his crown, which now
    cast on the ground doth lie.

40 His hedges thou hast broken down,[14]
  his strong holds down hast torn.
41 He to all passers-by a spoil,
  to neighbours is a scorn.
42 Thou hast set up his foes' right hand;
  mad'st all his en'mies glad:
43 Turn'd his sword's edge, and him to stand
  in battle hast not made.
44 His glory thou hast made to cease,
  his throne to ground down cast;
45 Shorten'd his days of youth, and him
  with shame thou cover'd hast.
46 How long, Lord, wilt thou hide thyself?
  for ever, in thine ire?
  And shall thine indignation burn,[15]
  as burns the flaming fire?
47 Remember, Lord, how short a time
  I shall on earth remain:
  O wherefore is it so that thou
  hast made all men in vain?
48 Where is the man possessing life,
  who death shall never see?
  Or from the grave's all-conquering power
  what man his soul shall free?
49 O where, O Lord, thy former love,
  and deeds of kindness now?
  Those which in truth and faithfulness
  to David sworn hast thou?
50 Mind, Lord, thy servant's sad reproach;
  how I in bosom bear
  The scornings of the people all,
  who strong and mighty are.
51 With what thy raging enemies
  reproach'd, O Lord, think on;
  With what they have reproach'd the steps
  of thine anointed one.

52 Though enemies may thus reproach,
   I'll ever praise the Lord :[16]
For ever and for ever be
   his blessed name adored.

PSALM XC.

1 LORD, thou hast been our dwelling-place
   in generations all.
2 Before thou ever hadst brought forth
   the mountains great or small ;
Ere ever thou hadst form'd the earth
   and world for man's abode ;
Ev'n thou from everlasting art
   to everlasting God.

3 Thou turnest to destruction man,
   to toil and trouble born ;
And unto them thou say'st, To dust [1]
   ye sons of men return.
4 Because a thousand years appear
   no greater in thy sight
Than seems a day, when it is past,
   or than a watch by night.

5 As with an overflowing flood
   thou carriest them away :
They're like a sleep—like changing grass,[2]
   which does so soon decay.
6 At morn it flourishes and grows,
   cut down at even doth fade.
7 For by thine anger we're consumed,
   and of thy wrath afraid.[3]

8 O Lord, thou our iniquities
   dost in thy presence place,
Thou sett'st our secret sins before [4]
   the brightness of thy face.
9 Beneath thy frown we pass our days,
   even to their very end ;

As passing tale, or fleeting thought,
  so we our years do spend.
10 Threescore and ten years now sum up
  our days and years, we see;
 Or if, from more enduring strength,
  in some fourscore they be:
 Yet does the strength of men so old
  but grief and labour prove;
 For it is soon cut off, and we
  with bird-like speed remove.
11 Who knows thine anger's awful power?
  according to thy fear
12 So is thine anger: Teach us, Lord,
  our end in mind to bear;
 And so to count our days, that we
  our hearts may still apply
 Thy wisdom thoroughly to learn,
  that we may live thereby.
13 Do thou, O Lord, to us return,
  how long thus shall it be?
 Revoke thy sentence pass'd on those
  who servants are to thee.
14 O with thy tender mercies, Lord,
  us early satisfy;
 So we shall all our days rejoice,
  and still be glad in thee.
15 According as have been the days,
  in which we grief have had,
 The years in which we ill have seen,
  so do thou make us glad.
16 Before thy servant's face, O let
  thy wondrous works appear;
 And evermore thy glory show
  unto their children dear.
17 And let the beauty of the Lord
  our God be us upon:

Our works perform'd establish thou,
establish them each one.

PSALM XCI.

1 HE who does in the secret place
   of the Most High reside,
Beneath the shade of him who is
   th' Almighty, shall abide.
2 I of Jehovah will declare,
   He is my refuge still;
He is my fortress, and my God,
   and trust in him I will.
3 He thee assuredly shall save,
   and give deliverance
From subtile fowler's snare, and from
   the noisome pestilence.
4 His feathers thee shall hide; thy trust
   beneath his wings shall be:
His faithfulness shall be a shield
   and buckler unto thee.
5 To thee no terrors of the night
   shall ever cause dismay;
And harmless shall the arrow be
   which cleaves the air by day.[1]
6 Safe thou from pestilence which walks[2]
   in darkness deep as night;
And from destruction which lays waste
   amid the noon-day light.
7 A thousand at thy side shall fall,
   on thy right hand shall lie
Ten thousand dead; yet unto thee
   it shall not once come nigh.
8 Unhurt, thou only with thine eyes[3]
   shalt a beholder be;
And thou the merited reward
   of wicked men shalt see.

9 Because the Lord, who ever is
  my refuge most secure,
 Even the Most High, is made by thee
  thy habitation sure ;⁴
10 No plague shall near thy dwelling come :
  no evil thee befall :⁵
11 For thee to keep in all thy ways
  his angels charge he shall.
12 They in their hands shall bear thee up,
  nor leave thee shall alone ;⁶
 Lest thou at any time shouldst dash
  thy foot against a stone.
13 Thou shalt upon the adder tread,
  and on the lions strong ;
 Thy feet on dragons trample shall,
  and on the lions young.
14 Because on me he set his love,
  I'll save and set him free ;
 Because my great name he has known,
  he shall exalted be.⁷
15 He'll call on me, I'll answer him ;
  I will be with him still
 In trouble, to deliver him,
  and honour him I will.
16 I'll give him such a length of days,
  as will him satisfy ;
 I also my salvation great⁸
  will cause his eyes to see.

PSALM XCII.

1 UNTO the Lord 'tis good our voice
  in thankful hymns to raise ;¹
 And to thy name, O thou Most High,
  to sing the songs of praise.
2 To show thy loving-kindness forth
  when shines the morning light :

And to declare thy faithfulness
  with pleasure every night,
3 Upon a ten-string'd instrument,
  upon the psaltery,
  And on the harp with solemn sound,
  and grave sweet melody.
4 For thou, Lord, by thy mighty deeds
  hast made me to be glad;
  And I will triumph in the works
  which by thine hands were made.

5 How deep, Lord, are thy thoughts! how great
  the doings of thy hand!²
6 These neither brutish man can know,
  nor fool can understand.
7 When those who practise wickedness³
  spring quickly up as grass,
  And workers of iniquity
  do flourish all apace;

  It is that they for ever may
  be overthrown and slain:
8 But thou, Jehovah, art Most High,
  for ever to remain.
9 For, lo, thine enemies, O Lord,
  thine en'mies perish shall;
  The workers of iniquity
  shall be dispersèd all.
10 But thou shalt, like unto the horn
  of the unicorn, exalt
  My horn on high: thou with fresh oil
  anoint me also shalt.
11 Mine eyes shall also see my wish
  upon mine enemies;
  Mine ear shall hear of wicked men,
  who up against me rise.
12 But like the palm tree flourishing
  shall be the righteous one;

He'll like the stately cedar grow
  Which is in Lebanon.
13 Those who within the house of God¹
    are planted by his grace,
  Shall still grow up, and flourish all
    in our God's holy place.

14 Unweaken'd by enfeebling age,
    they fruit still forth shall bring;
  They shall be fat, be full of sap,
    and still be flourishing;
15 To show that upright is the Lord:
    he is a rock to me;
  And he from all unrighteousness
    is altogether free.

PSALM XCIII.

1 JEHOVAH reigns; he is enrobed¹
    with majesty most bright;
  His works declare him clothed to be,
    and girt about with might.
  The world is also stablishèd,
    that it can not depart.
2 Thy throne is fix'd of old, and thou
    from everlasting art.

3 The floods, O Lord, have lifted up,
    have lifted up their voice;
  The floods have lifted up their waves
    and made a mighty noise.
4 The sovereign Lord, who dwells on high,²
    more powerful is by far
  Than noise of many waters is,
    or great sea-billows are.

5 Thy testimonies every one
    in faithfulness excel:
  For ever holiness, O Lord,
    thy house becometh well.

PSALM XCIV.

1 O LORD God, unto whom alone
    all vengeance doth belong;
  O God, whose province vengeance is,
    shine forth avenging wrong.
2 O thou who dost as sovereign Judge[1]
    o'er all the earth preside,
  Lift up thyself, give due reward
    unto the sons of pride.

3 How long, O mighty Lord, shall those
    whose deeds unrighteous be,
  How long shall men of wicked lives
    thus triumph haughtily?
4 How long shall things most hard by them
    with sland'ring tongues be told?[2]
  And all who work iniquity
    to boast themselves be bold?

5 The wicked crush thy people, Lord,[3]
    thy heritage oppress:
6 The widow and the stranger slay,
    and kill the fatherless.
7 Yet God, say they, shall not see this,
    nor God of Jacob know.
8 Ye brutish people! understand;
    fools! when wise will ye grow?

9 Shall God, who form'd the ear of man,
    to hear unable be?
  Shall he who form'd the human eye
    possess no power to see?
10 Has he, who nations does correct,
    no chastisement for you?[4]
  He teaches knowledge unto man,
    shall he himself not know?

11 Man's thoughts to be but vanity
    the Lord doth well discern.
12 Bless'd he whom thou dost chasten, Lord,[5]
    and mak'st thy law to learn:

13 That thou may'st kindly give him rest[6]
　　from sad and troublous days,
　Until the pit be dug for those
　　who walk in wicked ways.

14 Because Jehovah from his saints
　　will not his favour take ;
　And those who are his heritage
　　he never will forsake :[7]

15 But judgment, now perplexing, shall
　　return to righteousness ;[8]
　And it shall follow'd be by all
　　who upright hearts possess.

16 Who will stand up for me against
　　those acting wickedly ?
　Who will me help against the men
　　who work iniquity ?

17 Unless the Lord had been my help
　　when I was sore oppress'd,
　My soul had almost in the house[9]
　　of silence been at rest.

18 When I, of strength despairing, said,
　　My foot doth slip away ;
　Thy mercy, Lord, was my support,
　　my never-failing stay.

19 Amid the crowd of vexing thoughts
　　Which in my spirit fight,[10]
　Thy consolations to my soul
　　impart supreme delight.

20 Shall ere a throne iniquitous[11]
　　have fellowship with thee,
　A throne which mischief by its laws
　　does wickedly decree ?

21 Against the righteous they conspire
　　they guiltless blood condemn.

22 But God, my refuge and my rock,[12]
　　will me defend from them.

23 On them their own iniquity
   the Lord our God shall lay,
And them in all their wickedness
   he certainly shall slay.

PSALM XCV.

1 O COME, and with a joyful noise
     sing praise unto the Lord ;
  The rock of our salvation should
     with praises be adored.¹
2 Before his presence let us come
     with praise and thankful voice ;
  To him sing psalms with grateful hearts,
     and make a joyful noise.

3 For God's a great God, and great King,
     above all gods he is.
4 The earth's great depths are in his hand,
     the towering hills are his.
5 To him belongs the spacious sea,
     the creature of his hand ;²
  And by his all-creating power
     was form'd the solid land.

6 O come, and let us worship him,
     and bow with rev'rence down ;
  Before the Lord our Maker kneel,
     and thus his greatness own.
7 For he's our God, the people we
     of his own pasture are,
  And of his hand the sheep ; to-day,
     if ye his voice will hear,

8 Then harden not your hearts, nor me
     provoke, as did the race ³
  Who by temptations greatly sinn'd
     in desert's pathless ways :
9 When me your fathers tempted, proved,⁴
     and did my working see ;

10 Throughout the space of forty years
    this race has grievèd me.

   I said, This people errs in heart,
    my ways they do not know:
11 To whom I swore in wrath, that to [5]
    my rest they should not go.

PSALM XCVI.

1 O WITH a new and grateful song, [1]
    sing praise unto the Lord.
  To celebrate Jehovah's praise,
    let all the earth accord.
2 Unto Jehovah praises sing,
    bless ye his holy name;
  And his salvation let your lips
    from day to day proclaim.
3 Among the heathen nations all [2]
    his glory great declare;
  And unto every people show
    his works which wondrous are.
4 For great's the Lord, and greatly he
    is to be magnified;
  Most worthy to be fear'd is he
    Above all gods beside.
5 For powerless idols are the gods [3]
    which blinded nations fear;
  But our God is the Lord, by whom
    the heav'ns created were.
6 Great honour is before his face,
    and majesty divine;
  Strength is within his holy place,
    and there doth beauty shine.
7 O glory give unto the Lord,
    ye men of every tribe, [4]
  Ascribe ye glory to the Lord,
    and mighty power ascribe.

PSALM XCVII.

8 Give ye the glory to the Lord
   which to his name is due;
Come ye into his courts, and bring
   an offering with you.

9 In beauty of true holiness,
   O do the Lord adore;
Let every quarter of the earth[5]
   tremble his face before.

10 Among the heathen say, God reigns;[6]
   the world shall stablish'd be
Immovably; the Lord shall judge
   his people righteously.

11 Let heav'ns be glad before the Lord,
   and let the earth rejoice;
Let seas, and all which they contain
   lift up their deafening voice.[7]

12 Let fields rejoice, and every thing[8]
   which in the fields is found;
Let all the trees, of every wood,
   send forth a joyful sound

13 Before the Lord; because he comes,
   he comes to judge the earth:
He'll judge the world with righteousness,
   he'll show his justice forth.

PSALM XCVII.

1 THE Lord is universal King,[1]
   let all the earth rejoice;
Let all the multitude of isles
   lift up for joy their voice.

2 Though round him be a robe of clouds
   and darkness deep as night,
Yet bright his throne with righteousness,
   and firm with judgment right.

3 Before him goes the fire, which burns
   his en'mies all about;

4 His lightnings lighten did the world ;
    th' earth saw, and shook throughout.
5 Hills, at the presence of the Lord,
    did melt, like wax, away [2]
  Before the Lord, who o'er the earth
    holds universal sway.

6 The heav'ns declare his righteousness,
    all men his glory see.
7 Let all who worship images [3]
    put to confusion be.
  Let those, who idols make their boast,
    into dishonour fall :
  Ye who are callèd gods, see that
    ye do him worship all.

8 On hearing, Sion joyful was,
    glad Judah's daughters were ;
  They much rejoiced, because, O Lord,
    thy judgments did appear.
9 Because, above all things on earth,
    thou, Lord, art very high ;
  And far above all gods thou art [4]
    exalted gloriously.

10 Hate evil, ye who love the Lord : [5]
    his saints' souls keepeth he ;
   Them from the hands of wicked men
    he sets entirely free.
11 For those who truly righteous are,
    sown is a joyful light ;
   And gladness for all those who love
    and follow what is right. [6]

12 Ye righteous, in the Lord rejoice ; [7]
    your thankfulness express,
   When ye into your memory
    recall his holiness.

PSALM XCVIII.

1 O SING a new song to the Lord,
    for he hath wonders done :
His right hand and his holy arm
    him victory has won.
2 The Lord God his salvation great[1]
    hath causèd to be known ;
His justice in the heathen's sight
    he openly hath shown.

3 He mindful of his grace and truth
    to Israel's house has been ;
And the salvation of our God
    all ends of th' earth have seen.
4 Let all the earth unto the Lord
    send forth a joyful noise ;
Lift up your voice aloud to him,
    sing praises, and rejoice.

5 To magnify Jehovah's name
    let harpers strike the lyre ;
Let harp, and let the voice of psalms,
    together joy inspire.
6 Blow trumpets, let the cornets sound,
    let all with sweet accord
Unite to make a joyful noise
    before the King the Lord.

7 Let seas with all their fulness roar ;
    the world, and dwellers there ;
8 Let floods clap hands, and let the hills
    in concert joy declare
9 Before the Lord ; because he comes,
    he comes for judgment forth :[2]
He'll judge with equity his saints,
    with righteousness the earth.

PSALM XCIX.

1 THE Lord eternal reigns as king,[1]
    let all the people quake ;

PSALM C.

He sits between the cherubim,
  let th' earth before him shake.
2 The Lord, who is in Sion great,
  above all people is;
3 Thy name, which dreadful is and great,[2]
  and holy, let them bless.

4 This powerful king, who judgment loves,[3]
  makes justice firm to stand;
  In Jacob righteous judgment thou
  maintain'st throughout the land.
5 Extol ye, then, Jehovah's name,[4]
  our God's name be adored;
  In worship at his footstool bow,
  since holy is the Lord.

6 Thus Moses, Aaron, Samuel did
  invoke God's holy name.
  On God these priests, this prophet call'd,
  to them an answer came.
7 He from the cloudy pillar did
  make known to them his will;
  His testimonies they observed,[5]
  and kept his statutes still.

8 Thou, Lord our God, didst answer them,
  thou didst forgive their sin;
  Yet by thy hand, for their misdeeds,
  they've sore afflicted been.
9 Do ye exalt the Lord our God,
  and at his holy hill
  Him worship ye; because the Lord
  our God is holy still.

PSALM C. L. M.

1 LET all who dwell in every land,[1]
  Sing to the Lord with cheerful voice.
2 Him serve with gladness, sing his praise,[2]
  Come ye before him and rejoice.

3 Know that the Lord is God indeed ;
Without our aid he did us make :
We are his flock, he doth us feed,
And for his sheep he doth us take.

4 O enter ye his gates with thanks,
Within his courts his praise proclaim ;
Be grateful to the source of good ;[3]
For ever bless his holy name.

5 Because the Lord our God is good,[4]
His mercy is for ever sure ;
His truth at all times firmly stood,
And shall from age to age endure.

PSALM C. C.M.

1 O ALL ye lands, unto the Lord
make ye a joyful noise.
2 Serve God with gladness, him before
come, and with praise rejoice.
3 Know that the Lord is God indeed ;
not we, but he us made :
We are his people, and the sheep
within his pasture fed.

4 O enter ye his gates with praise,[1]
his courts with thankfulness ;
To him express your gratitude,
his name together bless.

5 Because the Lord our God is good,
his mercy never ends ;
And down to generations all
his faithfulness extends.

PSALM CI.

1 OF mercy I'll and judgment sing,[1]
I'll sing, O Lord, to thee.
2 With wisdom in a perfect way
shall my behaviour be.

O when, in kindness unto me,
　　wilt thou be pleased to come?
I with a perfect heart will walk
　　within my house at home.

3 I will not cause a wicked thing[2]
　　before mine eyes to be :
Their work who turn aside I hate,
　　it shall not cleave to me.

4 The man who is of froward heart
　　depart quite from me shall ;
A person given to wickedness
　　I will not know at all.

5 I'll cut him off who slandereth[3]
　　his neighbour privily :
I will not bear the haughty heart
　　nor him whose look is high.

6 Upon the faithful of the land
　　mine eyes shall be, that they
May dwell with me : me serve shall he
　　who walks in upright way.

7 The man who practises deceit
　　with me shall never dwell ;
And banish'd from my sight shall be
　　the man who lies doth tell.

8 I'll early to destruction doom
　　the wicked of the land ;
To rid God's city from all those
　　who spurn at his command.

PSALM CII. C.M.

1 O LORD, unto my prayer give ear,
　　my cry let come to thee ;
2 And in the day of my distress
　　hide not thy face from me.
Give ear to me ; what time I call,
　　to answer me make haste :

3 For, as a hearth, my bones are burn'd,
    my days, like smoke, do waste.

4 My heart within me smitten is,
    and it is witherèd
  Like very grass; so that I do
    forget to eat my bread.
5 By reason of my groaning voice
    my bones cleave to my skin.
6 Like pelican in wilderness
    forsaken I have been:

  I like an owl in desert am,
    which there does nightly moan;
7 I watch, and like a sparrow am
    on the house-top alone.
8 From bitter en'mies all the day
    I have reproaches borne;[1]
  And foes, who frantic are with rage,
    to ruin me have sworn.

9 Because I ashes eaten have
    as if they were my bread;
  And largely mingled was my drink
    with tears which I have shed.
10 This grief, alas, comes from thy wrath,[2]
    and thine indignant frown;
   For thou, who once didst lift me up,
    again hast cast me down.

11 My days are like the shadow long,
    which doth declining pass;
   And I'm entirely witherèd,[3]
    ev'n like the very grass.
12 But thou, Jehovah, shalt endure
    to ages without end;
   And thy remembrance also shall[4]
    to endless years extend.

13 Thou shalt arise, and mercy have
    upon thy Sion yet;
   The time to favour her is come,
    the time which thou hast set.
14 For in her rubbish and her stones
    thy servants pleasure take;
   Nay, they regard her very dust
    with favour for her sake.
15 Thus heathen nations rev'rence shall
    Jehovah's holy name;
   And all the kings on earth shall fear
    the glory of thy fame.
16 When Sion by Jehovah's power
    built up again shall be,
   In all his glorious majesty
    to men appear shall he.
17 The prayer of those who helpless are,[5]
    he surely will regard;
   Their prayer he never will despise,
    by him it shall be heard.
18 For generations yet to come
    this shall on record be:[6]
   So shall the Lord be still extoll'd
    by late posterity.
19 He from his sanctuary's height
    has downward cast his eye;
   The Lord beheld the earth from heaven,
    his glorious throne on high.[7]
20 To hear the pris'ner's mournful groan,
    to catch his deep-drawn sigh,
   To raise to freedom those whom men
    appointed have to die.
21 That they in Sion may declare
    Jehovah's holy name,
   And in Jerusalem to all
    his praises may proclaim.

PSALM CII.

22 When people congregated are
    in tribes with one accord,
And kingdoms shall assembled be
    to serve the sovereign Lord.

23 The measure of my strength he has³
    abated in the way,
And he my days hath shortenèd :
24   Thus therefore did I say,
In mid-time of my days, O God,
    O take me not away :
Thy years through endless ages last,
    remote from all decay.

25 The firm foundation of the earth
    thou hast of old time laid ;
The heavens also are the work
    which by thy hands were made.
26 Thou shalt for evermore endure,
    but they shall perish all ;
Yea, every one of them wax old,
    like to a garment, shall :

Thou them shalt as a vesture change,
    and they shall changèd be :
27 But thou the same art, and thy years
    are to eternity.
28 The children of thy servants shall
    continually endure ;
And in thy presence, Lord, their seed
    shall be establish'd sure.

PSALM CII.   L.M.

1 O THOU, Jehovah, hear my prayer,
    And let my cry ascend to thee ;¹
2 In time of my calamity
    O hide not thou thy face from me.
Hear when I call on thee ; that day
    An answer speedily return :

3 My days, like smoke, consume away,
 And, as a hearth, my bones do burn.

4 My heart is wounded very sore,
 And withered, like the grass, does fade:
 And therefore I can mind no more [2]
 To take and eat my daily bread.
5 By reason of my pain within,
 And voice of my most grievous groans,
 My flesh consumèd is, my skin,
 All parch'd, now cleaves unto my bones.

6 To pelican in wilderness,
 To owl in desert, I'm a match;
7 And sparrow-like, companionless,
 I lonely on the house-top watch.
8 Reproach'd by my malicious foes, [3]
 I've all day long to bear their scorn;
 And en'mies, who against me rose,
 As madmen are against me sworn.

9 I've therefore ashes eaten up,
 As if they were my daily bread;
 And with the contents of my cup
 I bitter tears a mixture made.
10 Because thy wrath was not appeased,
 And dreadful indignation's frown: [4]
 For me thou formerly hadst raised,
 And thou again hast cast me down.

11 My days are like the transient shade,
 Which doth declining swiftly pass:
 And me to wither thou hast made,
 Much like the quickly fading grass.
12 But thou, O Lord, shalt still endure,
 From changes all for ever free, [5]
 And to all generations sure
 Shall thy remembrance ever be.

13 Thou shalt arise, and mercy yet
   Thou shalt upon mount Sion have :
   Arrived the period which was set,
   When thou, O Lord, shalt Sion save.
14 Thy saints take pleasure in her stones,
   Her very dust to them is dear.
15 So heathen lands and kingly thrones
   On earth thy glorious name shall fear.
16 Jehovah glorious shall appear,
   When Sion's ruins he repairs.
17 He shall regard and lend his ear
   Unto the needy's humble prayers :
   Th' afflicted's prayer he will not scorn.
18 All times this shall on record be :[6]
   And generations yet unborn
   Shall magnify, Jehovah, thee.
19 He from his holy place look'd down,
   Beheld the earth from heaven on high ;
20 To hear the pris'ner's piteous groan,
   And free those who are doom'd to die :
21 That Sion, and Jerus'lem too,
   God's name and praise may well record,[7]
22 When people and the kingdoms do
   Assemble there to serve the Lord.
23 My strength he weaken'd in the way,
   My days of life he shortenèd.
24 Me let not, O my God, decay
   In mid-time of my life, I said :
   Thy years throughout all ages last.
25 Thou hast of old establishèd
   The earth's foundation firm and fast :
   Thy forming hands the heavens have made.
26 They perish shall, as garments do,
   But thou the same shalt still endure ;
   As vestures, thou shalt change them so ;
   And they shall all be changèd sure :

27 But from all changes thou art free ;
  Thine endless years know no decay.³
28 Thy saints, and their posterity,
  Establish'd shall before thee stay.

PSALM CIII.

1 BLESS, O my soul, the Lord thy God,
  and all which in me is
  Be stirrèd up his holy name
  with praises due to bless.
2 Bless, O my soul, the Lord thy God,
  and not forgetful be
  Of all the gracious benefits
  which he bestows on thee :¹
3 Who doth all thine iniquities
  most graciously forgive :
  Who thy diseases all and pains
  doth heal, and thee relieve :
4 Who doth redeem thy life, that thou
  to death shouldst not go down ;
  Who thee with loving-kindness doth
  and tender mercies crown :
5 Who with abundance of good things
  doth satisfy thy mouth ;
  Whence thou art, as the eagle, fresh
  with renovated youth.
6 God righteous judgment executes
  for all oppressèd ones ;
7 His ways he made to Moses known,
  his acts to Israel's sons.
8 The Lord is merciful, and he
  is gracious ever found ;²
  Long-suffering, and slow to wrath,
  his mercy doth abound.
9 He will not chide continually,
  nor keep his anger still.

10 He dealt not with us, as we sinn'd,
   nor did requite our ill.
11 For as the heaven in its height
   the earth surmounteth far;
   So great to those who fear the Lord
   his tender mercies are:
12 As far as th' east is distant from
   the west, so far has he
   In mercy great removed from us
   all our iniquity.
13 Such pity as a father has
   upon his children dear;
   Like pity shows the Lord to those
   his name who truly fear.
14 For he remembers that we're dust,
   and well our frame he knows.
15 Frail man, his days are but as grass,
   as flower in field he grows:
16 For over it the wind doth pass,
   and it is quickly gone;
   And by the place where late it was
   it shall no more be known.
17 But unto those who fear the Lord,
   his mercy never ends;
   And to their children's children still
   his righteousness extends:
18 To those who keep his covenant,
   and mind from day to day[3]
   The rules of his most just commands
   that they may them obey.
19 Jehovah in the heavens high
   prepared has his throne;[4]
   And the dominion over all
   belongs to him alone.
20 O ye his angels, who excel
   in strength, bless ye the Lord;

Ye who obey what he commands,
    attending to his word.⁵
21 O bless and magnify the Lord ;
    ye glorious hosts of his ;
  Ye ministers, who do fulfil
    whate'er his pleasure is.

22 O bless the Lord, all ye his works,
    with which is richly stored,⁶
  In every place, his kingdom vast.
    My soul, bless thou the Lord.

PSALM CIV.

1 BLESS God, my soul. O Lord my God,
    thou art exceeding great ;
  With honour and with majesty
    thou clothèd art in state.
2 With light, as with a robe, thyself
    thou coverest about ;
  Like far-extending curtain, thou
    the heavens stretchest out.
3 Who does his chambers' high-raised beams
    within the waters lay ;
  Who makes the clouds his chariot make,
    on wing'd winds speeds his way.
4 Who fire his ministers, and winds
    his messengers doth make :
5 Who earth's foundation firm did lay,¹
    that it should never shake.

6 Thou didst it cover with the deep,
    as with a garment spread ;
  The waters standing o'er the hills,
    a shoreless ocean made.²
7 But at the voice of thy rebuke
    they, awe-struck, would not stay ;³
  They at thy thunder's dreadful voice
    did speed their flight away.

8 By mountains and by valleys they[4],
   rush on with thund'ring sound;
Retreating to that very place
   which thou for them didst found.
9 A bound, which they may not transgress,[5]
   is fix'd, Lord, by thy hand,
That waters may no more return
   to overflow the land.

10 He to the valleys sends the springs,
   which run among the hills:
11 All beasts, even asses wild, have drink
   from these refreshing rills.
12 Near them is found the dwelling-place
   of birds of every wing,[6]
Where perch'd among the branches, they
   in strains melodious sing.
13 He from his chambers watereth
   the hills, when they are dried:
By fruits of these thy wondrous deeds,
   the earth is satisfied.
14 He makes for cattle grass to grow,
   he makes the herb to spring
For sustenance of man, that food[8]
   he from the earth may bring;
15 And wine, which to the heart of man
   does cheerfulness impart;
He gives anointing oil, and bread
   which strengtheneth his heart.
16 The trees of God are full of sap;
   the cedars high which stand
On Lebanon, all planted were
   by his almighty hand.
17 Upon their boughs birds of the air
   are taught their nests to make;
As for the stork, the fir-tree she
   doth for her dwelling take.

18 The lofty mountains for wild goats
   a place of refuge be ;
The conies to the craggy rocks,
   their place of safety, flee.
19 He sets in heav'n the moon, thereby
   the seasons to discern :
From him the sun his proper time
   of going down doth learn.
20 Thou darkness mak'st,—'tis night ; then beasts
   of forests creep abroad.
21 The lions young then roar for prey,
   and seek their meat from God.
22 The sun arises, home they flock,
   and in their dens they lie.
23 Man goes to work, his labour he
   does till the evening ply.
24 How manifold, Lord, are thy works !
   by perfect wisdom's rule [9]
Thou every one of them hast made ;
   earth's of thy riches full :
25 So is this great and spacious sea,
   in which things creeping are,
Which number'd cannot be ; and beasts
   both great and small are there.
26 There ships go ; there thou mak'st the great
   leviathan to play.[10]
27 These all wait on thee, to receive
   their food from day to day.
28 Whatever thou on them bestow'st,
   they gather for their food ;
Thine hand thou open'st lib'rally,
   they fillèd are with good.
29 Thou hid'st thy face ; they troubled are,
   thou tak'st their breath away ;
They die, and to their kindred dust
   return again do they.

30 Thou send'st thy quick'ning spirit forth,
    whence rise another race;[11]
And thus by thee renewèd is
    the earth's decayèd face.
31 The glory of the mighty Lord
    for evermore shall stand;[12]
JEHOVAH shall rejoice in all
    the doings of his hand.

32 Th' earth, as affrighted, trembleth all,
    if he on it but look;
If he the mountains only touch,
    they presently do smoke.
33 I'll sing unto the Lord most high,
    so long as I shall live;
So long as I have being, I
    to God will praises give.

34 Of him my meditation shall
    delight to me afford;
I glad for evermore shall be
    in God, my only Lord,
35 Consumed be sinners from the earth,
    let ill men no more be.
O thou my soul, Jehovah bless.
    Praise to the Lord give ye.

PSALM CV.

1 O GIVE unto Jehovah thanks;[1]
    call ye upon his name;
The wondrous doings of his hand
    to people all proclaim.
2 With cheerful voice sing ye to him,
    show forth in psalms his praise;
And let your subject of discourse
    be still his wondrous ways.

3 To glory in his holy name,[2]
    ye people, all accord;

And let the heart of every one
  rejoice who seeks the Lord.
4 The Lord Almighty, and his strength,
  with steadfast hearts seek ye :
  His blessèd and his gracious face
  seek ye continually.
5 To all his many wondrous works
  attentively give heed ;[3]
  His wonders, and the judgments all
  which from his mouth proceed ;
6 O ye his servant, Abr'ham's race,
  who these his works have known ;[4]
  And ye who Jacob's children are,
  whom he chose for his own.
7 He is the high almighty Lord,
  he also is our God ;
  The God whose righteous judgments are
  in all the earth abroad.
8 His cov'nant he remember'd has,
  that it may ever stand :
  To thousand ages he will keep
  his promise and command.[5]
9 Which covenant with Abraham[6]
  most solemnly he made ;
  And unto Isaac, by an oath,
  confirm'd what he had said.
10 And this to Jacob, for a law,
  he did establish sure :
  To Israel for a cov'nant which
  for ever should endure.
11 He said, I Canaan's land will give[7]
  for heritage to you ;
12 While yet they were but strangers there,
  and few, nay, very few :
13 While yet they went from land to land
  without a fix'd abode ;

PSALM CV.

And while through sundry kingdoms they
  were wand'ring far abroad ;
14 He suffer'd none to do them wrong,[8]
  still guarding them in love ;
Yea, he to shield them from all ill,
  did mighty kings reprove.
15 Thus said he, Do not injure those
  who mine anointed be,
Nor do the prophets any harm
  who do belong to me.
16 He call'd for famine on the land,[9]
  he broke the staff of bread :
17 But yet he sent before a man,
  by whom they should be fed ;
Ev'n Joseph, whom unnat'rally
  sell for a slave did they ;
18 Whose feet with fetters they did hurt,
  and who in irons lay ;
19 Until the time when his word came
  to give him liberty ;
When the prophetic word of God
  did him in prison try.
20 Then came the king's command, that he
  no longer bound should be :
He who the people's ruler was
  did send to set him free.
21 To rule his family and court,
  he him appointed lord ;
And gave into his charge the wealth[10]
  throughout his kingdom stored.
22 That he might at his pleasure bind
  the princes of the land ;
And might instruct his senators[11]
  wisdom to understand.
23 The people then of Israel's house
  down into Egypt came ;

And Jacob was a sojourner
   within the land of Ham.
24 And he did greatly by his power
   increase his people there;
And stronger than their enemies
   they by his blessing were.
25 He turn'd their en'mies' hearts to hate[12]
   his people bitterly,
With those who his own servants were
   to deal in subtilty.
26 His servant Moses he did send,
   Aaron his chosen one;
27 By them his signs and wonders great
   in Ham's land were made known.
28 He darkness sent, and made it dark;
   they did his word obey.
29 He turn'd their waters into blood,
   and he their fish did slay.
30 The land in plenty brought forth frogs
   in chambers of their kings.
31 His word all sorts of flies and lice
   in all their borders brings.
32 He hail for rain, and flaming fire
   into their land he sent:
33 He did their vines and fig-trees smite;
   trees of their coasts he rent.
34 He spoke, and caterpillars came,[13]
   much locusts did abound;
35 Consuming in their land all herbs,
   and produce of the ground.
36 He smote all first-born in their land,
   chief of their strength each one.
37 With gold and silver brought them forth,
   weak in their tribes was none.[13]
38 Glad Egypt was, when forth they went,
   their fear on them did light.

39 He spread a cloud for covering,
   and fire to shine by night.
40 They ask'd, and he brought quails : with bread
   of heav'n he fillèd them.
41 He open'd rocks, floods gushing ran
   in deserts like a stream.
42 For on his holy promise he,
   and servant Abr'ham, thought.
43 With joy his people, his elect
   with gladness forth he brought.
44 He for possession gave to them [14]
   the heathen's pleasant lands;
   And added for a heritage
   the labour of their hands.
45 That they the statutes might observe
   recorded in his word;
   And might his holy laws obey.
   Give praise unto the Lord.

PSALM CVI.

1 PRAISE God; O to the Lord give thanks,
     for bountiful is he;
  His tender mercy will endure
     unto eternity.
2 Who utter can God's mighty works?
     who show forth all his praise?
3 They blessèd are who judgment keep,
     and justly do always.

4 Me, Lord, remember with the love [1]
     which thou to thine dost bear;
  With thy salvation, O my God,
     to visit me draw near:
5 That I thy chosen's good may see,
     may in their joy rejoice;
  And may with thine inheritance
     in triumph raise my voice. [2]

6 We with our fathers sinnèd have,
    and of iniquity
We have too long the workers been;
    we have done wickedly.
7 The wond'rous works which thou, O Lord,
    didst do in Egypt land,
Our fathers, though they saw them, yet
    they did not understand:

Thy multitude of mercies they
    kept not in memory;
But at the sea, ev'n the Red sea,
    provoked him grievously.
8 He notwithstanding savèd them,
    even for his own name's sake;
That so he might to be well known
    his power almighty make.[3]

9 When he the Red sea did rebuke,
    then dried its channel was:[4]
Through depths, as through the wilderness,
    he made them safely pass.
10 From hands of him who hated them[5]
    he did his people save;
And from the foe's oppressing hands
    to them redemption gave.
11 The waters overwhelm'd their foes;
    not one was left alive.
12 Then they believed his word, and praise
    to him in songs did give.
13 They quickly did his mighty works[6]
    ungratefully forgot,
Nor on his counsel and his will
    did they with patience wait;

14 But God they much in desert tried,
    nor did their lust control.[7]
15 He gave them their desire, yet sent
    he leanness to their soul.

16 And toward Moses in the camp
    their envy did appear;
At Aaron, servant of the Lord,
    they envious also were.[8]
17 The earth did therefore open wide,[9]
    and Dathan did devour,
And all Abiram's company
    did cover in that hour.
18 Against their rebel company
    a kindled fire was turn'd;[10]
By whose devouring flame to death
    these wicked men were burn'd.
19 A calf-shaped idol they did make[11]
    on Horeb's very hill;
Before a molten image they
    in adoration fell.
20 Thus both their glory, and their God,
    absurdly changèd they
Into the likeness of an ox
    which eateth grass or hay.
21 They soon forget the mighty God,
    who had their saviour been,
By whom so wondrous things perform'd
    they had in Egypt seen.
22 In Ham's land he did wondrous works,
    things terrible did he,
When he did his almighty arm
    stretch out at the Red sea.
23 They therefore had to death been doom'd,
    had not, his wrath to stay,
His chosen Moses interposed,[12]
    that them he should not slay.
24 Yea, they despised the pleasant land,
    believèd not his word:
25 But in their tents they murmurèd,
    not heark'ning to the Lord.

26 In desert, therefore, them to kill [13]
    he lifted up his hand :
27 'Mong nations to o'erthrow their seed,
    and scatter in each land.
28 At Baal's shrine on Peor's hill [14]
    they did for worship meet ;
And victims offer'd to the dead
    they did profanely eat.
29 Thus, by their lewd inventions, they [15]
    his anger did provoke ;
And in upon them suddenly,
    – as fire, the pest'lence broke.
30 Then Phin'has rising, justice did, [16]
    which caused the plague to cease ;
31 This to all ages counted was
    to him for righteousness.
32 And at the waters, where they strove,
    they him did angry make,
To such degree, that it went ill [17]
    with Moses for their sake :
33 Because they there his spirit meek
    did bitterly provoke, [18]
So greatly, that in anger he
    words unadvisèd spoke.
34 Nor, as the Lord commanded them,
    did they the nations slay :
35 But mingling with the people round,
    soon learn'd of them their way.
36 And served their idol gods which did
    a snare unto them turn.
37 To demons they their daughters did,
    and sons, as victims, burn.
38 In their own children's guiltless blood
    their hands they did imbrue,
Whom they to Canaan's idol gods [19]
    for sacrifices slew :

So was the land defiled with blood.
39　They stain'd with their own way,
　　And with their own inventions vile [20]
　　　they did a whoring stray.
40　Against his people therefore was
　　　God's wrath inflamed so sore, [21]
　　That even his own inheritance
　　　he greatly did abhor.
41　He gave them to the heathen's hand;
　　　their foes did them command.
42　Their en'mies them oppress'd, they were
　　　made subject to their hand.
43　He many times deliver'd them;
　　　but with their counsel so
　　They him provoked, that for their sin
　　　they were brought very low.
44　Yet he their suff'rings did regard, [22]
　　　when he did hear their cry:
45　And he for them his covenant
　　　did call to memory;

　　After his mercies' multitude
46　　he did repent: And made
　　Them to be pitied by all those [23]
　　　who had them captive led.
47　Us save, and gather, Lord our God, [24]
　　　the heathen from among,
　　That we thy holy name may praise
　　　in a triumphant song.
48　Bless'd be JEHOVAH, Israel's God,
　　　to all eternity:
　　Let all the people say, Amen.
　　　Praise to the Lord give ye.

PSALM CVII.

1　O GIVE unto Jehovah thanks, [1]
　　　for great his goodness is;

Because his mercy still endures,
   his name with praises bless.
2 Let them say so, whom he redeem'd
   from chains in foreign land ;
Whom he most graciously set free
   from foes' oppressive hand.

3 And gather'd them from distant lands,
   both in the east and west ;
From kingdoms to the north and south,
   where was for them no rest.
4 They wander'd in the wilderness,
   where they could find no way,
No city for a dwelling-place,
   where they in peace might stay.

5 For thirst and hunger in them faints
6   their soul. When straits them press,
They cried unto the Lord, and he
   them freed from their distress.
7 Them also in a way to walk
   which right is he did guide,
That they might to a city go,
   in which they might abide.

8 O that men to the Lord would give
   praise for his goodness then,
And for his works of wonder done
   unto the sons of men !
9 For he the fainting longing soul
   doth fully satisfy ;
With goodness he the hungry soul
   doth fill abundantly.

10 The men who sit in darkness deep,
   and in death's shade abide,
Whom troubles great have strongly bound,
   and irons fast have tied :
11 Because against the word of God
   they wrought rebelliously,

And since they scorn'd the counsel wise
   of him who is most High:
12 Their haughty heart he therefore brought ²
      with grief and labour down;
   Bereft of strength they prostrate fell;
      to help them there was none.
13 Then in their trouble to the Lord
      they did their cry address;
   And he to them a Saviour was
      from all their sore distress.

14 By him they were from darkness brought,
      from death deliv'rance found;
   And he asunder broke the bands
      with which they had been bound. ³
15 O that men to the Lord would give
      praise for his goodness then,
   And for his works of wonder done
      unto the sons of men!

16 Because the massive gates of brass ⁴
      he did in pieces tear,
   By him asunder also cut
      the bars of iron were.
17 For sin, and for iniquities,
      fools sore affliction bear;
18 Abhorring every kind of food:
      to death's gates they draw near.

19 In grief they cry to God; he saves
      them from their miseries.
20 He sends his word, them heals, and them
      from their destructions frees.
21 O that men to the Lord would give
      praise for his goodness then,
   And for his works of wonder done
      unto the sons of men!

22 Thank-off'rings too let them to him
    present in sacrifice ;[5]
  And let them show abroad his works
    in songs with thankful voice.
23 The men who go to sea in ships,
    and foreign traders be,
24 Behold, while on the deep, God's works,
    and there his wonders see.
25 For he commands, and forth in haste
    the raging tempest flies,
  Which makes the sea with swelling waves
    in foamy mountains rise.[6]
26 They mount to heav'n, then deep are plunged
    amid the yawning wave ;
  Their souls, with trouble melting, deem
    each surge a watery grave.
27 They reel and stagger like one drunk,
    at their wit's end they be :
28 Then they in trouble cry to God,[7]
    who them from straits doth free.
29 The storm is changed into a calm
    when such his sovereign will ;[8]
  So that the waves, which raged before,
    now silent are and still.
30 Then glad are they, because at length
    they now in stillness be ;
  So them he to the haven brings,
    which they much long'd to see.
31 O that men to the Lord would give
    praise for his goodness then,
  And for his works of wonder done
    unto the sons of men !
32 Let them in the assemblies great
    exalt his glorious name ;
  Amid assembled elders spread
    his most renownèd fame.

33 He streams turns into wilderness,
   to deserts water-springs;⁹
34 O'er fruitful lands, for wickedness,
   sterility he brings.
35 He turns to pools the wilderness,
   long waterless and burn'd;
   By him the ground, dried up before,
   to water-springs is turn'd.
36 And there, for dwelling, he a place
   doth to the hungry give,
   That they may cities build in which¹⁰
   they may with comfort live;
37 And that from fruitful fields and vines¹¹
   rich stones may never cease.
38 His blessing multiplies themselves,
   nor lets their stock decrease.
39 Again they are diminishèd,
   again brought very low,
   Through sorrow and the train of ills¹²
   which from oppression flow.
40 He upon princes pours contempt,
   and causes them to stray,
   Far off amid the wilderness,
   in which there is no way.
41 Yet setteth he the poor on high
   from all his miseries,
   And he, like an increasing flock,
   doth make him families.
42 The righteous, when they this behold,¹³
   shall very joyful be;
   And, as ashamèd, stop her mouth
   shall all iniquity.
43 Whoso is wise, and will these things
   observe, and them record,
   Even they shall understand the love
   and kindness of the Lord.

PSALM CVIII.

1 MY heart is fix'd, Lord; I will sing,
    I'll with my glory praise.
2 Awake both psaltery and harp;
    myself I'll early raise.
3 O Lord, among the people I
    will praise thy holy name;[1]
  And I, among the nations all,
    thy praises all proclaim.
4 For great thy tender mercy is,
    above the heavens high;
  Aloft thy faithfulness doth reach
    unto the very sky.
5 Be thou, O God, above the heav'ns[2]
    exalted gloriously;
  Thy glory above all the earth
    be lifted up on high.
6 That thy belovèd people may
    from ills deliver'd be,
  Salvation bring with thy right hand,
    and answer give to me.
7 God in his holiness hath said,—[3]
    ne'er will his promise fail;
  I Shechem will divide; my line
    will measure Succoth's vale.
8 I Gilead claim as mine by right;
    Manasseh mine shall be;
  While Ephraim is my tower of strength;
    laws Judah gives for me;
9 I'll Moab make my slave; my shoe
    I'll over Edom throw;
  And over Palestina's land
    I will in triumph go.
10 O who will kindly bring me to
    the city fortified?
  O who to Idumea's land
    will deign to be my guide?

11 O God, who hast rejected us,
    this thing wilt thou not do?
  And wilt not thou, ev'n thou, O God,
    forth with our armies go?
12 Do thou from trouble give us help,
    for vain is human aid.
13 Through God we shall do valiantly;
    he shall our foes down tread.

PSALM CIX.

1 O GOD, to whom address'd my praise,
    do thou not hold thy peace;
2 For mouths of wicked men to speak
    against me do not cease:
  The lips of vile deceitful men
    against me open'd be;
  And they with falsehood in their tongue [1]
    have been accusing me.
3 These slanderers beset me round [2]
    with words of hateful spite; [3]
  And though I gave to them no cause,
    they did against me fight.
4 They for my love became my foes,
    but I me set to pray.
5 They ill for good, and for my love, [4]
    they hatred did repay.
6 Set thou the wicked over him;
    and upon his right hand
  Let Satan, as accusing foe,
    permission have to stand.
7 When he before thee shall be judged,
    let him condemnèd be;
  And let his prayer be turn'd to sin,
    if he shall call on thee.
8 Few be his days, and in his room
    his charge another take.
9 His children let be fatherless,
    his wife a widow make.

10 His children let be vagabonds,
   and beg continually;
 Let them from places desolate
   seek bread for their supply.
11 Let covetous extortioners
   snatch all he has away:
 And let the fruit of all his toil
   to strangers be a prey.
12 Let there be none to pity him,
   let there be none at all
 Who to his children fatherless
   extend his mercy shall.
13 Let all his offspring from the earth
   cut off for ever be;
 In coming ages let their name
   be blotted out by thee.
14 Let God his father's wickedness
   into remembrance call;
 And never let his mother's sin
   be blotted out at all.
15 Before Jehovah let them still
   appear continually,
 That he may wholly from the earth
   cut off their memory.
16 For mercy he forgot to show,
   but persecuted still
 The poor and needy, that he might
   the broken-hearted kill.
17 As cursing was to him delight,
   let curses on him fall;
 As he no joy in blessing had,
   him never bless at all.
18 As he put cursing on as clothes,
   into his bowels so,
 As water, and into his bones,
   as oil, down let it go.

PSALM CIX.

19 Let cursing cover him as robes
   which clothe the body round;
And as the girdle is with which
   he constantly is bound.
20 From God be this reward to those
   who en'mies are to me,
To those also who speak against
   my soul maliciously.
21 But be a friend, O God the Lord,
   for thy name's sake to me;
Since bountiful thy mercy is,
   from trouble set me free.
22 For I am indigent and poor,
   I am afflicted sore,[6]
Nor in my deeply wounded heart
   is soundness any more.
23 I pass like a declining shade,
   am like the locust tost:
24 Through fasting weaken'd are my knees,
   my flesh has fatness lost.
25 I also from mine enemies
   have sore reproaches borne;
And those who at me cast a look
   did shake their heads in scorn.
26 O thou, who art the Lord my God,
   to me a helper be:[7]
According to thy mercy great
   deliv'rance grant to me.
27 That they thereby may know that this
   is thine almighty hand;
And that thou, Lord, hast done this deed[8]
   they well may understand.
28 Though they delight to curse, yet, Lord,
   bless thou with friendly voice:
Let them, when they arise, be shamed;[9]
   thy servant let rejoice.

29 Let thou mine adversaries all
    be clothed throughout with shame ;[10]
And, as a mantle, let their own
    confusion cover them.

30 But as for me, I with my mouth
    will greatly praise the Lord ;
Yea, I among the multitude
    his praises will record.

31 For God will be a shield to him[11]
    who is in poverty,
To save him from all those who would
    condemn his soul to die.

PSALM CX.

1 JEHOVAH said unto my Lord,
    Sit thou at my right hand,
Until I make thy foes a stool
    on which thy feet may stand.[1]

2 Jehovah shall from Sion send
    the rod of thy great power :
In midst of all thine enemies
    be thou the governor.

3 A willing people in thy day
    of power shall come to thee,
In holy beauties from morn's womb ;
    thy youth like dew shall be.

4 The Lord hath sworn, nor will repent,
    I thee a priest ordain,[2]
Of th' order of Melchisedec
    for ever to remain.

5 The glorious and mighty Lord,
    who sits at thy right hand,
Shall, in his day of wrath, strike through
    the kings who him withstand.[3]

6 He shall among the heathen judge,
    he shall with bodies dead

The places fill : o'er many lands
 he wound shall every head.
7 The brook which runneth in the way [4]
 with drink shall him supply;
 And therefore he in triumph shall
 lift up his head on high.

PSALM CXI.

1 PRAISE ye the Lord : with my whole heart
 God's praise I will declare,
 Where the assemblies of the just
 and congregations are.
2 The whole works of Jehovah are
 above all measure great,
 Sought out they are by all who love
 on them to meditate.[1]
3 His work most honourable is,
 most glorious and pure,
 And his untainted righteousness
 for ever doth endure.
4 His works of wonder he hath made
 still to be kept in mind;
 The Lord is gracious, and he is
 compassionate and kind.[2]
5 He giveth meat unto all those
 who truly do him fear;
 And evermore his covenant
 he will in mem'ry bear.
6 The power of his amazing works [3]
 he to his people show'd,
 When he on them for heritage
 the heathen's land bestow'd.
7 His works are righteousness and truth :[4]
 all his commands are sure :
8 And, done in truth and uprightness,
 they evermore endure.

9 His people he redemption gave ;[5]
   laws evermore the same,
  A cov'nant too ;—thrice holy is,
   and reverend is his name.

10 The spring of wisdom is God's fear:
   to walk in righteous ways
  Is proof of understanding good ;
   eternal is his praise.[6]

PSALM CXII.

1 PRAISE ye the Lord. The man is bless'd
   who fears the Lord aright,
  And who does his commandments pure[1]
   account his chief delight.

2 His offspring raised to signal power
   shall be upon the earth :[2]
  And bless'd the children who derive
   from upright men their birth.

3 Abundant wealth shall ever be[3]
   within his house in store ;
  And his unspotted righteousness
   endures for evermore.

4 Unto the upright doth arise,
   amid the darkness, light ;
  He gracious is, and merciful,
   and follows what is right.[4]

5 A good man doth his favour show,
   and doth to others lend :
  He with discretion his affairs
   will guide unto the end.

6 There surely is not any thing
   which him shall ever move :[5]
  The righteous man's memorial
   shall everlasting prove.

7 Though he should evil tidings hear,
   he shall not be afraid :

His heart is fix'd, his confidence
    upon Jehovah stay'd.
8 His heart is firmly stablishèd,
    afraid he shall not be,
Until upon his enemies
    he his desire shall see.

9 He has dispersed, given to the poor;
    his righteousness shall be
To ages all; with honour shall
    his horn be raisèd high.
10 The wicked shall it see, and fret,
    his teeth gnash, melt away:
What wicked men do most desire
    shall utterly decay.

PSALM CXIII.

1 O GIVE ye praises to the Lord,[1]
    Jehovah's praise proclaim;
Ye servants of the Lord, do ye
    extol God's holy name.
2 O blessèd be Jehovah's name
    with joyful songs of praise,
Extending from the present time
    to everlasting days.

3 Ev'n from the rising of the sun
    unto his going down,
O let the praises of God's name
    be spread from town to town.
4 Above all nations of the earth,
    the mighty Lord is high;
And high his glory does extend
    unto the very sky.

5 Who's like unto the Lord our God,[2]
    whose dwelling is on high?
6 Yet deigns on things in heaven and earth
    to cast a gracious eye.

7 He raises from the dust the poor,[3]
   who low in sorrow lie;
 And from the dunghill lifts the man
   borne down with poverty;
8 That he may highly him advance,
   and may with princes set:
 With those who o'er his people have
   the power of princes great.
9 The barren woman house to keep
   he maketh, and to be
 Of sons a mother full of joy.
   Praise to the Lord give ye.

PSALM CXIV.

1 WHEN Israel out of Egypt went,
   his dwelling-place did change,
 And Jacob's house went out from those
   who were of language strange.
2 He Judah did his sanctuary,
   his kingdom Israel make:
3 The sea beheld, and quickly fled,
   Jordan was driven back.
4 The mountains from their seats were toss'd,
   as skip the bounding rams;
 And lightly leap'd the little hills,
   as bound the sportive lambs.
5 What power convulsed thee, O thou sea,
   that thou swift flight didst take?
 What, Jordan, drove thy swelling stream
   a backward course to make?
6 O wherefore did ye, mountains great,
   skip lightly, as do rams?
 And why did ye, O little hills,
   bound as do sportive lambs?
7 O at the presence of the Lord,
   earth, tremble thou for fear,

Whene'er the presence of the God¹
of Jacob doth appear :
8 Who from the hard and stony rock
did pools of water bring ;
Who by his power did turn the flint
into a water-spring.

PSALM CXV.

1 NO praise to us, Lord, none to us,¹
but do thou glory take
Unto thy name, ev'n for thy truth,
and for thy mercy's sake.
2 O wherefore should the heathen say,²
Where, where is now their God ?
3 Our God, who what him pleased has done,
in heav'n is his abode.
4 Their idols silver are and gold,
work of men's hands they be.
5 Mouths have they, but they cannot speak ;
and eyes, but cannot see ;
6 Ears have they, but they do not hear ;
noses, but savour not ;
7 Hands, feet, but handle not, nor walk ;
nor speak they through their throat.
8 Their makers like them are, and all
who on their help depend.³
9 O Israel, trust in God, thy help,
and who will thee defend.
10 Trust in the Lord, O Aaron's house,
their help and shield is he.
11 Trust in the Lord, ye fearing God,
their help and shield he 'll be.
12 The Lord of us has mindful been,
he 'll surely bless us still :
He will the house of Israel bless,
bless Aaron's house he will.

13 Both small and great, who fear the Lord,
   he will most surely bless.⁴
14 The Lord will you, you and your seed,
   still more and more increase.
15 O blessèd are you by the Lord,
   who made the earth and heav'n.
16 The heav'n, the heav'ns, are God's, but he
   th' earth to men's sons has giv'n.
17 The dead, and those in silent dust,⁵
   do not God's praise record.
18 But we henceforth for ever will
   bless God. Praise ye the Lord.

PSALM CXVI.

1 I LOVE the Lord, because my voice
   and prayers he deign'd to hear.
2 I, while I live, will call on him
   who bow'd to me his ear.
3 Death's overpowering sorrows did¹
   me sore distress'd surround;
   The pains of hell took hold on me,
   I grief and trouble found.
4 Then call'd I on Jehovah's name;²
   to him thus was my speech:
   Deliver thou my soul, O Lord,
   I humbly thee beseech.
5 God merciful and righteous is,
   yea, gracious is our Lord.
6 God saves the meek : I was brought low,
   he help did me afford.
7 O thou my soul, do thou return
   unto thy wonted rest;
   Because Jehovah largely thee³
   has with his bounty bless'd.
8 For my distressèd soul from death
   deliver'd was by thee:

Thou didst my weeping eyes from tears,
   my feet from falling, free.

9 So long as I have strength and life,[4]
   I'll walk the Lord before.
10 I did believe, I therefore spoke :[5]
   I was afflicted sore.
11 I said, when I was in my haste,
   that all men faithless be.
12 What shall I render to the Lord
   for all his gifts to me?
13 I'll joyful take salvation's cup,[6]
   on God's name I will call :
14 I'll pay my vows now to the Lord
   before his people all.
15 In God's sight precious his saints' death.
16   Thy servant, Lord, am I ;
   Thy servant and thy handmaid's son :[7]
   my bands thou didst untie.

17 Thank-off'rings I'll to thee present,
   I on the Lord will call,
18 I'll pay my vows now to the Lord
   before his people all ;
19 Within the courts of God's own house,
   and in the midst of thee,
  O city of Jerusalem.
   Praise to the Lord give ye.

PSALM CXVII.

1 O ALL ye nations of the earth,
   give praise unto the Lord ;[1]
  To magnify his holy name,
   ye people, all accord.
2 For great are always toward us [2]
   his loving-kindnesses :
  His truth endures for evermore.
   Jehovah do ye bless.

PSALM CXVIII.

1 O PRAISE the Lord, for he is good;[1]
   his mercy's ever sure.
2 His mercy now, let Israel say,
   does evermore endure.
3 His mercy, say, O Aaron's house,
   does evermore endure.
4 Let all who fear the Lord now say,
   His mercy's ever sure.

5 I in distress call'd on the Lord;
   the Lord me answer gave:
He in a large place did me set,
   from trouble did me save.
6 The mighty Lord is on my side,
   I will not be afraid;
For anything which man can do,
   why should I be dismay'd?

7 Jehovah takes my part with those
   who help to succour me:
I therefore my desire on those[2]
   who do me hate shall see.
8 To trust in God is better far[3]
   than trust in man's defence;
9 Far better trust in God than make
   princes our confidence.

10 Confederate nations compass'd me
   with purpose to annoy:[4]
But in Jehovah's holy name
   I shall them all destroy.
11 These enemies encompass'd me,[5]
   me straitly did enclose:
But in Jehovah's name I'll bring
   destruction on these foes.
12 Like swarming bees they compass'd me;
   like thorns which fiercely flame
They quenchèd are: for I'll destroy
   them in Jehovah's name.

13 To cause my fall, thou sore hast thrust,
   but God assisted me.⁶
14 Jehovah my salvation is,
   my strength and song is he.
15 In dwellings of the righteous still ⁷
   is heard the melody
   Of joy and health : the Lord's right hand
   doth ever valiantly.
16 The right hand of the mighty Lord
   exalted is on high ;
   The right hand of the mighty Lord
   doth ever valiantly ;
17 I shall not die, but live, and shall ⁸
   God's works to others show.
18 The Lord has me chastisèd sore,
   but not in death laid low.
19 O set ye open unto me
   the gates of righteousness ;
   I will rejoicing enter them,
   and will Jehovah bless.
20 This is the gate of God, by which
   the righteous shall go in.
21 I'll praise thee, for thou heard'st me ; thou
   hast my salvation been.
22 The stone is made head corner-stone,
   which builders did despise :
23 This is the doing of the Lord ;
   'tis wondrous in our eyes.
24 In this day, glorious made by God,
   we'll joy triumphantly.
25 Save now, I pray thee, Lord ; I pray,
   send now prosperity.
26 Bless'd he who in Jehovah's name ⁹
   now cometh us to save :
   We, from the house which to the Lord
   pertains, you blessèd have.

27 God is the Lord, who made to us
    this joyful light to rise:
  Bind ye unto the altar's horns
    with cords the sacrifice.
28 Thou art my God, I'll thee exalt;
    my God, I thee will praise.
29 Give thanks to God, for he is good:
    his mercy lasts always.

PSALM CXIX.

ALEPH. *The 1st Part.*

1 BLESSED are they who undefiled,[1]
    and straight are in the way;
  Who in the Lord's most holy law
    do walk, and do not stray.
2 Blessèd are they who do not from[2]
    his statutes' way depart;
  And who do seek the living God
    with all their mind and heart.

3 Such in his ways do walk, and they
    do no iniquity.
4 Thou hast commanded us to keep
    thy precepts carefully.
5 O that thy statutes to observe
    thou wouldst my ways direct!
6 Then shall I not be shamed, when I
    thy precepts all respect.

7 Then with integrity of heart
    I'll thee with praises bless,[3]
  When I have learn'd the judgments all
    of thy pure righteousness.
8 To keep thy righteous precepts all
    I will my study make:[4]
  O do not then, most gracious God,
    me utterly forsake.

PSALM CXIX.

BETH. *The 2d Part.*

9 By what means shall a young man learn
      to purify his way?⁵
    If he the precepts of thy word
      attentively obey.
10 I thee unfeignedly have sought⁶
      with all my soul and heart:
    O let me not from the right path
      of thy commands depart.
11 Thy word I in my heart have stored,⁷
      that I offend not thee.
12 Thou, O Jehovah, blessèd art,
      thy statutes teach thou me.
13 The judgments of thy mouth each one
      my lips declarèd have:
14 More joy thy testimonies' way
      than riches all me gave.
15 I will thy holy precepts all
      my meditation make;⁸
    And all thy ways, as perfect rules,
      I as my guides will take.
16 Upon thy statutes my delight
      shall still be chiefly set:
    And, by thy grace, I never will
      thy holy word forget.

GIMEL. *The 3d Part.*

17 With me thy servant, in thy grace,
      deal bountifully, Lord;
    That by thy favour I may live,
      and keep with care thy word.
18 Open mine eyes, that in thy law
      I wondrous things may see.
19 I am a stranger in the earth,
      hide not thy laws from me.
20 My soul within me breaks, and does
      much fainting still endure,

Through longing which it always has
  unto thy judgments pure.
21 Thou hast rebuked the cursèd proud,
  who from thy precepts stray.
22 Reproach and shame remove from me,
  for I thy laws obey.

23 Against me did the princes speak,⁹
  while they in council sat :
  But I thy servant did upon
  thy statutes meditate.
24 The sources of my chief delight,
  thy testimonies be ;
  And they, in all my vexing doubts,
  are counsellors to me.

DALETH. *The 4th Part.*

25 I to the dust cleave : quicken me
  according to thy word.
26 I've shown my ways, and me thou heardst :
  me teach thy statutes, Lord.
27 The way of thy commandments pure ¹⁰
  make me aright to know ;
  So all thy many wondrous works
  I shall to others show.

28 My vexèd spirit sinks beneath
  the burden of my grief :
  To me, according to thy word,
  give strength, and send relief.
29 The way of false and guileful words,
  do thou remove from me ;¹¹
  The wish and power to keep thy law,
  O grant me graciously.

30 The perfect way of truth divine
  I for my choice have made :¹²
  Thy judgments, which most righteous are,
  I have before me laid.

31 I to thy testimonies cleave ;
   Lord, keep me from disgrace.[13]
32 When thou enlargèd hast my heart,
   I'll run thy precepts' ways.

He. *The 5th Part.*

33 O Lord, instruct me in the way
   of thy precepts divine ;
   To keep it to the end of life[14]
   I shall my heart incline.
34 Give understanding unto me,
   so keep thy law shall I ;
   Yea, ev'n with my whole heart I shall
   observe it carefully.

35 In thy law's path make me to go ;
   for I delight therein.
36 My heart unto thy statutes, Lord,[15]
   and not to greed, incline.
37 Turn thou away my wand'ring eyes[16]
   from viewing vanity ;
   And be thou pleased to quicken me
   while walking in thy way.

38 To me confirm thy gracious word,
   which I did gladly hear ;
   To me, thy servant, Lord, who am
   devoted to thy fear.
39 Turn thou away my fear'd reproach ;
   for good thy judgments be.
40 Lo, I have for thy precepts long'd ;
   in thy truth quicken me.

Vau. *The 6th Part.*

41 Let thy sweet mercies also come
   to visit me, O Lord ;
   Let thy benign salvation come,[17]
   according to thy word.

42 So shall I furnish'd be with means
    to give an answer just
  To him who casts reproach on me ;
    for in thy word I trust.

43 O take not quite out of my mouth [18]
    thy true and faithful word ;
  For on thy righteous judgments I
    have placed my trust, O Lord.

44 So shall I keep for evermore
    thy law continually.
45 And since thy precepts pure I seek, [19]
    I'll walk at liberty.

46 I'll speak thy word to kings, and I
    shall not with shame be moved ;
47 And always will delight myself [20]
    in thy laws, which I loved.
48 Thy loved commandments to obey, [21]
    my hands employ I will ;
  And will with pleasure meditate
    upon thy statutes still.

ZAIN. *The 7th Part.*

49 The promise keep in mind, which thou
    didst to thy servant make, [22]
  The word which, Lord, as ground of hope,
    thou causedst me to take.
50 This word of thine my comfort is
    in mine affliction great : [23]
  For it alone revives my soul
    in each perplexing strait.
51 The men whose hearts with pride are fill'd, [24]
    did greatly me deride ;
  Yet from the way of thy commands
    I have not turn'd aside.
52 The judgments which thou didst, O Lord,
    in bygone ages give, [25]

I did remember, and from them
  much comfort did receive.
53 Me horror seized, for wicked men
  thy righteous law forsake.
54 I in my house of pilgrimage
  my songs thy statutes make.
55 Thy laws I kept, and, Lord, thy name,
  I call'd to mind by night,
56 And as I kept thy word with care,[26]
  it yields me this delight.

CHETH. *The 8th Part.*

57 Thou art alone the portion sure
  which I did choose, O Lord:
I've solemnly declared that I
  would keep thy holy word.
58 With my whole heart I did entreat
  in prayer thy favour free:[27]
According to thy gracious word
  be merciful to me.
59 Reflecting on my former ways,
  I did my life well try;
And to thy testimonies pure
  my feet then turnèd I.
60 I lost not by delay the time,
  as those who slothful are;
But quickly thy commands to keep
  I did myself prepare.
61 Though bands of wicked men me robb'd,
  I ne'er thy law did slight.
62 I'll rise at midnight thee to praise,
  for all thy judgments right.
63 I'm a companion of all those
  who fear thee, and obey.
64 O Lord, thy mercy fills the earth;
  me teach thy laws, I pray.[28]

TETH. *The 9th Part.*

65 Well hast thou with thy servant dealt,
   as thou didst promise give;
66 Good judgment me, and knowledge teach,
   for I thy word believe.
67 Ere I afflicted was, I stray'd;
   but now I keep thy word.
68 Both good thou art, and good thou dost:
   Me teach thy statutes, Lord.
69 The men whose minds are filled with pride,[29]
   against me forged a lie;
   Yet thy commandments all obey
   with my whole heart will I.
70 Through worldly ease and wealth their hearts
   like grease in fatness be:[30]
   But in thy holy law I take
   delight continually.
71 It fruitful was of good to me
   that I afflicted was,
   That I the knowledge might acquire[31]
   of all thy holy laws.
72 The word proceeding from thy mouth
   is better far to me
   Than many thousands and great sums
   of gold and silver be.

JOD. *The 10th Part.*

73 Teach me, the creature of thy hands,
   to know thy precepts, Lord.
74 Those fearing thee shall joy to see
   me trusting in thy word.
75 That righteous are thy judgments, Lord,
   I know, and do confess;
   And that my troubles have been sent
   by thee in faithfulness.
76 O let thy kindness merciful,
   I pray thee, comfort me,

As to thy servant faithfully
  was promisèd by thee.
77 And let thy tender mercies come
  to me, that I may live;
Because supreme delight to me
  thy holy precepts give.³²

78 Be shame the portion of the proud;
  for they, without a cause,
With me perversely dealt: but I
  will muse upon thy laws.
79 Let those who fear thee, and have known
  thy statutes, turn to me.
80 Sound in thy statutes be my heart,
  that shamed I may not be.³³

CAPH. *The 11th Part.*

81 My soul for thy salvation faints:
  yet I thy word believe.
82 Mine eyes fail for thy word: when wilt
  thou consolation give?
83 For like a bottle I'm become,
  which in the smoke is set:³⁴
Though black, and shrunk with grief; yet I
  thy laws do not forget.

84 How many are thy servant's days?³⁵
  when will thy hand uproot
In judgment just the wicked men
  who do me persecute?
85 The proud have diggèd pits for me,
  thus trampling on thy laws.³⁶
86 All faithful are thy words: help me,
  pursued without a cause.

87 They so oppress'd me, that on earth
  my life they scarce did leave:
Thy precepts yet forsook I not,
  but close to them did cleave.

88 After thy loving-kindness, Lord,
    preserve and quicken me :
  So of the words which thou didst speak,[37]
    I shall observant be.

LAMED.   *The 12th Part.*

89 Thy word for ever is, O Lord,
    in heaven settled fast ;
90 And unto generations all[38]
    thy faithfulness doth last :
  Thou hast establishèd the earth,
    and it abides by thee.
91 All things remain as thou ordain'dst ;[39]
    for all thy servants be.
92 Unless in thy most perfect law
    my soul had found delight,
  I surely should have perishèd,[40]
    in trouble's dismal night.
93 Thy precepts I will ne'er forget ;
    they quick'ning to me brought.
94 Lord, I am thine ; me save, because[41]
    thy precepts I have sought.

95 The wicked have for me laid wait,
    me seeking to destroy :
  But I thy testimonies all
    consider will with joy.
96 Perfection's very end and height[42]
    I here have seen, O God :
  But as for thy commandment pure,
    it is exceeding broad.

MEM.   *The 13th Part.*

97 O how love I thy laws ! they are
    my study all the day :
98 They make me wiser than my foes ;
    for still they with me stay.

99 Than all my teachers now I have
    more understanding far ;
  For oft the subject of my thoughts [43]
    thy testimonies are.

100 In understanding I excel
    the elders of the land ; [44]
  Because in all my deeds I strive
    to follow thy command.
101 From every evil I've refrain'd,
    that I may keep thy word.
102 I have not from thy judgments swerved ;
    for thou hast taught me, Lord.

103 How sweet unto my taste, O Lord,
    are all thy words of truth !
  I find them to be sweeter far
    than honey to my mouth.
104 I through thy precepts, as my guide, [45]
    do understanding get ;
  I therefore each deceitful way
    with all my heart do hate.

Nun. *The 14th Part.*

105 Thy word is to my feet a lamp,
    and to my path a light.
106 I've made an oath, which I'll perform, [46]
    to keep thy judgments right.
107 I am with tribulation sore [47]
    quite overwhelm'd, O Lord :
  In mercy raise and quicken me
    according to thy word.

108 The free-will off'rings of my mouth
    accept, I thee beseech :
  And unto me, thy servant, Lord,
    thy judgments clearly teach.
109 Though still my life be in my hand, [48]
    thy laws I'll not forget.

110 I stray'd not from them, though for me
    the wicked snares did set.

111 Thy precepts are above all things [49]
    the object of my choice,
To be my endless heritage;
    for they my heart rejoice.

112 Depending on thy help, I strove [50]
    my heart and thoughts to bend;
That I thy statutes may obey
    till life itself shall end.

SAMECH. *The 15th Part.*

113 I hate the thoughts of vanity,
    but love thy laws, O Lord.
114 Thou art my shield and hiding-place:
    I rest upon thy word.
115 Ye workers of iniquity, [51]
    from me far hence depart;
For to obey my God's commands
    I've purposed in my heart.

116 Be thou, according to thy word,
    a sure support to me,
That I may live, and of my hope
    ashamèd never be.

117 Hold thou me up, and I shall be
    in perfect safety still;
And to thy statutes have respect
    continually I will.

118 Thou trodden in the dust hast all [52]
    who from thy precepts stray;
For thou hast made themselves to feel
    the falsehood of their way.

119 The wicked thou hast cast like dross,
    from this and other lands;
I therefore more intensely love
    and value thy commands.

120 For fear of thee my very flesh
　　doth tremble, all dismay'd;
　And of thy righteous judgments, Lord,
　　my soul is much afraid.

AIN. *The 16th Part.*

121 I judgment have, and justice done,
　　by giving each his right;[53]
　Then leave me not a prey unto
　　my fierce oppressors' might.
122 For good unto thy servant, Lord,
　　a friendly surety be:
　From the oppression of the proud
　　do thou deliver me.
123 Mine eyes do fail with looking long
　　for thy salvation, Lord,[54]
　While waiting with enfeebled hope
　　upon thy righteous word.
124 Thy statutes to thy servant teach,[55]
　　thy wonted mercy show;
125 To me, thy servant, wisdom give,
　　that I thy laws may know.

126 'Tis time to work, Lord; for they have[56]
　　made void thy law divine.
127 I therefore love thy precepts more
　　than gold, yea, gold most fine.
128 I therefore judge all thy commands
　　to be entirely right,[57]
　And every false and wicked way
　　is hateful in my sight.

PE. *The 17th Part.*

129 Since wonderful thy statutes, Lord,
　　my soul them keeps with care.
130 The entrance of thy words gives light,
　　makes wise who simple are.

131 My mouth I open'd wide, and with
  much earnestness did pant;⁵⁸
 I long'd to know thy perfect laws,
  O satisfy this want.

132 Look on me, Lord, and merciful
  do thou unto me prove,
 As thou art wont to do to those
  who thee sincerely love.
133 O let my footsteps in thy word
  still rightly order'd be:
 Let no iniquity obtain
  dominion over me.

134 From man's oppression set me free;
  so keep thy laws I will.
135 Thy face make on thy servant shine;
  me teach thy statutes still.
136 The tears in rivers from mine eyes⁵⁹
  run down, while sad I see
 The wicked trampling on thy law
  without all fear of thee.

          TSADDI.   *The 18th Part.*
137 Thou righteous art, and upright are⁶⁰
  thy judgments all, O Lord;
138 Most faithful too, and righteous are
  the precepts of thy word.
139 My zeal has ev'n consumèd me,
  because mine enemies
 Thy holy words forgotten have,
  and do thy laws despise.
140 Since very pure thy word, on it⁶¹
  thy servant's love is set.
141 Nor do I, though despised and small,
  thy precepts pure forget.
142 Thy righteousness is righteousness
  which ever doth endure :

PSALM CXIX.

    Thy law, by thee establish'd, is
      the very truth most pure.
143 Sore trouble and excessive grief[62]
      have taken hold on me:
    Yet my delight and main support
      thy just commandments be.
144 Eternal righteousness is in
      thy testimonies all:
    Give understanding unto me,
      and ever live I shall.

Koph. *The 19th Part.*

145 I cried with my whole heart, Lord, hear;
      thy word I will obey.
146 To thee I cried; me save, and I
      will always keep thy way.[63]
147 Before the dawn I raised to thee
      my supplicating cry;
    For all mine expectation still[64]
      did on thy word rely.
148 Mine eyes did timeously prevent
      the watches of the night,
    That on thy word with pious care
      then meditate I might.
149 Hear, in the kindness of thy love,
      my voice, which calls on thee:
    According to thy judgment, Lord,
      be pleased to quicken me.[65]
150 The mischievous beset me round,[66]
      they from thy law are far:
151 But thou art near, O Lord; and truth
      all thy commandments are.
152 As for thy testimonies all,
      this I of old have tried,
    That thou hast surely founded them
      for ever to abide.

RESH. *The 20th Part.*

153 Consider mine affliction great,[67]
    and me in safety set;
    Deliver me, O Lord, for I
    thy laws do not forget.
154 After thy word revive thou me;
    me save, and plead my cause.
155 Salvation is from sinners far;
    for they seek not thy laws.

156 O Lord, both great and manifold
    thy tender mercies be:
    According to thy judgments just,
    be pleased to quicken me.
157 My persecutors many are,
    and foes who me malign;
    Yet from thy testimonies pure
    my heart doth not decline.

158 I saw transgressors, and was grieved;
    for they keep not thy word.
159 See how I love thy law! as thou
    art kind, me quicken, Lord.
160 Thy word from the beginning has
    been only truth most pure:
    Thy righteous judgments every one
    for evermore endure.

SCHIN. *The 21st Part.*

161 Though princes have without a cause
    me persecuted, Lord;
    Yet still my heart doth stand in awe
    of thy most holy word.
162 I at thy word rejoice, as one
    who finds of spoil great store.[68]
163 Thy law I love; but falsehood all
    I hate, and I abhor.

164 Seven times a day it is my care
    to give due praise to thee;
Because of all thy judgments, Lord,
    which righteous ever be.
165 Great peace have those who love thy law;
    offence they shall have none.
166 I've hoped for thy salvation, Lord,
    and thy commands have done.

167 My soul thy testimonies pure [69]
    did carefully obey;
And them, with all my heart and soul,
    I love exceedingly.
168 Thy testimonies and thy laws
    I've kept with special care;
Rememb'ring that my ways each one
    before thee open are.

Tau. *The 22d Part.*

169 O let my supplicating cry
    come near before thee, Lord:
Give understanding unto me,
    according to thy word.
170 Let my request before thee come:
    after thy word me free.
171 My lips shall sing thy praise, when thou
    hast taught thy laws to me.

172 I of thy word with joy will speak,
    and thee for it will bless;
Because all thy commandments are [70]
    unspotted righteousness.
173 Let thy strong hand my helper be;
    thy precepts are my choice.
174 I long'd for thy salvation, Lord,
    and in thy law rejoice.

175 O let my soul live, and it shall
    give praises unto thee;

  And let thy judgments gracious be [71]
   still helpful unto me.
176 I, like a lost sheep, went astray;
   thy servant seek, and find:
  For thy commands I suffer'd not
   to slip out of my mind.

PSALM CXX.

1 IN my distress I cried to God,
   and he gave ear to me.
2 From lying lips, and guileful tongue,
  O Lord, my soul set free.
3 What shall be giv'n to thee, false tongue?
  or what to thee be done?
4 Fierce, lasting fires, and arrows sharp,
  from the Almighty One.[1]

5 Woe's me that I in Mesech am
  a sojourner so long;[2]
  And that I dwell in Kedar's tents,
   fierce enemies among.
6 My soul with him who hateth peace
  has long a dweller been.
7 I plead for peace; but when I speak,
  they are for battle keen.

PSALM CXXI.

1 I'LL lift mine eyes unto the hills,
  whence cometh all mine aid.
2 My safety from Jehovah comes,
  who heav'n and earth has made.
3 Thy foot he'll not let slide, nor will
  he slumber who thee keeps.
4 Behold, he who keeps Israël,
  ne'er slumbers—never sleeps.[1]

5 The Lord thee keeps, the Lord thy shade
  on thy right hand doth stay:

6 The moon by night thee shall not smite,
   nor yet the sun by day.
7 The Lord shall keep thy soul; he shall
   preserve thee from all ill.
8 Henceforth thy going out and in
   he keep for ever will.

PSALM CXXII.

1 I JOY'D when to the house of God,
   Go up, they said to me.
2 Jerusalem, within thy gates
   our feet shall standing be.
3 Jerus'lem as a city is,
   which does compactly stand:[1]
4 To it the tribes of God go up,
   the tribes throughout the land:

   To Israel's testimony, there
   to give due thanks to God.
5 There too the seats of judgment are,[2]
   there David's throned abode.
6 Pray that Jerusalem may have
   felicity and peace:[3]
   To those who love thee and thy good
   may blessings never cease.

7 I therefore wish that peace may still
   within thy walls remain,
   And ever may thy palaces
   prosperity retain.
8 I'll say, for friends and brethren's sake,
   Within thy gates be peace.
9 And for Jehovah's house I'll pray
   thy good may still increase.

PSALM CXXIII.

1 O THOU who in the heav'ns dost dwell,
   I lift mine eyes to thee.

2 Behold, as servants' eyes attend [1]
   their masters' hands to see,
As handmaid's eyes her mistress' hand ;
   so do our eyes attend
Upon the Lord our God, till he
   to us his mercy send.

3 O Lord, be merciful to us, [2]
   to us most gracious be ;
Because replenish'd with contempt
   exceedingly are we.
4 Our soul is fill'd with scorn of those
   who at their ease abide,
And with the insolent contempt
   of those who swell in pride.

PSALM CXXIV.

1 HAD not the Lord, may Israel say,
   been kind to interpose ;
2 Had not Jehovah proved our friend,
   when men rose up as foes ;
3 They had us soon devour'd, when burn'd [1]
   their wrath beyond control ;
4 The spreading floods, and rising stream
   had swallow'd up our soul.
5 In swelling waters we had sunk,
   bereft of every stay ; [2]
6 Bless'd be the Lord, who to their teeth
   us gave not for a prey.
7 Our soul's escapèd, as a bird
   escapes the fowler's snare ; [3]
The snare asunder broken is,
   and we deliver'd are.
8 Our all-sufficient, only help,
   is in JEHOVAH'S name ;
Who by his power did heav'n create,
   and who the earth did frame.

PSALM CXXIV.

1 NOW Israel
    may say, and that truly,
If that the Lord
    had not our cause maintain'd;
2 If that the Lord
    had not our right sustain'd,
When cruel men
    against us furiously
Rose up in wrath,
    to make of us their prey;

3 Then certainly
    they had devour'd us all,
And swallow'd quick,
    for aught that we could deem;
Such was their rage,
    as we might well esteem.
4 And as fierce floods
    before them all things drown,
So had they brought
    our soul to death quite down.

5 The raging streams,
    with their proud swelling waves,
Had then our soul
    o'erwhelmèd in the deep.
6 But bless'd be God,
    who doth us safely keep,
And hath not giv'n
    us for a living prey
Unto their teeth,
    and bloody cruelty.

7 Ev'n as a bird
    out of the fowler's snare
Escapes away,
    so is our soul set free:
Broke are their nets,
    and thus escapèd we.

8 Therefore our help
   is in the Lord's great name,
 Who heav'n and earth
   by his great power did frame.

PSALM CXXV.

1 THOSE firmly trusting in the Lord,[1]
   shall be like Sion hill,
 Which never can removèd be,
   but stands for ever still.
2 As round Jerusalem a range
   of circling mountains stand,
 So round his people ever is[2]
   the Lord's protecting hand.

3 For ill men's rod upon the lot
   of just men shall not lie;
 Lest righteous men stretch forth their hands
   unto iniquity.
4 To all the truly good do thou[3]
   thy goodness, Lord, impart;
 And do thou good to those who have
   integrity of heart.

5 But those who, leaving righteous paths,
   pursue a crooked way,
 God shall lead forth with wicked men:
   on Israel peace shall stay.

PSALM CXXVI.

1 WHEN Sion's bondage God turn'd back,
   as men who dream were we.[1]
2 Then fill'd with laughter was our mouth,
   our tongue with melody:
 The very heathen said, The Lord[2]
   has great things for them wrought.
3 The Lord has done for us great things,
   whence joy to us is brought.

4 As streams of water in the south,
   our bondage, Lord, recall.
5 Who sow in tears, a reaping time
   of joy enjoy they shall.
6 The man who, bearing precious seed,
   in going forth doth mourn,
Shall doubtless, bringing back his sheaves,[3]
   with joyful heart return.

PSALM CXXVII.

1 WE build in vain, unless the Lord
   the building shall sustain,[1]
Unless the Lord the city keep,
   the watchmen watch in vain.
2 For you to rise betimes is vain,
   or late from rest to keep,
To feed on sorrow's bread; sure he[2]
   gives his belovèd sleep.

3 Lo, children are God's heritage,
   the womb's fruit his reward.
4 Since youthful sons, as arrows are,
   for strong men's hands prepared.
5 O happy is the man who has
   with these his quiver fill'd;[3]
When foes assail him in the gate,
   their words will be his shield.

PSALM CXXVIII.

1 BLESS'D every one who fears the Lord,
   and walketh in his ways;
2 For of thy labour thou shalt eat,
   in many happy days.[1]
3 Thy wife shall as a fruitful vine
   by thy house' sides be found:
Thy children as the olive-plants
   shall be thy table round.

4 Behold, the man who fears the Lord.
  thus blessèd still shall live.²
5 The Lord his blessing unto thee,
  shall out of Sion give.
  Thou shalt Jerus'lem's good behold,
  while thou on earth shalt dwell.
6 Thou shalt thy children's children see,
  and peace on Israël.

PSALM CXXIX.

1 THEY 've often vex'd me from my youth,¹
     may Israel now declare;
2 They've often vex'd me from my youth,
  yet not victorious were.
3 The ploughers plough'd upon my back;
  they long their furrows drew.
4 The righteous Lord did cut the cords
  of this unrighteous crew.

5 Let Sion's haters back be turn'd,
  into confusion thrown :²
6 Be they as grass on houses' tops,
  which fades ere fully grown :
7 Of which enough to fill his hand³
  the mower cannot find;
  Nor fill his bosom can the man,
  whose work is sheaves to bind.

8 Nor is it said by passers-by,⁴
  God's blessing on you rest:
  We wish you in Jehovah's name
  to be with plenty bless'd.

PSALM CXXX.

1 TO thee, Lord, from the depths I cried.
2   My voice, Jehovah, hear;
  Unto my supplication's voice
  give an attentive ear.

3 Lord, who shall stand, if thou, O Lord,
    shouldst mark iniquity?
4 But yet with thee forgiveness is,
    that fear'd thou mayest be.

5 For God I wait, my soul does wait,
    my hope is in his word.
6 More than they who for morning watch,[1]
    my soul waits for the Lord;
  I say, more eagerly than they
    who morning watch to see.
7 Let Israel in Jehovah hope,
    for with him mercies be;

  And ever will redemption be[2]
    in plenty found with him.
8 And from all his iniquities
    he Israel shall redeem.

PSALM CXXXI.

1 O LORD, not haughty is my heart,[1]
    nor lofty is mine eye;
  Nor meddle I with matters great,
    or things for me too high.
2 I surely have myself behaved
    with spirit calm and mild,[2]
  As child by mother wean'd: my soul
    is like a weanèd child.
3 Let Israel's hope entirely rest
    upon the Lord most high,
  Extending from the present time[3]
    unto eternity.

PSALM CXXXII.

1 LORD, David to remembrance call,
    and all his trouble's load;
2 How to the Lord he swore, and vow'd
    to Jacob's mighty God.

3 I will not come into my house,[1]
    nor rest at all in bed ;
4 I'll not in slumber nor in sleep,
    recline at night my head ;
5 Till for the Lord I find a place,
    where he may make abode ;
  A place of habitation sure[2]
    for Jacob's mighty God.
6 We heard of it near Ephratah ;[3]
    its destined site there found,
  Amid the fields which long had been
    with trees and forests crown'd.
7 We'll to his tabernacles go,[4]
    and at his footstool bow.
8 Arise, O Lord, into thy rest,
    th' ark of thy strength, and thou.
9 O let thy priests be clothèd, Lord,
    with truth and righteousness ;
  And let thy servants shout for joy,
    and thee with praises bless.[5]
10 Now for thy servant David's sake.
    O hear me from on high ;
  Nor to thine own anointed one[6]
    what he requests deny.
11 The Lord in truth to David swore.
    his oath he'll not disown :[7]
  I of thy body's fruit will make
    to sit upon thy throne.
12 If thy sons keep my covenant,
    and laws to them made known,
  Their children also shall be placed
    for ever on thy throne.
13 For Sion is Jehovah's choice ;
    he there desires to dwell.
14 This is my rest, here still I'll stay ;
    since I do like it well.

15 I'll greatly bless her food ; her poor
    with bread will satisfy.
16 I'll with salvation clothe her priests ;
    her saints shall shout for joy.
17 And there will I make David's horn
    to bud forth pleasantly :
For him who mine anointed is
    a lamp ordain'd have I.

18 As with a garment I will clothe
    with shame his en'mies all :
But yet the crown which he doth wear
    upon him flourish shall.

PSALM CXXXIII.

1 BEHOLD how pleasant, and how good,[1]
    and how becoming well,
Together such as brethren are
    in unity to dwell !
2 'Tis like rich ointment on the head,[2]
    which down the beard did flow.
Ev'n Aaron's beard, and to the skirts
    did of his garments go.
3 As Hermon's dew, the dew which does
    on Sion's hills descend :
For there the blessing God commands,
    life which shall never end.

PSALM CXXXIV.

1 BEHOLD, bless ye the Lord, all ye
    who his attendants are,
Who in Jehovah's temple wait,[1]
    and praise him nightly there.
2 Your hands within God's holy place
    lift up, and praise him still.
3 The Lord who made the heav'n and earth,[2]
    thee bless from Sion hill.

1 UNTO Jehovah sing ye praise,¹
    praise ye Jehovah's name ;
  O ye who servants are to him,
    Jehovah's praise proclaim.
2 Ye standing in Jehovah's house,
    sing praises unto God ;
  And ye, who in his sacred courts
    enjoy a blest abode.
3 Praise ye the Lord, for he is good ;
    in songs your voices raise :
  Sing praises to his name, because
    it pleasant is to praise.
4 For Jacob to himself the Lord²
    did choose of his good will,
  For his peculiar treasure he
    has chosen Israël.
5 Because I know the Lord to be
    above all measure great,
  And that our Lord above all gods
    in glory hath his seat.
6 The Lord with powerful hand performs³
    whate'er his pleasure be,
  In heav'n and earth, all places deep,
    and in the spacious sea.
7 He makes the vapours be exhaled
    from th' earth's remotest end ;
  He lightnings makes with rain, and wind
    doth from his treasures send.
8 Egypt's first-born of man and beast
9   he smote. Strange tokens he⁴
  On Pharaoh and his servants sent,
    Egypt, in midst of thee.
10 He smote great nations, slew great kings :
11   Sihon of Heshbon king,
  With Og of Bashan, and to nought
    did Canaan's kingdoms bring :

12 And for a rich inheritance
   their land to Israel gave,
A land which his own people might
   in sure possession have.⁵

13 Thy name, O Lord, shall still endure,⁶
   and thy remembrance shall
With glory still continued be
   to generations all.

14 Because the righteous Lord will judge
   his people righteously;
Concerning those who do him serve,
   himself repent will he.

15 The idols of the nations round⁷
   of silver are and gold,
And from the hands of men proceed
   their workmanship and mould.

16 They mouths possess, but do not speak:⁸
   and eyes, but do not see;

17 Ears, but they do not hear; and in
   their mouths no breathing be.

18 Their makers are like them; and all⁹
   who do on them rely.

19 O Israel's, and, O Aaron's house,
   bless God, the Lord most high.

20 O bless Jehovah, Levi's house,
   ye who his praise record;
All ye who fear Jehovah's name,
   give praises to the Lord.

21 From Sion be Jehovah bless'd,
   his name be still adored,
Who dwelleth at Jerusalem.
   Give praises to the Lord.

PSALM CXXXVI. C.M.

1 GIVE thanks to God, for he is good:
   his mercy's ever sure.

2 Give thanks unto the God of gods ;
   his grace doth still endure.
3 Give thanks unto the Lord of lords :
   his mercy's ever sure.
4 Who only wonders great can do ;
   his grace doth still endure.
5 Who by his wisdom made the heav'ns ;
   his mercy's ever sure.
6 Who stretch'd the earth above the sea ;
   his grace doth still endure.
7 To him who made the great lights shine ;
   his mercy's ever sure.
8 Who made the sun to rule by day :
   his grace doth still endure.
9 The moon and stars to rule by night ;
   his mercy's ever sure.
10 Who Egypt's first-born all cut down ;
   his grace doth still endure.
11 And Israel out of Egypt brought ;
   his mercy's ever sure.
12 With out-stretch'd arm, and powerful hand ;
   his grace doth still endure.
13 By whom divided was the sea ;
   his mercy's ever sure.
14 And through it made all Israel pass ;
   his grace doth still endure.
15 Who drown'd both Pharaoh and his host ;[1]
   his mercy's ever sure.
16 Who through the desert Israel led ;
   his grace doth still endure.
17 To him who overthrew great kings ;
   his mercy's ever sure.
18 Who famous kings in battle slew ;
   his grace doth still endure.
19 Ev'n Sihon king of th' Amorites ;
   his mercy's ever sure.

PSALM CXXXVI.

20 And Og, who did o'er Bashan rule;
   his grace doth still endure.

21 Their land in heritage to have;
   his mercy's ever sure.
22 His servant Israel right he gave;
   his grace doth still endure.
23 Who did not us, when low, forget;
   his mercy's ever sure.
24 And from our foes our freedom wrought;
   his grace doth still endure.

25 Who doth all flesh with food relieve;
   his mercy's ever sure.
26 Thanks to the God of heaven give;
   his grace doth still endure.

PSALM CXXXVI.   P.M.

1 PRAISE God, for he is kind:[1]
   His mercy lasts for aye.
2 Give thanks with heart and mind
   To God of gods alway:
     For certainly
       His mercies dure
       Most firm and sure
     Eternally.

3 The Lord of lords praise ye,
   Whose mercies still endure.
4 Great wonders only he
   Doth work by his great power:
     For certainly, &c.

5 Which God omnipotent,
   By might and wisdom high,
   The heav'n and firmament
   Did frame, as we may see:
     For certainly, &c.

PSALM CXXXVI.

6 To him who did outstretch
This earth so great and wide,
Above the waters' reach
Making it to abide :
For certainly, &c.

7 Great lights he made to be ;
For his grace lasteth aye :
8 Such as the sun we see,
To rule the lightsome day :
For certainly, &c.

9 Also the moon so clear,
Which shineth in our sight ;
The stars that do appear,
To guide the darksome night :
For certainly, &c.

10 To him that Egypt smote,
Who did his message scorn ;
And in his anger hot
Did kill all their first-born :
For certainly, &c.

11 Thence Israel out he brought ;
For his grace lasteth ever.
12 With a strong hand he wrought,
And stretch'd-out arm deliver :
For certainly, &c.

13 The sea he cut in two ;
For his grace lasteth still.
14 And through its midst to go
Made his own Israël :
For certainly, &c.

15 But overwhelm'd and lost
Was proud king Pharaoh,
With all his mighty host,
And chariots there also :
For certainly, &c.

PSALM CXXXVII.

16 To him who powerfully
His chosen people led,
Ev'n through the desert dry,
And in that place them fed :
 For certainly, &c.

17 To him great kings who smote ;
For his grace hath no bound.
18 Who slew, and sparèd not
Kings famous and renown'd :
 For certainly, &c.

19 Sihon the Am'rites' king ;
For his grace lasteth ever :
20 Og also, who did reign
The land of Bashan over :
 For certainly, &c.

21 Their land by lot he gave ;
For his grace faileth never,
22 That Israel might it have
In heritage for ever :
 For certainly, &c.

23 Who hath rememberèd
Us in our low estate ;
24 And us deliverèd
From foes which did us hate :
 For certainly, &c.

25 Who to all flesh gives food ;
For his grace faileth never.
26 Give thanks to God most good,
The God of heav'n, for ever :
 For certainly, &c.

PSALM CXXXVII.

1 BY Babel's streams we sat and wept,[1]
when we of Sion thought.

2 To tune our harps on willows hung
    no captive lyrist sought.
3 For there a song required they,
    who did us captive bring:
Our spoilers call'd for mirth, and said,
    A song of Sion sing.

4 How shall we sing Jehovah's song
    within a foreign land?
5 If thee, Jerus'lem, I forget,
    skill part from my right hand.
6 My tongue to my mouth's roof let cleave,
    if e'er I thee forget,
Jerusalem, and thee above
    my chief joy do not set.

7 Remember Edom's children, Lord,
    who in Jerus'lem's day,
Said, Raze it, raze it, and quite bare
    its deep foundations lay.
8 O daughter thou of Babylon,
    so near to ruin run;
Bless'd shall he be who does to thee,
    as thou to us hast done.

9 Nay, surely happy shall he be
    who shall thy little ones
Seize with unpitying hand, and them
    shall dash against the stones.

PSALM CXXXVIII.

1 I'LL thee extol with all my heart,
    I'll praises sing to thee
2 Before the gods: I worship will
    towards thy sanctuary.
Thy loving-kindness and thy truth,
    I will in songs proclaim;
For thou thy word hast magnified
    above all thy great name.[1]

3 Thou didst me answer in the day
    when I to thee did cry ;
And thou my soul with needed strength
    didst strengthen inwardly.
4 All kings who are upon the earth [2]
    shall give thee praise, O Lord ;
What time they from thy mouth shall hear
    thy true and faithful word.
5 Yea, in Jehovah's righteous ways
    they shall with gladness sing : [3]
For great's the glory of the Lord,
    who is for ever King.
6 The Lord, though high, does yet respect
    all those who lowly are ;
Whereas the lofty and the proud
    beholdeth he afar. [4]
7 Though I in midst of trouble walk,
    I life from thee shall have ;
'Gainst wrathful foes thou 'lt stretch thine hand ;
    thy right hand shall me save.
8 Surely whate'er concerneth me
    the Lord will perfect make :
Lord, still thy mercy lasts ; do not
    thine own hands' works forsake.

PSALM CXXXIX.

1
2 O LORD, thou hast me search'd and known.
    Thou know'st my sitting down,
And rising up ; yea, all my thoughts
    afar to thee are known.
3 Thou compassest my path by day ;
    my lying down by night ; [1]
And thoroughly are all my ways
    laid open to thy sight.
4 For in my tongue, before I speak,
    not any word can be,

Which is not, O Jehovah, known,
  lo, fully known to thee.
5 Thou hast beset behind, before,
  and laid on me thy hand.
6 Such knowledge is for me too strange,
  too high to understand.

7 From thy sp'rit whither shall I go?
  or from thy presence fly?
8 Ascend I heav'n, thou, Lord, art there;
  there, if in hell I lie.
9 Take I the morning wings, and dwell
  in utmost parts of sea;
10 Ev'n there, Lord, shall thy hand me lead,
  thy right hand hold shall me.

11 Were I to say that darkness shall
  me cover from thy sight,
Then surely shall the very night
  about me be as light.
12 Yea, darkness hideth not from thee,
  but night doth shine as day:
To thee the darkness and the light
  are both alike alway.

13 For thou possessèd hast my reins,
  and thou hast cover'd me,
When I within my mother's womb
  enclosèd was by thee.
14 I'll thee extol; for fearfully
  and strangely made I am;
Thy works are wondrous, and full well
  my soul doth know the same.

15 My substance was not hid from thee,
  what time in secret I [2]
Was made; and in earth's lowest parts
  was wrought most curiously.
16 My substance, when devoid of form, [3]
  thine eyes did clearly see;

And in thy book my members all
    recorded were by thee.

These after, in the course of time,
    were fashion'd every one,
Although before they shapeless were,
    and of them there was none.

17 How precious also are thy thoughts.
    O gracious God, to me!
And in their sum how passing great,
    how numberless they be!

18 If I should count them, than the sand
    they more in number be:
What time soever I awake,
    I ever am with thee.

19 Thou, Lord, wilt sure the wicked slay:
    hence from me, bloody men.

20 Thy foes against thee loudly speak,
    and take thy name in vain.

21 Do not I hate, O Lord, all those
    who hatred bear to thee?
With those who up against thee rise
    can I but grievèd be?

22 With perfect hatred them I hate,
    I them my en'mies hold.

23 O God, search me, and know my heart,
    me try, my thoughts unfold:

24 And see if any wicked way
    at all be found in me;[4]
And in thine everlasting way
    to me a leader be.

PSALM CXL.

1 LORD, from the man of wickedness[1]
    do thou deliver me;
And from the vi'lent man by thee
    may I preservèd be;

2 Who deeds of mischief in their hearts
 still meditating are : [2]
And they continually in bands
 assembled are for war.

3 Much like unto a serpent's tongue
 their tongues they pointed make ;
Conceal'd beneath their lips there is [3]
 the poison of a snake.

4 Lord, keep me from the wicked's hands,
 from vi'lent men me save ;
Who utterly to overthrow
 my goings purposed have.

5 The proud have hid for me a snare,
 and cords ; yea, they a net
Have by the way-side spread for me ;
 they gins for me have set.

6 I said unto the Lord, Thou art
 my God ; unto the cry
Of all my supplications, Lord,[4]
 do thou thine ear apply.

7 That thou my strength and Saviour art,
 O God the Lord, I'll say ; [5]
For oft my head thou cover'd hast
 in battle's doubtful day.

8 O Lord, unto the wicked man
 his wishes do not grant ;
Nor prosper thou his wicked plot,
 lest they themselves should vaunt.

9 As for the head and chief of those
 who now encompass me,[6]
Let them by mischiefs of their lips
 completely cover'd be.

10 Let burning coals upon them fall,
 them cast into the flame,[7]
And pits so deep, that they no more
 may rise out of the same.

11 Let not an evil speaker be
    on earth establishèd :
  Mischief shall hunt the vi'lent man,
    till he be ruinèd.
12 God will, I know, th' afflicted's cause [8]
    maintain, and poor men's right.
13 Thee surely shall the upright praise ;
    the just dwell in thy sight.

PSALM CXLI.

1 O LORD, to thee I raise my cry,
    make haste to succour me,
  O give thine ear unto my voice,
    when I cry unto thee.
2 As incense let my earnest prayer [1]
    on high before thee rise ;
  And the uplifting of my hands
    as th' evening sacrifice.
3 Set, Lord, a watch before my mouth,
    keep of my lips the door.
4 And never let my heart incline [2]
    to what I should abhor,
  To practise wickedness with men
    who work iniquity ;
  Nor let their delicacies prove
    ensnaring unto me.
5 Let him who righteous is me smite,
    it shall a kindness be ;
  Let him reprove, I shall it count
    a precious oil to me ;
  Such smiting shall not break my head :
    for yet will come the day, [3]
  When I in their calamities
    to God for them will pray.
6 What time their rulers down shall be [4]
    in rocky places cast.

Then shall they hear my words; which shall
  be sweet unto their taste.
7 About the grave's devouring mouth
    our bones are scatter'd found,
  As wood which workmen cut and cleave [5]
    lies scatter'd on the ground.

8 But unto thee, O God the Lord,
    uplifted are mine eyes:
  My soul do not leave destitute;
    my trust on thee relies.
9 Me keep in safety from the snares
    which they for me prepare;
  And from the subtile gins of those
    who wicked workers are.

10 Let workers of iniquity
    into their own nets fall,
  While I by thy support escape [6]
    the danger of them all.

PSALM CXLII.

1 I TO Jehovah with my voice [1]
    sent up my earnest cry;
  My supplication with my voice
    I made to God most high.
2 Before him I pour'd out in prayer
    my sad complaint and grief;
  Before him all my trouble spread,
    imploring some relief.

3 When overwhelm'd my spirit was,
    then well thou knew'st my way;
  They, in the way in which I walk'd,
    their snares for me did lay.
4 I look'd on my right hand and view'd,
    but none me wish'd to know; [2]
  Me refuge fail'd, none to my soul
    would care or pity show.

5 I cried to thee; I said, Thou art
    a refuge, Lord, to me;
  And my sure portion in the land
    of those who living be.³
6 Because I am brought very low,
    attend unto my cry:
  Me from my persecutors save,
    for stronger they than I.⁴

7 O me, in close confinement kept,⁵
    to freedom do thou bring;
  That I new songs of thanksgiving
    unto thy name may sing.
  The men who practise righteousness
    I yet shall round me see;
  For thou shalt yet in mercy show
    thy bounteousness to me.

PSALM CXLIII.

1 O LORD, my supplications hear.
    unto my prayer attend.
  In righteousness and in thy truth
    do thou an answer send.¹
2 And do not into judgment bring
    thy servant to be tried:
  Because no living man can be
    in thy sight justified.

3 For foes, me persecuting, do²
    my life to ground down tread:
  In darkness make me dwell, like those
    long number'd with the dead.
4 Whence overwhelm'd my spirit is³
    with sore perplexity;
  Within me does my very heart
    in desolation lie.

5 I call to mind the days of old,
    to meditate I use

On all thy works ; upon the deeds
　　by thee perform'd I muse.
6 My hands to thee I stretch ; my soul
　　thirsts, as dry land, for thee.
7 Haste, Lord, to hear, my spirit fails :[4]
　　hide not thy face from me ;

Lest I resemblance bear to those
　　descending to the dust.
8 At morn let me thy kindness hear ;
　　since placed in thee my trust.
Me teach the way where I should walk :
　　I lift my soul to thee.
9 Lord, free me from my foes ; to thee
　　I for protection flee.

10 Because thou art my God, to do
　　thy will do me instruct :
Thy Sp'rit is good, me to the land
　　of uprightness conduct.
11 O thou, Jehovah, quicken me,
　　even for thine own name's sake ;
Do thou, Lord, for thy righteousness,
　　my soul from trouble take.

12 And in thy mercy slay my foes ;
　　let all destroyèd be.
Who now afflict my soul : for I
　　a servant am to thee.

PSALM CXLIII.

1 OH hear my prayèr, Lord,[1]
　　And unto my desire
To bow thine ear accord,
　　I humbly thee require ;
And, in thy faithfulness,
　　Unto me answer make,
And, in thy righteousness,
　　Upon me pity take.

2 In judgment enter not
  With me thy servant poor;
  For why, this well I wot,
  No sinner can endure
  The sight of thee, O God:
  If thou his deeds shalt try,
  He dare make none abode
  Himself to justify.

3 Behold, the cruel foe
  Me persecutes with spite,
  My soul to overthrow:
  Yea, he my life down quite
  Unto the ground hath smote,
  And made me dwell full low
  In darkness, as forgot,
  Or men dead long ago.

4 Therefore my sp'rit, much vex'd,
  O'erwhelm'd is me within;
  My heart right sore perplex'd
  And desolate hath been.

5 Yet I do call to mind
  What ancient days record,
  Thy works of every kind,
  I think upon, O Lord.

6 Lo, I do stretch my hands
  To thee, my help alone;
  For thou well understands
  All my complaint and moan:
  My thirsting soul desires,
  And longeth after thee,
  As thirsty ground requires
  With rain refresh'd to be.

7 Lord, let my prayer prevail,
  To answer it make speed;
  For, lo, my sp'rit doth fail:
  Hide not thy face in need;

Lest I be like to those
That do in darkness sit,
Or him that downward goes
Into the dreadful pit.

8 Because I trust in thee,
O Lord, cause me to hear
Thy loving-kindness free,
When morning doth appear:
Cause me to know the way
Wherein my path should be;
For why, my soul on high
I do lift up to thee.

9 From my fierce enemy
In safety do me guide,
Because I flee to thee,
Lord, that thou may'st me hide.
10 My God alone art thou,
Teach me thy righteousness:
Thy Sp'rit's good, lead me to
The land of uprightness.

11 O Lord, for thy name's sake,
Be pleased to quicken me;
And, for thy truth, forth take
My soul from misery.
12 And of thy grace destroy
My foes, and put to shame
All who my soul annoy;
For I thy servant am.

PSALM CXLIV.

1 O BLESSED let Jehovah be,
the source of all my might,[1]
My teacher in the art of war,
who trains my hands to fight.
2 My good, my fortress, my high tower,
my saviour, and my shield,

In whom I trust: who under me
the people makes to yield.

3 Lord, what is man, that thou of him
dost so much knowledge take?
Or son of man, that thou of him
so great account dost make?
4 Man is like vanity; his days,
as shadows, pass away.
5 Lord, bow thy heav'ns, come down, touch thou
the hills, and smoke shall they.

6 Cast forth thy lightning, scatter them;
thine arrows shoot, them rout.
7 Thine hand send from above, me save;
from great depths draw me out;
And from the hand of children strange,
8 Whose mouth speaks vanity;
And whose right hand is a right hand [2]
which works deceitfully.

9 A new song I will sing to thee,
Lord, on a psaltery;
I on a ten-string'd instrument
will praises sing to thee.
10 Even he it is who unto kings
deliverance doth send;[3]
Who his own servant David doth
from hurtful sword defend.

11 O free me from strange children's hand,
whose mouth speaks vanity;
And whose right hand a right hand is [2]
which works deceitfully.
12 That so our sons may be as plants,
which high their branches rear;[4]
Our daughters like the corner-stones
which grace some palace fair.

13 That with abundance of all stores
  our garners may be fill'd;
 That fruitful flocks, ten thousands may
  throughout our sheep-walks yield.[5]
14 That strong our oxen be for work,
  that no in-breaking be,
 Nor going out; and that our streets
  may from complaints be free.
15 O blessèd are the people whose
  condition is like this;
 Yea, blessèd are the people all,
  whose God JEHOVAH is.

PSALM CXLV. C. M.

1 I'LL thee extol, my God, O King;
  thine endless praise proclaim;[1]
2 Thee will I bless each day, and will
  for ever praise thy name.
3 Great is the Lord, much to be praised;
  his greatness search exceeds.
4 Race unto race shall praise thy works,
  and show thy mighty deeds.
5 I of thy glorious majesty
  the honour will record;
 I'll speak of all thy mighty works,
  which wondrous are, O Lord.
6 Men of thine acts the might shall show,
  thine acts which dreadful are;
 And I, thy glory to advance,
  thy greatness will declare.
7 The mem'ry of thy goodness great
  they largely shall express;
 With songs of praise they shall extol
  thy perfect righteousness.
8 Most gracious is the mighty Lord,[2]
  in him compassions flow;

He is in mercy very great,
   and is to anger slow.

9 The Lord JEHOVAH unto all
   his goodness doth declare;
  And over all his countless works³
   his tender mercies are.
10 Thee all thy works shall praise, O Lord,
   and thee thy saints shall bless;
11 They shall thy kingdom's glory show,
   thy power by speech express:

12 To make the sons of men to know
   his acts done mightily,
  To know his kingdom's excellent⁴
   and glorious majesty.
13 Thy kingdom shall for ever stand,
   thy reign through ages all.
14 God raises all who are bow'd down,⁵
   upholdeth all who fall.

15 The eyes of all things wait on thee,
   the giver of all good;
  And thou, in time convenient,
   bestow'st on them their food:
16 Thou open'st lib'rally thy hand,⁶
   and givest of thy good
  What meets the wants of every thing
   which looks to thee for food:

17 The Lord is just in all his ways,
   holy in his works all.
18 God's near to all who call on him,
   in truth who on him call.
19 He will accomplish the desire
   of those who do him fear:
  He also will deliver them,
   and he their cry will hear.

20 The Lord preserves all who him love,
    that nought can them annoy :
But all who work iniquity
    he'll utterly destroy.
21 My mouth the praises of the Lord[7]
    will evermore proclaim :
And let all flesh through ages all
    extol his holy name.

PSALM CXLV.   L. M.

1 O LORD, thou art my God and King ;
    Thee will I magnify and praise :
I will thee bless, and gladly sing
Unto thy holy name always.
2 Each day I rise I will thee bless,
Will praise thy name time without end.
3 Much to be praised, and great God is ;
His greatness none can comprehend.

4 Race shall thy works praise unto race,
The mighty acts show done by thee.
5 I will speak of thy glorious grace,
And honour of thy majesty ;
Thy wondrous works I will record.
6 By men the might shall be extoll'd
Of all thy dreadful acts, O Lord :
And I thy greatness will unfold.

7 They utter shall abundantly
The mem'ry of thy goodness great ;
And shall sing praise with cheerfulness,
While they thy righteousness relate.
8 Most gracious is the Lord our God,
Compassionate is he also ;
In mercy he abundant is,[1]
But is to indignation slow.

9 Good unto all men is the Lord :
O'er all his works his mercy is.

10 Thy works all praise to thee afford:
　　Thy saints, O Lord, thy name shall bless.
11 They shall thy kingdom's glory show,[2]
　　And of thy power unbounded tell;
12 That sons of men his deeds may know,
　　And kingdom's grace which doth excel.

13 Thy kingdom has no end at all,[3]
　　But does through ages all remain.
14 The Lord upholdeth all who fall,
　　The cast-down raiseth up again.
15 The eyes of every thing which lives[4]
　　On thee with expectation wait,
　　And what they need thy goodness gives,
　　In season due, and measure great.

16 Yea, thou thine hand dost open wide,
　　And every thing dost satisfy
　　Which lives, and doth on earth abide,
　　Of thy great liberality.
17 The Lord is just in his ways all,
　　And holy in his works each one.
18 He's near to all who on him call,
　　Who call in truth on him alone.

19 God will the just desire fulfil
　　Of such as do him fear and dread:
　　Their cry regard, and hear he will,
　　And save them in the time of need.
20 The Lord preserves all, more and less,
　　Who bear to him a loving heart:
　　But workers all of wickedness
　　Destroy will he, and clean subvert.

21 My mouth and lips I'll therefore frame
　　To speak the praises of the Lord:
　　To magnify his holy name
　　For ever let all flesh accord.

PSALM CXLVI.

1 PRAISE God. The Lord praise, O my soul.
2 I'll praise God while I live;
   While I have being, to my God
     in songs I'll praises give.
3 In those of princely power and rank,[1]
     repose not ye your trust;
   Nor aid expect from son of man,
     the helpless child of dust.
4 For soon bereft of breath, he turns
     back to his kindred clay;
   And all his thoughts and power to help,
     will perish in that day.
5 O truly blessed is the man[2]
     whom Jacob's God doth aid;
   Whose hope upon Jehovah rests,
     and on his God is stay'd:
6 Who made the earth and heavens high,
     who made the swelling deep,
   And everything which it contains;[3]
     who truth doth ever keep;
7 Who righteous judgment executes
     for those oppress'd who be;
   Jehovah doth the hungry feed,
     and sets the pris'ners free.
8 Jehovah gives the blind their sight,
     the bowèd down doth raise:
   Jehovah dearly loves all those[4]
     who walk in righteous ways.
9 The stranger's shield, the widow's stay,
     the orphan's help is he:
   But by the Lord, turn'd upside down
     the wicked's way shall be.
10 The Lord shall reign for evermore:
     thy God, O Sion, will
   Be King to generations all.[5]
     O praise Jehovah still.

PSALM CXLVII.

1 PRAISE ye the Lord; for it is good
    praise to our God to sing:
For it is pleasant, and to praise
    is a most comely thing.[1]
2 The Lord builds up Jerusalem;
    and he it is alone
Who Israel's outcasts from afar[2]
    is gath'ring into one.
3 Those who are broken in their heart,
    and grievèd in their minds,
And those who have been wounded sore,
    he tenderly up-binds.
4 He counts the number of the stars;
    he names them every one.
5 Great is our Lord, and of great power,
    his wisdom search can none.
6 The Lord lifts up the meek; and casts
    the wicked to the ground.
7 Sing to the Lord, and give him thanks;
    on harp God's praises sound;[3]
8 Who covereth the heav'n with clouds,
    who for the earth below
Prepareth rain, who maketh grass
    upon the mountains grow.
9 He gives the beast his food; he feeds
    the ravens young which cry.
10 His pleasure, nor in horses' strength,[4]
    nor in man's legs, doth lie.
11 But in all those who fear his name
    the Lord does pleasure take;
In those who to his mercy great
    by hope themselves betake.
12 Jerus'lem, praise the Lord; to God.
    O Sion, praise express:[5]
13 For thy gates' bars he maketh strong:
    thy sons in thee doth bless.

14 He makes throughout thy borders peace ;
   with fine wheat filleth thee.
15 He sends forth his command on earth,
   his word runs speedily.
16 The hoar-frost he like ashes spreads ;
   he snow like wool doth give :
17 He casts like morsels forth his ice ;
   who in its cold can live ?
18 He sendeth out his mighty word,
   and melteth them again ;
   He makes his wind to blow, and then
   the waters flow amain.
19 The doctrine of his holy word
   he doth to Jacob show ;
   His statutes and his judgments he
   makes Israël to know.
20 To any nation never he
   such favour did afford ;
   For they his judgments have not known.
   Give praise unto the Lord.

PSALM CXLVIII.

1 PRAISE God. From heavens praise the Lord,
   in heights praise to him be.
2 All ye his angels, sound his praise ;[1]
   his hosts all, praise him ye.
3 Proclaim, O sun and moon, his praise ;
   him praise, all stars of light.
4 Him praise, ye heav'ns of heav'ns, and clouds
   which move through heavens' height.
5 Let them extol with praise the name[2]
   of our Almighty Lord :
   For they at his command arose,
   the creatures of his word.
6 He too, to generations all[3]
   has them establish'd sure ;

They still shall keep his fix'd decree
    still do his high command.

7 Ye depths, and monsters of the deep,
    praise ye the earth's great Lord;
8 Fire, hail, snow, vapour, stormy wind,
    accomplishing his word:
9 All hills and mountains, fruitful trees,
    and all ye cedars high:
10 Beasts, cattle all, with creeping things,
    and all ye birds which fly:
11 Kings of the earth, ye nations all,
    princes, earth's judges all:
12 Young men and maidens, and with them
    old men, and children small:—
13 Praise ye the Lord's name; for his name
    alone is excellent:
    His glory is above the earth,
    above the firmament.

14 His people's horn, the praise of all
    his saints, exalteth he;
    Ev'n Israel's seed, a people near
    to him. The Lord praise ye.

PSALM CXLVIII. P.M.

1 THE Lord of heav'n confess,[1]
    On high his glory raise.
2 Him let all angels bless,
    Him all his armies praise.
3   Him glorify
        Sun, moon, and stars;
4   Ye higher spheres,
        And cloudy sky.

5 From God your beings are,
    Him therefore famous make;
    You all created were,
    When he the word but spake.

PSALM CXLIX.

6 And from that place,
  Where fix'd you be
  By his decree,
  You cannot pass.

7 Praise God from earth below,
  Ye dragons, and ye deeps:
8 Fire, hail, clouds, wind, and snow,
  Whom in command he keeps:
9   Praise ye his name,
    Hills great and small,
    Trees low and tall;
10   Beasts wild and tame;

All things that creep or fly:
11 Ye kings, ye vulgar throng,
  All princes mean or high;
12 Both men and virgins young,
  Ev'n young and old,
13   Exalt his name;
    For much his fame
    Should be extoll'd.

O let God's name be praised
  Above both earth and sky;
14 For he his saints hath raised,
  And set their horn on high;
    Even those that be
    Of Israel's race,
    Near to his grace.
  The Lord praise ye.

PSALM CXLIX.

1 PRAISE ye Jehovah; to him sing
  a new song, and his praise
In the assembly of his saints
  in psalms melodious raise.
2 In him who their Creator is
  let Israel rejoice;

PSALM CL.

　　Let Sion's children to their King
　　　lift up their joyful voice.
3 O let them to his glorious name
　　give praises in the dance;
　Let them, with timbrel and with harp,
　　in songs his praise advance.
4 For God doth pleasure take in those
　　who his own people be;
　And he with his salvation great[1]
　　the meek will beautify.
5 In glory so surpassing great
　　let all his saints rejoice;
　Let them to him upon their beds
　　lift up aloud their voice.
6 Let in their mouth aloft be raised
　　the praises of the Lord,
　And let them have in their right hand
　　a sharp two-edgèd sword;
7 To execute the vengeance due
　　upon the heathen all;
　To make deservèd punishment
　　upon the people fall.
8 And even with chains, as pris'ners, bind
　　their kings who them command;[2]
　And chain, with iron fetters strong,
　　the nobles of the land.
9 To execute on them the doom
　　recorded in his word:
　This honour is to all the saints.
　　Give praise unto the Lord.

PSALM CL.

1 PRAISE ye the Lord. God's praise within
　　his sanctuary raise;
　In heav'ns, where shines his glorious power,[1]
　　proclaim in songs his praise.

2 For all his deeds of wondrous might
   with praise him magnify:
Great be his praise, as he excels
   in glorious majesty.

3 To praise him let the trumpet sound;
   him praise with psaltery:
And let the sweetly-sounding harp
   enrich the melody.

4 By damsels be the timbrel struck,
   and led the sacred dance;
Let organs and string'd instruments
   the harmony advance.

5 Let cymbals with their louder tones
   a bolder concord raise;
With these combine the cymbals used
   on solemn holidays.

6 Let every being bless'd with breath,
   unite in sweet accord
To celebrate JEHOVAH's praise.
   For ever praise the Lord.

NOTES.

NOTES.

*** *The figure preceding each note refers not to the verse of the psalm, but to the reference figures used throughout.*

PSALM I.—1. This line more literal than that in the common version.

2. 'Sits' for 'sitteth,' and 'places' for 'placeth,' prevent the too frequent repetition of the termination *eth*.

3. 'On' for 'upon,' to put the preposition 'on' in a syllable of the line not emphatic, and the word 'God' in a place more emphatic.

4. The change in this stanza is to rectify the redundant measure of the common version in lines 2 and 4, 'ri*ver*,' 'ne*ver*.'

5. 'Does' for 'doth,' more modern.

6. In line 1, 'Because' for 'For why?' now obsolete.

PSALM II.—1. By this alteration we get rid of the expletive 'do,' and the word 'rulers' seems preferable to 'princes,' as foretelling the opposition to Christ by the Jewish rulers; 'rulers,' besides, is the term by which our translators have rendered the original word.

2. By the change made in this line, the word 'cords'—an important term here, is placed in a more prominent position, and the pronoun 'us' in a less conspicuous place.

3. 'Who' is here put for 'that.' In modern language, *who* has greatly and justly gained upon *that* as a relative pronoun.

4. This stanza has been changed to remedy the redundant syllable in its second and fourth lines, 'appoint*ed*,' 'anoint*ed*.'

5. This line was changed to get rid of the particle 'of,' which occupied too prominent a place in the line. The harmony of the line seems improved by the change.

6. The 'and' which was in this line was put there by

Rous, but has no corresponding word in the original; by putting out the 'and,' we can substitute 'vessel' for the less poetical term 'sherd.' 'To pieces' seems better than the expression 'in pieces.'

7. The change of 'ire' into 'wrath' was made because 'ire' is now little used. The expression, '*from* the way,' seeming obscure, I substituted '*in* the way.' If it be thought that the word 'wrath,' occurring twice in the same stanza, is objectionable, the third line may be turned—
'If once his anger kindled be.'

PSALM III.— 1. In Rous's version this line is neither elegant nor harmonious; hence the attempt to improve it.

2. In the second line, the expression, 'thou hast *stroke*,' is very poor, and obviously ungrammatical. It is now at least correct in point of grammar. Rous here sacrificed grammar to rhyme. This was improper, sense being superior to sound.

3. In ver. 8, line 1, 'salvation,' according to a practice common with Rous, is considered a word of four syllables; 'doth,' as there used, is nearly an expletive; hence the attempt to amend the line. The last two lines are turned into a prayer, on the authority of Patrick, Horne, and Orton.

PSALM IV.— 1. Rous, in translating this second verse, changed the order of its clauses; they are here restored to their primitive order.

2. Changed to avoid the expletive 'do,' and to use a word of two syllables, viz., 'implore.' Rous's version superabounds with monosyllables.

3. The design in changing this line was to improve its construction and its harmony.

4. 'Alway,' in line 4 of this stanza, in Rous, is both an unfashionable word, and has no corresponding word in the original.

PSALM V.— 1. Bishop Horne, *in loco*, translates the original word by 'meditations,' or 'dove-like *mournings*;' and Bishop Patrick by 'silent *groans*,' or 'sighs.' It was therefore thought that Rous's word, 'meditation,' should be changed into 'mournful musings,' to bring out clearly the plaintive, pensive character of David's thoughts.

2. The arrangement of the words in this line might be altered thus:—

'My loud cry hear, my King, my God;'

thereby making 'my' less, and 'loud' more, emphatic than before.

3. 'Dayspring' and 'dawn' have been put for Rous's word 'early,' a term which does not necessarily mean the *morning*, but may also mean at a time not long after some period referred to. The expression, 'come early,' means merely, 'do not be late.' Let me have an *early* reply, that is, Do not delay long your answer.

4. In vers. 4, 5, 6, 'that,' as a relative, has been changed into 'who,' for a reason given in p. 7 of the Prefatory Remarks.

5. Rous's rendering, 'their inward part is ill,' seems greatly too weak to express the full force of the corresponding expression in the prose translation, 'their inward part is *very wickedness;*' hence the attempt to strengthen Rous's line. The inspired poet represents the wickedness of those referred to, to be like the wickedness of Satan in Milton, 'Evil, be thou my good.'

6. Rous's expressions, 'let all joy,' and 'make shouting noise,' being considered deficient in elegance, an attempt was made to amend them.

7. The expression in this stanza, 'compass him about as with a shield,' is both tautological and incorrect; tautological, in having both 'compass' and 'about;' incorrect, as a shield only defends, but does not compass the warrior.

PSALM VI. (L.M.)— 1. One object in attempting to amend this version of Psalm vi., was to reduce the number of its monosyllables—a kind of words to the use of which Rous seems to have been partial. Of this the first eight lines of Rous's version furnishes a proof. In these eight lines he uses forty-eight monosyllables, and only seven words of more than one syllable. One bad effect of a superabundance of little words, is a perceptible deficiency in the rhythmical flow of the verse.

2. Rous uses the words 'hot rage;' *rage* does not seem happily used in the circumstances as applied to God.

3. In the end of ver. 3 there is a thought only partially expressed, 'but thou, O Lord, how long?' Such expres-

sions are quite characteristic of strong feeling and passion.

4. The arrangement of the words in this line has been changed from that of Rous, to remove 'weary' from being immediately before 'am;' '*weary am*' is a collocation causing an *hiatus*.

5. Rous's expression, 'caused for to swim,' seems feeble by the use of the expletive 'for.' The 'for' has therefore been dropped in the attempted emendation.

6. The thought expressed in ver. 7 has been slightly modified, whether with, or without success, I presume not to determine.

7. In Rous's concluding stanza there is no rhyme, since 'gracious*ly*' and 'sudden*ly*' end with a syllable completely alike; hence the attempt to remedy this.

PSALM VI. (C.M.)—1. The change in this line is to supply the want of a syllable.

2. The accent being on the first syllable of 'therefore,' the line, as Rous has it, is inharmonious; hence the change of 'therefore' into 'since.'

3. In the last two lines of the fifth stanza in Rous's version, there are as many words as there are syllables; there is also an expletive, 'do.' To increase the harmony, and to remove the expletive, the words, 'now lying,' were used.

4. One of the parallelisms which occur so frequently in the poetical portions of the Old Testament seems to be in this sixth verse: 'the bed swims,'—'the couch is watered;' similar to that, 'he was wounded for our transgressions, —he was bruised for our iniquities.' (Isa. liii.)

5. In this line Rous, according to his custom, makes the *tion* in 'supplication' stand for two syllables; hence the attempted emendation. For a similar reason, 'prayer,' which Rous uses as a word of two syllables, is changed so as to count one. Strictly it has two, but in poetry it is not now used as a dissyllable.

PSALM VII.—1. The word 'that,' in Rous's line, is an inelegant redundance; hence the change.

2. To get rid of the untasteful parenthesis which occurs in this fourth verse, a different turn has been given to lines 3, 4. This turn to the thought, while it hurts not, but

rather brings out more forcibly the writer's meaning, does away with the parenthesis of Rous.

3. That by the word 'place' in this verse of Rous's version is meant a 'seat' or 'throne of judgment,' appears evident, both from the preceding and subsequent context; hence the attempted amendment.

4. In Rous this line is ungrammatical, by the two nominatives 'Lord' and 'he.' Our translators have not so rendered this verse. Rous sometimes has recourse to this expedient to eke out a line.

5. The pronoun 'he' has been changed into the noun for greater clearness.

6. In the last line of ver. 14, Rous, in opposition to our translators, has turned a past tense into a future, '*shall bring forth.*' That Rous in doing this was in error, appears from ver. 15, which is an explanation of the preceding verse. The conception referred to in the former verse was the making of the pit in the latter; the birth in the former verse corresponds to his fall into his own pit in the latter. The fall was a thing *past*, and not future; hence the change in the fourth line.

7. The word 'pate' has always appeared an unpoetical vulgarism; hence the attempted emendation.

PSALM VIII.—1. Rous's *didest*, as a word of two syllables, appearing feeble, is, by the attempted emendation, made a monosyllable, as it is now pronounced by all.

2. In Rous's third stanza there is no rhyme, as no one can say that 'framed' rhymes with 'ordained.' To remedy this defect was the object of the change.

3. The change of 'a' into 'but' modifies, but it is hoped improves the thought.

4. Rous's expressions, 'hands' works,' and 'under's feet,' are inelegant, also the expression 'do stray.' If by the changes made the language be improved, the meaning does not seem to be impaired.

PSALM IX.—1. In Rous this sixth verse is objectionable in having no rhyme, since the final syllables in the rhyming words are the very same. This verse in Rous is also ungrammatical in the words 'thou cities raz*ed*,' which should be 'thou cities raz*edst*.'

2. In ver. 7 Rous has left out the important word 'But;' and in the same line he has used a word, 'aye,' which is now obsolete, or nearly so. The amended form of the verse remedies both these faults.

3. In vers. 9, 10 the emendations are the change in three instances of *that* as a relative pronoun into *who*.

4 As given by Rous, there are two faults in this line, first, that of 'nations' being used as a word of three syllables, a mode of pronouncing the word which in our time is followed by no good speaker; and, secondly, the too prominent position of the word 'among;' hence the alteration made.

5. Here an emendation has been tried, to get rid of the obsolete term 'folk,' and also of the awkward arrangement, 'he not forgets.'

6. In the third line of this verse, the word 'always' is by Rous so placed as to lead naturally to a wrong pronunciation. In the amended form of the line this evil is remedied.

7. In ver. 16, Rous uses an expression which is at least doubtful as to its being good English, I mean, 'to work judgment.' One may use the phrase 'do, or execute judgment;' but 'to work judgment' is not to be imitated. To improve this English led to the emendation of this stanza.

8. Rous, in ver. 17, has a very imperfect rhyme, namely, 'be' with 'high.' It was the aim of the emendation to improve the rhyme without impairing the meaning of the stanza.

9. The concluding word in ver. 18, line 2, and also in line 4, 'alway' and 'aye,' are both words unsanctioned by modern usage.

PSALM X.—1. Rugged in Rous; hence changed.

2. In this line the construction not good, by the want of a relative; in the amended line the relative has been introduced.

3. In Rous the word 'blesseth' is apt to convey a wrong meaning; and Rous's expression, 'that's,' is not tasteful; hence the proposed emendation.

4. The second line of this stanza is encumbered with the expletive 'he;' hence the proposed emendation.

5. Rous has a double nominative in this line, arising from the Hebrew idiom. The emendation removes the superfluous pronoun 'they.'

6. In line 3 of this stanza Rous uses 'underneath,' an unpoetical word, at least now; and in his fourth line the word 'mischief' has a wrong position; hence the emendation.

7. In line 3, the expression, 'draws him *in* his net,' seems bad English. The 'in' should be 'into,' which is accordingly used in the emendation.

8. As the first half of this stanza contains a question, to which the last half is an answer, the third line might be read thus:—

'That God will ever be his judge.'

9. Rous's unhappy position of the word 'mischief' gave occasion to the emendation in this stanza.

10. In the first two lines of this verse Rous gives a specimen of awkward construction, a construction better adapted to the Latin than to the English language. The word 'desire' should rather be placed *before* the words 'of those,' than five words *after* these two. To remove this Latinized form of collocation, and to give to the clause the usual English mode of arrangement, gave occasion to this emendation.

11. For Rous's words, 'of earth,' are put 'from dust,' as somewhat more humbling to the oppressor's pride.

PSALM XI.—1. In this first stanza Rous has given a bad rhyme, 'ye,' 'high,' which has been amended. In the second line of the third verse, he appears to have given a wrong meaning to the question in that line; see Prefatory Remarks, pp. 11, 12. As will be there seen, Rous should have rendered the line in question as above, 'What can the righteous do?' This question, and most of the preceding context, is to be considered as spoken by David's timid friends. All the remaining part of the Psalm is to be regarded as the heroic and pious answer given by David to their question, and their well-meant but ill-judged advice.

PSALM XII.—1. The object of the emendation in the first eight lines is to add harmony and vigour to the style, by exchanging little words, such as 'do' and 'doth,' for words which are longer. Rous too frequently uses the resolved or divided form of the verb; as, I do write, I do sing, etc.

2. In this stanza 'be' has been changed into 'are,' 'that' into 'which,' and 'hath' into 'has.'

PSALM XIII.—1. In the first stanza of this Psalm Rous has failed, by putting unimportant words in prominent places, as at the close of lines 2 and 4, the words 'be' and 'me;' the design of the emendation was to remedy this.

2. Rous's expression, 'consider well,' seems too vague; and in the second line of the same stanza he seems to mistake the meaning; the petition there put up is '*hear* me,' not '*answer* me.'

3. In Rous's phrase, 'Lest *that*,' etc., the word *that* is unnecessary, and should therefore be left out.

4. In this stanza, in Rous's version, there are two faults: one is the putting of the preposition 'upon' after the word 'mercy,' and at the *end* of the line; a second fault is, that the fourth line wants a syllable, so that the word 'salvation' must be pronounced sal-va-*ti*-on. This latter fault (at least it is *now* one, whatever it might be in the days of Rous) occurs very frequently in the Psalms of this author. Both these faults are removed by the emendation.

5. As happens frequently in Rous, there is no rhyme in this stanza, 'cheerful*ly*,' 'abundant*ly*,' having in their final syllables the very same letters; hence the necessity for emendation.

PSALM XIV.—1. The emendation proposed seemed to the writer more poetical and more forcible than the line as given by Rous.

2. As given by Rous this verse is ungrammatical, by having two nominatives to one verb, namely, 'workers' and 'they;' the fourth line too is ill arranged, by the word 'on' being placed in a position of prominence. In Iambic verse, unemphatic words should not in general be put in the second, fourth, sixth, or eighth syllable of the line.

3. Instead of 'shame,' Rous's word in this line, the word 'mock,' or 'scorn,' seemed preferable.

PSALM XV.—1. In proposing the emendation in this 15th Psalm, the sole object was to improve the style, by suppressing or changing a number of Rous's auxiliary particles. In Rous's version of the above quotation, we have the word 'doth' four times in four consecutive lines. In the emendation two of these are struck out, and the other two modernized. In the first line of ver. 3, two monosyllables have been changed into the word 'neither.' In ver. 4, line 1, a similar change has been made, by putting 'wicked' for 'vile men;' in the second line 'the Lord' is put for 'God' in Rous, by which we get rid of the expletive *do* in the expression 'do fear.'

PSALM XVI.—1. Rous has tried to condense the matter of the first three verses into six lines. To remedy his apparently unsuccessful attempt, a stanza has been added in the emendation. Part of the obscurity occasionally met with in Rous's version may be traced to excessive condensation. He is very faithful in trying not to sink any thought; and he labours manfully, but not always with either clearness or elegance, to compress into two or four lines the matter of a verse.

2. In this fourth verse there is acknowledged difficulty in the meaning. Whether the emendation removes any portion of it I cannot be confident.

3. In the second line of this stanza, Rous's elongation of 'portion' into 'por-*ti*-on' gave occasion to the emendation.

4. 'The inheritance I got,' in the third line of this stanza, is not good English, unless the relative 'which' were put after the word 'inheritance;' the line as amended is free from this objection.

5. 'Since,' in this line, is put for 'sith,' obsolete.

6. Rous's word, 'corruption,' expanded into 'cor-rup-*ti*-on,' made an emendation necessary in the fourth line of this verse.

PSALM XVII.—1. 'That doth' superseded by the change in lines 3 and 4.

2. These lines seemed obscure in Rous; hence the attempt to make them clearer.

3. In Rous this line is rugged; 'visit'dst' is hardly pronounceable.

4. Rous translates a future as a past tense, 'found'st.' This has been altered in the emendation.

5. This line in Rous is obscure, especially the expression

'As for *men's* works.' Rous says nothing about these works. How far, or whether at all, the emendation improves this line, I shall not presume to say.

6. 'Hold up' changed into 'uphold,' and the word 'those' put out.

7. In this verse 'that,' as a relative, thrice changed into 'who.'

8. The expression in Rous, 'compassing round,' which is somewhat redundant, altered.

9. 'Which' changed into 'who;' the same in ver. 14, lines 1, 3.

10. 'Part and portion' seeming redundant, is the reason of the change into 'fleeting portion.'

11. 'Of their goods the rest,' unpoetical, therefore changed into 'remaining goods.'

PSALM XVIII.—1. 'That doth' changed into 'who does;' and in the sixth line of this verse, 'horn of my sal-va-*ti*-on,' has been changed.

2. The word 'there' changed into 'forth.'

3. 'Under his feet *attend*,' appearing an unpoetical expression, this stanza was modified.

4. The word 'thereon' is supplied by Rous himself, it was therefore considered allowable to put in its place the expression 'quick as thought.'

5. Perhaps the arrangement might be improved thus:
 'Discover'd were at thy rebuke.'

6. Perhaps the following arrangement might improve the harmony of the line:—
 'He me from many waters drew.'

7. The meaning, as the expression is given by Rous, is not clear. To make it clearer, 'beset' was put for 'prevented.'

8. As the word 'liberty' in this line is Rous's own, it has been dispensed with.

9. In Rous's arrangement the word 'upright' was in a wrong place of the line; hence the change.

10. I was obliged to alter the arrangement of the clauses to make it possible to pronounce the closing word, 'upright,' line 2, with the accent on the first syllable. In the

twenty-sixth verse Rous has failed here exceedingly, as his expression, ' froward thou kyth'st unto the froward wight,' is very unpoetical, and conveys also a wrong meaning. The word 'kythe' is not English, but Scotch; and the word 'wight' is far from dignity. See Bishop Horne, *in loco.*

11. By this emendation we are freed from Rous's expletive, '*do* lie.'

12. 'I scale,' is more in the military style than ' overleap.'

13. The second line of this verse is in Rous ungrammatical, from a redundant nominative, ' Lord ' and ' word.'

14. The relative 'that' discarded.

15. Lines 2 and 4 of this stanza have a redundant syllable, and, besides, do not rhyme; hence the emendation.

16. In line 1 Rous has ' sal-va-*ti*-on;' and in line 3 he separates without necessity the component parts of the compound verb to *uphold*. His version is too monosyllabic to be harmonious.

17. Rous's mode of expression seems obscure. The latter portion of the verse was a guide in attempting to amend the seeming obscurity of the former part.

18. Rous's ' destroy and slay,' in the third line, seems feeble; *slay* is not in the original.

19. ' Cried,' as a dissyllable, is feeble; hence the emendation.

20. The last two lines of this stanza seem badly arranged in Rous, by the relative ' that ' being placed too near the end of the sentence.

21. In Rous ' doth avenge,' changed into ' avenges.'

22. The word ' therefore' should not stand first in a line of Iambic verse.

PSALM XIX.—1. In the beginning of this Psalm. as in the beginning of the 16th, Rous, I apprehend, goes to an injudicious extent in condensing the meaning of the original. He attempts to render by six lines the entire meaning of the first three verses. I have endeavoured to amend this excessive compression by a little expansion.

2. ' Amid a blaze of light.'—Bishop Heber, in his work written in India, states it as his opinion, that the reference to the ' bridegroom in this verse does not point so much to

the personal adornment of the bridegroom as to the great light of his torch-bearing attendants.'

3. This Psalm, be it remembered, was written long before the date of the Copernican System of Astronomy.

4. Or, 'the soul enslaved by vice.' Perhaps this is preferable, in point of construction, to the line in the text; the meaning of the two lines seems the same; the learned reader will at once see that what follows 'soul' in either of the lines forms no part of the original.

5. In lines 2 and 4 of this verse Rous gives a syllable too much, and no rhyme; hence the emendation.

6. It is humbly apprehended that the proposed emendation in ver. 11 brings out the meaning of the inspired writer better than is done in the authorized version.

7. In stanza 13 of Rous, the word 'righteous' is by him made 'righ-*te*-ous;' hence the change.

PSALM XX.—1. In Rous 'sanctuary,' which is properly a word of four syllables, is squeezed into three. Besides, its final syllable is too feeble to be a good rhyming syllable.

2. The emendation leaves out 'and thoughts,' put in by Rous.

3. Rous makes 'prayers' a dissyllable. This word is not now used as such in poetry.

4. Rous makes 'chariots,' which is a word of three syllables, to be one of two; and in line 2 he closes the line with a preposition, thereby making the word 'upon' too emphatic.

5. Rous compresses vers. 8, 9, into four lines. This seemed to require some emendation and expansion; hence his four lines have been made eight.

PSALM XXI.—1. Rous here, as frequently, makes the word 'salvation,' sal-va-*ti*-on. This is rectified.

2. Rous makes 'bestowed' a word of three syllables. To do so makes a feebly-sounding line. The rhyme too, 'have' and 'crave,' is imperfect. The emendation was to remove these deficiencies.

3. To 'prevent with blessings,' is to a common audience not a clear expression; hence the amendment.

4. Rous's expression, 'Because that,' was considered unpoetical; hence a different turn was given to the phrase.

In the previous verse 'that' has been changed into 'the,' and the word 'comely' dropt, whether rightly or wrongly is another question. Neither 'that' nor 'comely' is in the original.

5. Rous's expression, to '*lay* confidence,' was deemed quite objectionable, we *put* or *place* confidence. To obtain a good rhyme, Rous in this case sacrificed good English.

6. Why Rous should allot only two lines to the tenth and eleventh verses, and four to every other verse of this Psalm, I cannot see; I have therefore tried to correct this excessive condensation on the part of the translator, by giving four lines to each verse.

7. In the second line of this verse, *for* 'WHEN arrows,' *read* 'THINE arrows;'—'when' is not in the original, neither is the word 'all' in line 3 of Rous.

8. In this line the expression, 'pow'r and strength,' appeared objectionable, on the ground that the words have nearly the same meaning, and because in the original there is only one word for the two. The word 'power,' besides, occurs in the fourth line, where, with no very great consistency, Rous uses it as a word of *two* syllables. The rhyme, 'high' and 'we,' is imperfect.

PSALM XXII.—1. Rous's 'All that' obviated.

2. The emendation gets rid of the expletive 'do.'

3. Rous's 'sith' changed into 'since.'

4. Rous has a bad custom of putting words between the antecedent and its relative; in the first two lines of this verse we have an example of this—antecedent 'thou,' or 'he,' separated from the relative 'that' by a whole clause.

5. Seemed more delicate than the line of Rous.

6. Ver. 15.—'My tongue it,' false construction.
Ver. 16.—'Compass'd about,' redundant.

7. In the fourth line of this stanza Rous has false grammar: 'thou gave,' for 'thou gavest;' hence the emendation.

8. 'Congregation,' made by Rous 'con-gre-ga-*ti*-on.'

9. Amended to unite the antecedent and its relative.

10. Faulty in Rous, by having too many little words.

11. In Rous badly constructed, by the relative 'that,' in line 3, being seven words after its antecedent 'they;'

and the unemphatic word 'do,' upon an emphatic or even place, namely, syllable six of the line.

12. It seemed an emendation to make the second line of this stanza end with the important word 'Lord,' in preference to the unimportant word 'unto.'

13. In Rous, the expression, 'appertain as his,' seemed an inelegant redundance of phraseology; we have also in this verse another specimen of na-*ti*-ons.

14. 'The rich,' instead of Rous's unpoetical phrase, 'fat ones.'

15. It appeared proper to amend the whole of this stanza, which, besides the defective measure of its third line, in 'gen-er-a-*ti*-on,' is altogether of an inferior character.

16. Rous begins the fourth line of this stanza with an 'and.' Query—What two words or clauses does this 'and' couple? In the original there is no corresponding word. The meaning of the verse seems to be, that those coming shall declare to a generation to be born God's truth and righteousness, manifested by his doing what is stated in the preceding context. If this be the sense, then the 'and' should become 'in,' as in the emendation.

Psalm XXIII.—1. Rous's word, 'again,' is redundant, there being no word for it in the original.

2. Rous writes 'none ill;' we do not say 'none' when its noun is expressed, as it is here.

Psalm XXIV.—1. Rous, in using the word 'remains,' did so probably because he needed a rhyme to 'contains.' Apart from this consideration, the word 'remains' does not either fully or accurately express the idea to be conveyed. To *remain* leads one to think of some who have *gone*, or been *taken away*. The inspired writer's notion is not this.

2. Rous, as usual, writes 'found-a-*ti*-ons,' as he afterwards, in vers. 5, 6, writes 'sal-va-*ti*-on' and 'gen-er-a-*ti*-on.' To attempt to rectify these faults in meaning and versification, I have been led to the above alterations.

3. Though the word 'God' is not in this sixth verse, yet it is so evidently understood, that it seems a proper, or at least an excusable liberty to supply it, especially when it is considered that, without the supplement, unlearned

readers may be at a loss to understand what is meant by 'seeking Jacob's face' with the whole desire of the heart.

4. Rous's somewhat antiquated word, 'aye,' has been left out. Though in the emendation the phraseology has been changed, the idea has been strictly retained.

PSALM XXV. (S.M.)—1. In the fourth line of this verse the word 'triumph,' as placed by Rous, destroys the harmony of the line; hence changed into 'rejoice.'

2. The third and fourth lines badly arranged by Rous; or rather ungrammatically constructed, by his giving the nominative 'those,' line 3, without any corresponding verb. The emendation was to rectify this.

3. The second and fourth lines of ver. 6 in Rous redundant measure, in 'remember,' 'ever;' hence the emendation.

4. Rous here couples the two prepositions, 'after' and 'for;' this changed for greater simplicity of construction.

5. Rous here, without necessity, contracted the word 'covenant' into 'cov'nant;' it seemed better to throw out the 'do,' and to restore 'cov'nant' to its uncontracted state.

6. Rous has in this stanza no rhyme, 'observe' and 'serve;' hence the emendation.

7. Rous writes 'Because *that*.' The latter of these two words better omitted.

PSALM XXV. (C.M.)—1. By this emendation the governing word, 'God,' is placed nearer the governed word, 'safety,' than in Rous, according to a general rule for the collocation of words.

2. Rous wants in this line a syllable, by his custom of making gracious 'gra-*ci*-ous;' the emendation rectifies this.

3. Rous in this stanza has no rhyme, 'alway' and 'way;' the word 'alway' is obsolete; its latter syllable, besides, is too feeble to be fit for a rhyming syllable.

4. Faulty in Rous, by ending with a preposition, a class of words quite unfit for rhyming syllables. In the department of rhyme, and in the selection of rhyming syllables, I remember no example of a writer so loose, defective, and careless as Rous is.

5. The arrangement, as given in the emendation, appeared to add force to the inspired poet's thought as compared with Rous's arrangement.

PSALM XXVI.—1. In this stanza, as given by Rous, two things seemed to require emendation: 'I trusted' should be made 'I've trusted,' to make it correspond with 'I have walked;' and in verse 3, with the verb 'I have trode,' which, by the way, should be 'trodden.' Another fault in the first stanza is, that its last word, 'I,' stands in a part of the line too prominent.

2. The change proposed is to rectify Rous's grammatical slip, 'I have trode,' which, as mentioned in the preceding note, should be 'trodden.'

3. 'Class' is put for Rous's word 'gather.' Line 3 in Rous inharmonious.

4. 'Con-gre-ga-*ti*-ons' in Rous; hence changed.

PSALM XXVII.—1. Rous's expression, 'saving health,' seems less definite and clear than the word 'safety' in the emendation. It is to be considered, too, that David, when he composed this Psalm, was, or had lately been, in danger from enemies.

2. Rous writes 'when as;' the 'as' is a cumberer of the sentence; 'what time' seems preferable.

3. Rous writes 'an host' wrongly, the *h* in 'host' being sounded. The change of Rous's 'is,' line 2, into 'were,' equivalent to 'would be,' improves the English of the expression, when we consider that the word 'though' is in the previous line. Line 3, the word 'this' is not more obscure in the emendation than in Rous.

4. The words in Rous, 'and admire,' and 'reverently,' are added by Rous himself.

5. Rous's expression, 'round encompass,' tautological; the next line also is ill arranged, and has a syllable too many. Rous's 'joyfulness' in the seventh line more vague than 'thanksgiving.'

6. Rous writes 'sal-va-*ti*-on,' *ut sæpe*. In next line, 'me leave not' more musical than 'leave me not' in Rous; so also 'me give not' in the first line of ver. 12.

7. Rous's phraseology in these lines not elegant; hence the attempted emendation.

Psalm XXVIII.—1. Rous's expression, 'hold not thy peace *to me*,' seemed neither very clear nor poetical.

2. Rous by leaving out the conjunction 'and,' connecting 'ill men' and the 'workers of iniquity,' has confounded two classes of bad men, that is, the negatively good, and the openly wicked. In the emendation the conjunction is restored.

3. Rous in this stanza has no rhyme, 'endeavour*ed*,' 'render*ed*.' The expression, 'handy works,' is unpoetical. To remedy these and other objectionable parts of the stanza, as given by Rous, the proposed emendation is given.

4. Our translators have rendered the verb in the original corresponding to the verb 'to regard,' by the present tense, indicative mood; Rous has turned it into a past tense. In the emendation, present tenses have been used in the verbs 'to understand,' and 'to regard.' Junius and Tremellius also use a present tense: *animadvertunt*.

5. Rous, in line 3, writes 'pe-ti-*ti*-ons;' and, in line 4, the feeble dissyllable 'pray-ers.' In the emendation it has been attempted to obviate these objections.

6. Ver. 7 has no rhyme, 're*ly*,' 'exceeding*ly*;' this deficiency amended.

Psalm XXIX.—1. Rous, in this stanza, as often in his version, has put the little words 'be' and 'ye' into prominent places. As his version of this sublime Psalm is not equal to several portions of his translations, the attempted amendments are unusually numerous.

2. Rous has given in this line a supernumerary syllable, so that the last syllable of the word 'beauty' must be cut off. In Milton such a practice is not very uncommon; but in lyric poetry it does not do well.

3. Rous in this stanza has no rhyme, 'Leban*on*,' 'Siri*on*;' this has been rectified in the emendation.

4. Rous has rendered the meaning of these two verses by four lines, while to all the rest, with one exception, he has given double the number of lines. In the emendation eight lines have been assigned to these two verses.

Psalm XXX.—1. To improve the harmony of the line was the design of the change.

2. Rous's expression, 'when *that* thou,' unpoetical.

3. This verse in Rous has neither rhyme nor proper measure; it wants rhyme, as the latter syllable of 'ascend' has the very same sound as the word 'send;' it wants proper measure, in 'sup-pli-ca-*ti*-on.'

4. While in Rous stanza eight has too few syllables, the tenth has too many, in 'gladness' and 'sadness.'

PSALM XXXI.—1. Rous's rhyme in this verse imperfect, *unce, fence;* and the fourth line inharmonious; hence the emendation.

2. The word 'therefore' should not begin an Iambic line.

3. Rous's composition is here bad, by a redundance of conjunctive particles, 'sith' and 'therefore;' and even though the latter of these two words had been useful, it should be at the end of a line.

4. Rous in this line has a 'for.' This word is one which Rous has put in, thereby hurting very much the music of the line.

5. From line 2 the 'and' has been struck out; in line 3, 'of those' changed into 'by those;' and in line 4, 'that' into 'who.'

6. In Rous this line is all monosyllables; the proposed emendation, 'on seeing me,' seems to improve the expression.

7. Rous writes, 'to lay trust;' not good English, and only used by him probably to rhyme with 'say.' Though Rous is very far from exact in the department of rhyme, yet in this example, and in others, he sacrifices good English from considerations of rhyme. We *lay a stone*, but we do not *lay*, but *put trust.*

8 Rous's measure, 'sal-va-*ti*-on,' amended.

9. The second line unmusical in Rous, and the rhyme 'have' and 'save' imperfect.

10. In the second and fourth lines of this verse, Rous has an expletive, 'do;' by the expulsion of these the style is invigorated.

11. This line in Rous has two faults, the word 'goodness' does not, I humbly think, express his idea so well as the word 'good,' used as a substantive noun. *Goodness* is an attribute of character; *good* denotes happiness to be enjoyed; a second fault in this line is the want of a relative, 'which,' before the word 'thou.'

12. Rous has in this stanza no rhyme, 'fied,' 'fied.' While by the emendation proposed the rhyme is amended, it is thought that David's meaning in reference to his escape from the city of Keilah is brought out more clearly than in the common version.

13. Invigoration of the style by the omission of two 'doths' was the object of this emendation.

14. The careful reader will observe that in this emendation the last part of Rous's stanza has been put first, it is hoped with some advantage, in regard to the natural arrangement of the thought which it conveys.

PSALM XXXII.—1. Rous in this stanza has no rhyme; by mistranslation, also, he has changed into 'sin,' in ver. 2, line 2, the word rendered 'iniquity' by our translators. One of the admitted beauties of these two verses is the variety of terms employed to mark moral evil, viz., 'transgression,' 'sin,' 'iniquity,' 'guile;' in Latin, *defectis, peccatum, iniquitas, dolus*. To the grieved penitent it is cheering to think that every kind of sin is to be pardoned and washed away.

2. Some change here made in Rous's style, such as 'when as,' into 'so long as,' and some changes of arrangement.

3. Or,—
'My very bones seemed age-worn from
my roaring all day long.'

4. Rous has in this stanza no rhyme.

5. Rous writes 'pray-er make;' better in sound, 'prayer address.'

6. Rous writes, 'horse or mule which do.' This expression not grammatical. Either the 'or' should be 'and,' or the 'do' should be 'does.' When two nominatives are connected by a disjunctive conjunction, we cannot, according to rule, use a plural verb.

7. Rous's style in this verse seemed inelegant in the expressions, 'his sorrows,' and 'compass round.'

PSALM XXXIII.—1. In these lines the style of Rous is quite grammatical and clear; but the emendation seemed somewhat superior in elegance.

2. The emendation more literal than the version of Rous,

both in the use of the term 'Lord,' and the suppression of the word 'is.'

3. Rous's expression, 'as it were,' is very flat.

4. In line 2 of this verse, Rous writes here, 'heathen folk ;' the latter of these words is obsolete.

5. 'O but ;' these words of Rous forming no part of the original, seem quite unnecessary.

6. Rous's rendering of this line, 'sees and beholds,' has much the appearance of repeating the same idea. The proposed emendation seems to remedy this. The Latin rendering is *intuetur* and *ridet*.

7. Rous has in this stanza no rhyme, 'serves,' 'serves.'

8. This line has in Rous only seven, instead of eight syllables, 'pre-ser-va-*ti*-on.'

9. The object of the emendation here was to improve the style by diminishing the number of auxiliaries.

10. It was thought that by changing Rous's word 'life' into the 'means of life,' the meaning would be clearer.

PSALM XXXIV.—1. It was thought that the insertion of the word 'at' before 'all' would improve the construction.

2. In the eight lines of these four verses (3-6), as given by Rous, there are two redundant syllables, 'faces,' 'distress*es* ;' and in the following stanza no rhyme, 'eth,' 'eth ;' hence the proposed emendations of these lines.

3. Rous's expression, to 'encompass round about,' is very tautological.

4. In Rous all monosyllables, hence the change, 'fearing him,' to improve the sound.

5. In Rous a bad rhyme, partly by the awkward contraction of the word 'spirit' into 'sp'rit,' and partly by the wrong position of 'contrite,' which is accented on the first syllable, and which therefore should not stand last in an Iambic line.

6. Rous has here in succession fourteen words of one syllable ; hence the substitution of 'Jehovah' for 'Lord,' for the purpose of improving the sound.

PSALM XXXV.—1. In these sixteen lines have been made the following changes :—In lines 1, 2, 'that,' as a relative, into 'who ;' in line 3, the position of 'take thou' altered, to put the word 'thou' in a more emphatic place of the line ; 'mine,' in line 4, changed into 'my,' because the *h* in 'help' is sounded. 'Also' has been changed into 'likewise' in line 5, to do away with the *hiatus* caused by 'also' coming after 'draw.' In ver. 4, changes in Rous's arrangement were made for the purpose of placing relatives immediately after antecedents, 'they who,' 'those who.' Rous very often improperly separates these.

2. Rous has put the word 'it,' which finishes this stanza, in a position far too prominent for the comparatively little importance of the word.

3. In the second line, to make good English, Rous should have put a 'which' after the word 'net ;' and he should have written 'into,' and not '*in* destruction.'

4. In Rous's English here there are two faults, one in the want of a relative after the word 'things,' and another in the improper arrangement of the words ' I not knew.'

5. Rous has in this stanza two redundant syllables, 'moth*er*,' 'broth*er* ;' and in stanza 15 the very same fault, 'togeth*er*,' 'gath*er*,'—and no rhyme.

6. Rous here also wants a relative after the word 'destructions.'

7. The last two lines of this verse contain an example of improper arrangement, in the antecedent 'them' being placed six words after its relative 'who' at the beginning of line 3. The statement of these faults in Rous's style forms my apology for attempting to amend them.

8. Rous writes, 'to *afford* judgment.' This, I suspect, is not good English ; we never read of a judge *affording* judgment in a case—he *gives* or *pronounces* judgment ; but the poet needed a rhyme to the word 'Lord.'

9. Rous's lines are grammatical, but far from poetical English. The object of the emendation was to make this language less flat, and to make the concluding line musical.

PSALM XXXVI.—1. There are two reasons for attempting to amend this stanza of Rous—the first line wants a syllable, 'trans-gres-*si*-on ;' and the rhyme is not good, as the word 'says' does not rhyme well with 'eyes.'

2. It seems at least doubtful whether, in the beginning of this stanza, Rous's word 'because' conveys properly the

notion of the original word. Bishop Patrick turns the expression, '*though* he flatter,' etc.

3. The first and second lines in this stanza, as given by Rous, seemed not tastefully expressed.

4. It was thought that Rous's arrangement of the first two words might be advantageously changed.

5. Rous writes '*in* heaven,' and such certainly is the literal rendering; but what is *in* heaven, is *above* the visible heavens, in so far as any beholder from our earth is concerned.

6. Rous has the word 'therefore' in a wrong position.

7. Rous's arrangement of this line is rather Latin than English arrangement.

8. In Rous the first two lines awkwardly arranged, and 'upright' in a wrong position.

9. Rous uses the word 'arise,' when he should have used 'rise.'

Psalm XXXVII.—1. Rous writes 'like unto the grass.' This seemed feeble.

2. In the second line of this verse, 'Cut off *and* fall;' this 'and' seemed better out.

3. 'Drawn out' changed into 'unsheathed,' combining two short words into one.

4. In the first word of this line the definite appeared preferable to the indefinite article.

5. Rous's word, 'same,' unpoetical in this way of using it.

6. Rous has here no rhyme, 'ly,' 'ly;' hence the proposed emendation.

7. Rous, in line 2, the word 'therefore' improperly last.

8. Rous improperly gives an interrogative arrangement to this line.

9. In Rous this stanza is redundant in measure, 'togeth*er*,' 'ev*er*,' and has no rhyme.

10. This line in Rous has nine syllables.

Psalm XXXVIII.—1. Rous wants here a syllable, 'in-dig-na-*ti*-on.'

2. Rous uses the expression 'to *do* sin.' Is this good English? We say '*do* evil,' or '*do* iniquity.' We say

'*commit* sin;' I do not remember any good authority for '*to do* sin.'

3. Rous's last word, 'me,' too prominently placed for its relative importance. The chief object here pointed at is the weight of the burden, not the bearer of it.

4. The word 'smell' more delicate than Rous's word.

5. Rous's arrangement here too Latinized.

6. In the second line Rous writes 'at distance,' before 'distance' should be made an *a* to make good English. Line 4 in Rous is rugged.

7. 'Mischievous' improperly placed by Rous.

8. The design of this emendation was to make the style more poetical. Rous, though in general a literal and a faithful translator, is not unfrequently unpoetical.

9. Rous in this part of the Psalm repeats four times, in four verses, the word 'for.' It is no doubt true that vers. 15-18 begin each with this particle. But for Rous to repeat this word so often in so short a space, is rather logical than poetical in style.

10. This line altered to bring the relative and its antecedent together, 'those who.' The last two lines, as given by Rous, awkwardly expressed.

PSALM XXXIX.—1. Perhaps the last clause of this verse might be more literally rendered—

. . . 'but silence stirr'd
My sorrow and my pain.'

2. Rous's expression, 'what is the *same*,' seemed flat. In the emendation the sense is retained, and an attempt made to obviate the ruggedness of the verse.

3. Rous writes 'work;' the word 'deed' seemed preferable, when in the prose version the expression is 'thou *didst* it'—not 'thou *wroughtst* it.'

4. Rous has here no rhyme, 'iniqui*ty*,' 'vani*ty*;' he violates also the laws of grammar in the expression, line 3, 'thou wastes,' instead of 'wast'st.'

5. Rous's expression, 'recover *again*,' is tautological, since the notion of 'again' is in the prefix of the word - recover. His expression, 'from hence,' is tautological also, as the word 'hence' means 'from this;' hence the proposed amendment.

PSALM XL.—1. As Rous in this stanza has no rhyme, 're*lies*,' '*lies*,' the proposed emendation was given.

2. Rous here splits into two parts the word 'towards.' This not very tasteful expedient has been by the amendment rendered not necessary.

3. Rous ungrammatical here in the words 'thou bor'd;' he probably did this, not in ignorance, but to avoid the roughness in sound of 'bored'st; not a good excuse, as grammatical accuracy is in composition essential.

4. Rous writes 'Behold and see.' The word 'see' seems more for the sake of the rhyme than of the meaning.

5. Has in Rous no rhyme, 'righteous*ness*,' 'faithful*ness*.'

6. Lines 3, 4 in Rous grammatically incorrect, by the nominatives 'lovingkindness' and 'truth' being without a verb; for the verb 'maintain' is the verb 'to let them.'

7. Rous writes in the second line 'confounded;' 'desolateness' is the idea.

8. In Rous this line has strictly only seven syllables. 'Saviour' being properly a dissyllable.

PSALM XLI.—1. Ver. 1 has in Rous, in lines 2, 4, a redundant syllable, 'consid*er*,' 'deliv*er*;' hence the emendation.

2. Rous writes 'for why?' changed into 'because.'

3. Rous's words, 'but then,' changed into 'meanwhile.' Rous writes 'heaps mischief to *it*'—to what? What *it*?

4. Rous writes 'mischief;' our translators write 'an evil disease.'

5. 'Triumph' cannot stand first in an Iambic line.

PSALM XLII.—1. Disliking Rous's word 'bray,' which applies rather to an ass than to a hart, I have tried to amend this stanza.

The design of the other changes was to improve the style in some places. In ver. 4, Rous ends line 2 with a preposition, a bad rhyming word, from the subordinate place which it holds in a sentence. Rous's word, 'heretofore,' scarcely poetical at least. Rous's word, 'multitude,' changed into 'tribes assembling,' as the word 'multitude' is soon repeated in the same verse.

2. Rous in this line has put the word 'the' into a place too prominent.

3. In Rous 'op-pres-*si*-on;' this changed.

4. In the second line of this verse Rous's arrangement changed for the sake of sound.

PSALM XLIII.—1. Rous in this stanza gives good rhyme, but bad measure, 'nation' and 'salvation.' Dr. Watts is a model for exactness, both in rhyme and measure; Rous the very reverse.

2. In this stanza Rous, as frequently, goes wrong in measure, in the word 'op-pres-*si*-on.' The last word, 'fro',' in line 2, is rather of the old school, one certainly which a poet of the present day would scarcely use.

3. Rous writes 'chief*est* joy,' an example of a double superlative; 'greatest' seems better.

4. In this verse Rous has made several supplements to the text; there was consequently the less need of excessive caution about altering his version of this stanza.

PSALM XLIV.—1. In the fourth line of this verse Rous writes, 'but them thou didst increase;' our translators write, 'and cast them out.'

2. To avoid the ambiguity often caused by the too abundant use of pronouns, it was deemed conducive to clearness to put in the first line the words, 'our fathers,' in place of 'their.'

3. Rous writes, 'go'st not with the same.' This last word, in this application of it, unpoetical.

4. Rous's rhyme imperfect, 'back,' 'take;' also line 4 is feeble, from the expletive 'do.'

5. In the fourth line Rous writes 'round about;' tautological.

6. In Rous flat, and somewhat obscure. Whether the proposed amendment makes what is bad any better, I am not sure.

7. In Rous not clear; nor am I sure about the emendation being any better, the Psalm being rather dark here.

8. The fourth line in Rous seeming objectionable, both in regard to the mode of expression and arrangement, a reconstruction of the stanza has been attempted.

9. Rous's expression, 'our heart not turned,' unpoetical; the 'not' should follow, not precede, 'turned.' 'Brak'st' changed into 'brok'st.'

10. 'Esteem'd' suited the beginning of the line better than Rous's word 'counted.'

11. As in the beginning of this verse the inspired poet refers to the soul being bowed down to the dust, and as 'belly' is joined by 'also' to the word 'soul,' it was thought proper to turn 'belly' into 'body,' as being opposed to the 'soul.'

PSALM XLV. (C.M.)—1. Rous's word, 'indite,' not now met with in poetry, so far as I remember.

2. Rous's word, 'ev'n,' changed into 'clothed,' as the sacred poet is speaking of the king's official ornaments.

3. In Rous a syllable wanting, 'sub-jec-*ti*-on.'

4. Rous writes 'for God.' Our translators write 'therefore God,' etc. See some notice taken of this in the Prefatory Remarks, p. 10. That Rous has here mistaken the sense of the passage seems very clear; and the mistake is most important, 'for' standing before the cause, and 'therefore' before the effect. 'Hence,' the word put in the emendation, corresponds nearly to 'therefore.'

5. Rous writes 'palaces.' As 'garments' are referred to, 'wardrobe' seemed the more appropriate term.

6. As the queen was the most conspicuous of the females referred to, it seemed an emendation of some consequence to close the stanza by the word 'queen.'

7. Rous writes 'then.' It is difficult to see the propriety of this word, no time being visibly referred to. The word 'so' seemed better, representing the king's vehement affection for the queen, as flowing in part from her forgetting her father's house and former friends, and transferring her love to her spouse.

PSALM XLV. (S.M.)—1. Line 3 wants a syllable, 'sub-jec-*ti*-on.'

2. See note 4 in common metre version, above.

3. 'Ophir's,' for 'Ophir' in Rous.

4. Rous's line appearing rather flat, the proposed amendment seemed preferable.

5. 'Mirth' changed into 'joy,' as the word 'mirth' seems deficient in gravity and sacredness.

PSALM XLVI. 1. In vers. 2-4, the changes proposed

are such as to make the emendation more of a strictly literal rendering than that of Rous.

2. It was supposed that by placing the word 'her' before 'nothing,' the sound of the line and force of the style would be improved.

3. In the third line Rous writes, 'the Lord God;' but as neither 'Lord' nor 'God' is in the text, it seemed an improvement to leave out the word 'God,' and to put in its place the word 'but,' as above.

4. Here, and also in ver. 11, the word 'refuge' ends the line in Rous. 'Refuge' cannot properly end an Iambic line.

5. In Rous a syllable wanting, 'de-so-la-*ti*-on.' The syllable wanting has been supplied.

PSALM XLVII.—1. Here, as frequently, Rous gives a line of seven syllables, by the word 'na-*ti*-ons.' This rectified.

2. This stanza, as given by Rous, is not perspicuous. The object of the emendation was to remove the seeming obscurity.

3. Ver. 9, lines 3, 4.—In Rous these lines not clearly expressed; and it appears doubtful whether the poet's thoughts be correctly conveyed. The design of lines 1, 2 was to make honourable mention of the princes who were present on the great occasion; and the object of lines 3, 4 was to bestow similar commendation on those of less elevated rank, of whom many thousands were present.

PSALM XLVIII.—1. See Bishop Patrick *in loco;* also Henry *in loco*, and on Psalm lxxv. sect. 2.

2. Rous seems to have expanded too much the sixth, and to have condensed too much the seventh verse. In ver. 6 Rous's first line is all his own; whereas, in rendering ver. 7, he has been so very laconic as to be, to ordinary readers, unintelligible. The design of the two verses is to picture by two expressive figures the consternation of the assembled kings. The woman in labour pictures their fear and pain, the shipwrecked sailors their despair either of victory or even of safety.

3. Rous allots to this verse five lines, here there are six. The first two lines bring out what had been told them of God's former doings; the third and fourth lines state what

they had just now seen of God's doings. The former and the latter were in complete harmony.

4. Rous's 'Sion mount' changed into 'Sion hill.'

5. As 'walk about' and 'go round' are so much alike, I with some hesitation modified the line as above, on the authority of Bishop Patrick.

PSALM XLIX.—1. The 'and' in Rous's first line not in the original.

2. In Rous, lines 3, 4 unpoetical and unintelligible. These four verses immediately following (6-9) contain only one sentence. In the emendation it will be seen that the word 'none' at the beginning of ver. 7 governs the words 'of those,' at the beginning of ver. 6.

3. Perhaps the following couplet would be preferable:—

'And when the honours of his house
    augmented greatly be.'

This would also improve the rhyme.

4. Vers. 19, 20.—Rous allots to these two verses only four lines; in the emendation the four have become eight, without, it is thought, any undue expansion.

PSALM L. (S.M.)—1. Rous's fourth line, 'hath his fall,' very flat.

2. Latinized construction, 'of excellency and beauty the perfection is.'

3. In line 2 the 'he' too prominently placed.

4. 'Heavens clear,' not elegant in expression.

5. Rous's style here seemed somewhat improvable.

6. Rous, to make good rhyme, wrote here bad grammar, 'thou went,' for 'thou went'st.'

7. In lines 2 and 4 Rous has a redundant syllable, and no rhyme; these rectified.

8. In line 3 a syllable wanting, 'sal-va-*ti*-on.'

PSALM L. (C.M.)—1. Rous writes 'hath spoke,' bad English for 'spoken.'

2. The words, 'from thence,' redundant.

3. Rous writes, 'compass about,' redundant.

4. By putting 'fowls' to the end of the line, it comes immediately before its relative 'which.'

5. Improvement of style the object of the change here.

6. Rous writes 'sith' twice, changed into 'since.'

7. In lines 2 and 4 Rous has redundant syllables, 'sal*vation*,' 'conver*sation*,' making the antepenult the rhyming syllables.

PSALM LI.—1. The proposed emendation, while it preserves the thought, seemed to improve the style.

2. In Rous has no rhyme, 'ness,' 'ness.'

3. In Rous badly constructed; the nominative, 'lips,' has no verb.

PSALM LII.—1. In Rous no rhyme, 'ly,' 'ly;' and bad arrangement in the word 'mischievous.'

2. 'For ever' has been put for Rous's 'for aye.'

3. The object of the proposed amendments was to give to the style somewhat more of a poetical cast, without materially changing the sense.

PSALM LIII.—1. Style weakened by the frequent use of substantive verbs. In Hebrew they are seldom used. By the proposed change one of the 'are's in this line got rid of.

2. Rous writes, 'if there was;' it should be 'were' after 'if.'

3. This stanza ungrammatical in Rous, by the nominative, 'workers,' having no verb.

4. To improve the mode of expression was the design of the modification here.

PSALM LIV.—1. 'Save me,' changed to 'me save,' since the word 'save' is here the more important term of the two, 'safety' being the thing prayed for.

2. Rous's arrangement not happy, 'mischief' standing at the beginning of line 2.

3. Rous writes 'free willingness;' unpoetical.

4. Rous writes 'his,' as applied to the eye; better 'its.' That in Hebrew there is no neuter gender, is no argument for the use of 'his' to the eye.

PSALM LV.—1. 'Nor' is the proper measure, or equivalent of 'and not,' the words of the text.

2. Rous writes 'hater that did 'gainst me ;' unpoetical.

3. Rous writes ' pray and make a noise ;' flat this.

4. Rous is here obscure, by separating the relative 'who' much too far from its antecedent 'Lord,' seven words intervening. It is hoped that by the proposed emendation the obscurity is removed, and the meaning fairly given. Or it may be given as follows :—

'Me hear, and them afflict, will God,
who hath of old abode ;
Because they never changes have,
they $\begin{Bmatrix} \text{have no} \\ \text{want the} \end{Bmatrix}$ fear of God.'

In this rendering the word 'therefore' in the last line of Rous has been left out intentionally, as uncalled for in our phraseology.

5. Rous writes ' more smooth' and ' more soft.' In monosyllabic adjectives the comparative degree is formed by adding *er*, in preference to prefixing more, going upon the Horatian rule, '*usus est norma*,' etc.

PSALM LVI.—1. As Rous in the first eight lines has twice the expression 'swallow,' the style was varied by 'devour.'

2. Rous writes ' thou took,' a grammatical blunder, to find a rhyme for ' book.'

PSALM LVII.—1. In Rous less literal than the emendation. In line 8 he uses the word ' overpass' in a sense not given in Johnson's Dictionary ; the rhyme imperfect, ' place,' ' pass.'

2. Rous writes ' digg'd,' passable, but inferior to ' dug.'

3. Rous writes ' above the heavens to stand,'—the meaning would have been better given without the last two words ; but the poet needed a rhyme to suit ' land,' line 4.

PSALM LVIII.—1. Rous writes 'congregation' here. It seems doubtful, at least, whether this word conveys the meaning ; when it is from the context evident that 'judges,' 'rulers,' and 'counsellors' are meant.

2. These two lines, as given by Rous, convey to me at least no definite meaning. It is not very clear even in the prose version. Whether the proposed amendment be any

improvement, I am not confident; but the view which it gives of an intentionally corrupt administration of justice seemed to agree with the preceding and following verses.

3. Rous writes 'cunning,' better 'skilful,' as the word cunning is now taken only *in malam partem*.

4. Not well arranged by Rous.

5. Rous writes 'still *do*,' better 'always,' as we thereby get quit of the expletive 'do.'

6. Ungrammatical, by a 'he' redundant in Rous.

PSALM LIX.—1. Rous has here no rhyme, 'ty,' 'ty;' this rectified.

2. Rous writes 'do combine;' this expletive got rid of by the emendation.

3. Rous's style is here unpoetical; and in the first line he mistranslates, as the notion is not that of 'walking to and fro,' but, as in verse 14, that of 'returning,' referring probably to the attempts of Saul to seize David, as related in 1 Sam. xix.

4. Rous writes, 'belch out with their mouth;' not tasteful this. Line 3 feeble by the 'do say.'

5. Latinized arrangement in Rous.

6. Rous writes 'folk;' changed into 'saints.'

7. To improve the mode of expression was the object of this emendation; such as 'words flying from the lips, etc.'

PSALM LX.—1. The text has here no 'and,' as in Rous.

2. Why 'earth' in line 1, and 'land' in line 4, as in Rous! This tends to confusion of ideas. It is no doubt true that in several languages the same word signifies land and earth. But in the second verse the land of Israel was probably meant; if so, the word 'earth' was unsuitable.

3. Rous writes 'delivered be from thrall;' unpoetical.

4. Lines 2, 4 in Rous have redundant syllables, 'plea*sure*,' 'mea*sure*.'

5. 'Of mine head the strength,'—construction too Latinized.

6. Rous, 'washing-pot;' unpoetical.

7. 'Who is he will' inelegant. Ver. 10, line 1, 'hadest' feeble in two syllables.

Psalm LXI.—1. Rous here writes 'refuge' and 'shelter,' in line 2. These two rather impair than increase the notion of security here conveyed. 'Refuge' is not in the text. It was therefore deemed proper to put for 'refuge' 'danger,' showing the need of a shelter.

2. Rous's rhyme imperfect, 'have,' 'save.'

3. Rous writes 'perform the same;' quite intelligible, but not poetical.

Psalm LXII.—1. In Rous a syllable wanting, 'ex-pec-ta-*ti*-on;' he has the same want in ver. 5, line 4; hence the proposed changes in both verses. The same want occurs also in verse 10, line 1, 'op-pres-*si*-on.' In ver. 10 also, we have, in line 3, the unpoetical expression, 'when as,' a favourite with Rous.

2. Rous uses the word 'power' as a dissyllable; this does not sound well in poetry.

Psalm LXIII.—1. Rous's word, 'wherein,' not now commonly used.

2. 'Power,' used as a dissyllable, not elegantly. In line 3 we find 'heretofore,'—fallen into desuetude.

3. Rous, strictly following the text, writes 'marrow and fat.' It appeared that the expression given in the proposed emendation is more tasteful and refined, and that it yet does not fail to convey the idea intended.

4. 'To spill the soul,' an expression unpoetical.

5. Not he who 'swears,' but he who keeps his oath, is opposed to the 'liars' in line 4,—meaning probably those who violate their oath by perfidy and disloyalty.

Psalm LIV.—1. Rous uses 'prayer' as a dissyllable too feeble to be so used.

2. Feeble and unpoetical, in Rous, '*do* lay.'

3. Rous's phraseology simplified in the emendation.

4. 'Upright' cannot well stand at the end of a line.

Psalm LXV.—1. Rous allots to these two verses only four lines. In the proposed emendation these four have been made eight. Rous's word, 'waits,' line 1, does not fully and adequately convey the sacred poet's idea.

2. Rous's 'purge away' changed into 'wash away;' and the syllable wanting in Rous's third line supplied.

3. Rous's 'sal-va-*ti*-on' rectified.

4. Rous's arrangement not good, both in the position of 'therefore,' and the 'who' in line 2.

5. The object of the proposed emendation is to improve Rous's phraseology.

6. In translating vers. 4, 5, Rous allots to each eight lines. Ver. 9 is about as long as either of these. In the emendation eight lines are given.

7. In this stanza Rous has no rhyme, as 'lie,' 'ly,' have the same sound in the initial consonant *l;* hence the emendation.

PSALM LXVI.—1. By changing Rous's position of 'cheerfully,' the *hiatus* caused by 'cheerfully' coming before the word 'unto' is avoided.

2. The text has no 'and' at the beginning of this line, nor 'ev'n' at the beginning of line 3.

3. The change made in this line improves the rhyme, 'eye,' 'high.'

4. To 'speak the voice of his praise,' was thought objectionable in expression.

5. 'Bands' changed into 'loads,' referring to the burdens laid on the backs of the enslaved and oppressed Israelites in Egypt.

6. In line 2, Rous's style seemed improvable.

PSALM LXVII. (S.M.)—1. In comparing Rous's two versions of this Psalm, it seems unaccountably strange that in the short metre he should, to the first two verses, give only four lines; while in the common metre he allots to the same two verses eight lines. In the short metre he allots twenty-six syllables to these two verses. In the common metre fifty-six syllables, that is, more than double the number. Hence, in the emendation of the short metre, Rous's four are made eight lines.

PSALM LXVIII.—1. Rous's 'all' not in the text, nor his word 'and.'

2. Syllable wanting, ' ri h-*te*-ous.'

3. To improve the style is the design of the change.

4. No 'and' in the text here, as in Rous.

5. 'By which' more modern than Rous's 'whereby.'

6. No 'and' at the beginning of this line in the text. Rous's 'did distribute' better 'distributed,' as to accent.

7. Rous's 'and in triumph'—no 'and' in the text; the word 'triumph' accented on the first syllable.

8. Order of the musicians—first, vocal band of men; secondly, females with tabrets; thirdly, an instrumental band. Rous's 'among' improper. Rous writes 'to *take* way;' not good English.

9. In Rous line 1 is defective, by 'con-gre-ga-*ti*-ons;' line 3 is obscure.

10. Rous writes '*and* silver'—no 'and' in the text, nor has the text any word answering to the 'and,' line 8.

11. Rous's 'for' not in the text.

Psalm LXIX.—1. By the change made, the expletive 'do' is got rid of. A similar change for the same reason has been made in ver. 4, line 1.

2. Rous writes 'who search do make, and seek thee.' To fill up this stanza, the poet is here very tautological.

3. Rous writes 'spake,' obsolete,—now 'spoke;' hence the change.

4. Rous writes, 'hath broke.' The past participle is 'broken,' not 'broke.' In Rous line 4 ill arranged; this rectified.

5. Rous here, as occasionally, writes 'when as.' The 'as' is merely to eke out the line, but has here no meaning.

6. Wants a syllable, 'in-dig-na-*ti*-on.'

7. Wants a syllable, 'ha-bi-ta-*ti*-on.'

8. Rous writes, 'be raz'd and blotted quite.' There is here redundance. The text has merely 'blotted;' the 'quite' was intended, no doubt, for a rhyme to 'writ,' line 4. But the word 'writ' is to the word 'quite' not a good rhyme; and it is still more objectionable as a specimen of good English, in our days at least.

9. 'The humble men.' As in the text there is no word answering to 'men,' this word has been left out in the proposed emendation.

10. Rous writes 'inherit shall the *same*.' Tame phraseology this. Hence the attempt to amend it.

PSALM LXX. (S.M.)—1. Rous has a syllable redundant, 'deliv*er*.'
2. Rous's arrangement, and his relative 'that,' changed. In line 2, 'insults' appeared preferable to 'shaming.'
3. In the text there is a word answering to 'but;' but there is none answering to 'am.' Of the two, 'but' seemed here the more needful, and therefore restored.

PSALM LXXI.—1. In Rous a syllable wanting, 'con-fu-*si*-on.' This supplied by the proposed amendment.
2. As the word 'rock' occurs in line 4, and as in the text there is no word for 'rock' in the first clause, a rendering more literal than that of Rous is given.
3. The object of the change in this stanza was greater delicacy.
4. Rous gives here redundant syllables.
5. The design of the emendation was to unite the separated antecedent and relative, 'those who;' in Rous, 'they that.' The same design gave rise to the proposed amendment in ver. 13, 'those who;' in Rous, 'they that.'
6. Wants a syllable, 'sal-va-*ti*-on.'
7. Rous's word, 'thereof,' obscure. To make the expression clearer dictated the change made.
8. Rous should have had a relative after 'wonders;' rectified.
9. By the amendment are united the separated antecedent and relative, 'those who;' in Rous, 'they that.'

PSALM LXXII.—1. Rous in this stanza has no rhyme, 'ness,' 'ness;' hence the emendation.
2. Rous writes 'the same,'—flat this; rectified.
3. Rous's arrangement changed, to unite antecedent and relative, 'those who.'
4. 'Do last,' changed into 'remain,' to get rid of the 'do.'
5. Rous writes, 'doth the,' changed into 'does the,' for better sound.
6. To make this monosyllabic version less so, the word 'dwellers' was preferred to Rous's line.

7. Rous's 'that hath' modernized into 'who has.'

8. Rous's rhyme imperfect, 'spare,' 'are,' rectified; and to improve the sound of line 2, Rous's arrangement modified.

9. Rous wants here a syllable, 'pre-*ci*-ous;' rectified.

10. The word 'shake,' as applied to corn, seems infelicitous, as, in the agricultural sense of the term, it denotes a partial loss of the crop by wind. Will the word 'wave' do better?

PSALM LXXIII.—1. Ill arranged by Rous, in putting 'I' before 'envious;' and the stanza flat in the manner of expression.

2. Has in Rous a syllable redundant, 'con-tin-u-eth.'

3. Rous writes, *ut sæpe*, 'compasseth about;' redundant.

4. Rous wrong, 'blasphemous' being accented on the first syllable.

5. Rous writes 'wealth and riches,'—a pleonasm.

6. An unmusical, unpoetical line; hence the attempt to improve the stanza.

7. To have 'daily' in this line, and 'every morning' in line 3, tends to confound and perplex the reader.

8. Or, 'new stripes did me await.'

9. 'Sanctuary' gives a syllable too many; hence 'dwelling-place.'

10. In Rous, 'upon' is a bad word for the end of a line which rhymes; and line 4 wants a syllable, 'de-struc-*ti*-on.'

11. To 'consume *away*,' in Rous, a pleonasm.

12. Rous wants the word 'vain;' but it, or some similar word, seems required to balance the word 'despise' in line 4.

13. In Rous 'beast' rhymes not well with 'oppress'd;' hence the change.

14. In Rous the measure is redundant in lines 2 and 4, 'never' and 'ever.' It is tedious to be so often referring to his irregularities of measure and rhyme. But still I deem it proper, as my apology for changing his stanzas. When verses are to be sung, as the Psalms are, their measure should be exact, to suit the notes of a psalm tune.

PSALM LXXIV.—1. Stanzas 2-5 are defective in measure, in 'con-gre-ga-*ti*-on,' 'de-so-la-*ti*-ons,' 'con-gre-ga-

ti-ous,' ' es-ti-ma-*ti*-on.' The translation of this Psalm, as a whole, seems one of Rous's least happy productions; hence the emendations are so many as to amount to nearly a new version. In Rous, vers. 15-17 are very good.

2. Rous writes 'defil'd the same;' unpoetical.
3. Rous ends the line with a preposition, 'among.'
4. Rous writes ' deliv'rance' sake;' inelegant.
5. Rous writes 'all the earth,'—'all' not in the text.
6. In Rous doubly ungrammatical, first, by 'thou brake,' instead of 'thou brakest;' then 'brake' should be 'brokest,' —with an *o*, not an *a*. 'Brake' in desuetude.
7. Rous puts the word 'leviathan' in a wrong position; and, contrary to the inspired poet, gives the monstrous animal only one head.
8. Rous writes 'keep it in record,'—'record' is accented on the first syllable, and cannot therefore well stand where placed.
9. Lines 2 and 4 have each a supernumerary syllable, 'deliv*er*,' 'ev*er*.'
10. Rous writes 'return again,'—pleonastic; as the idea conveyed by 'again' is in the prefix of '*re*turn.' Instead, therefore, of putting the word 'again,' I considered it better to put the word 'unheard,' as giving a reason for the shame felt on returning, namely, that the prayer of the oppressed for relief was not listened to.
11. This stanza, especially lines 3 and 4, as given by Rous, is by no means clear as to its meaning. The design of the proposed emendation is to bring out with more perspicuity the meaning of the sacred poet.

Psalm LXXV.—1. In Rous these lines are rather obscure, and line 2 wants a syllable, 'con-gre-ga-*ti*-on.'
2. Rous's expression, 'bear up and stablish well,' flat, and rather pleonastic.
3. In Rous obscure, as there is nothing declared.
4. Rous's 'lewd' and 'just' changed into 'bad' and 'good.'

Psalm LXXVI.—1. Rous has in this line nine syllables.
2. Rous writes 'brake;' changed into 'broke.'

3. In Rous this line all monosyllables, and, with one xception, the whole stanza.

4. Rous writes 'in a dead sleep,' changed to 'into,' etc.

5. Rous writes 'thou caus'd,' should be 'causedst.'

6. Rous writes 'remnant.' This word commonly means something small and inconsiderable.

7. In Rous the meaning not clear; nor can one see why he made 'spirit,' 'sp'rits.'

PSALM LXXVII.—1. Rous's word, 'Lord,' not in this verse; and the word 'God,' belonging to the second clause, he has put in the first clause.

2. The design of the amendment was to elucidate the meaning.

3. The object of this emendation was to point out, as is done in line 3, the probable subject of meditation, and to improve the mode of expression; such as, 'years agone.'

4. Following Bishop Patrick, I have pluralized 'song.' 'Commune' is accented on the second syllable; and 'spirit' cannot well be made a monosyllable.

5. In Rous 'gra-*ci*-ous.'

6. In Rous 'yea,'—no 'yea' in the text.

7. Rous writes 'the na-*ti*-ons among;' rectified.

8. In Rous the relative improperly placed.

9. Rous's 'did flee,' changed into 'fled.'

PSALM LXXVIII.—1. As in Rous line 2 seemed nearly a repetition of line 1, it appeared proper to make the proposed emendation.

2. Wants in Rous a syllable, 'gen-er-a-*ti*-on.'

3. Rous writes 'spirit' in one syllable; an inelegant contraction.

4. As Ephraim seemed intended for an instance of unsteadfastness, the word 'like' has been thrown in.

5. 'Brake' changed into 'broke.' In line 1, ver. 11, the arrangement changed to bring together the antecedent and relative.

6. The emendation unites two assertions into one. Rous's words, 'and ev'n,' in line 4, not in the text; 'fertile' seemed more natural to complete the line.

NOTES. 327

7. Rous's 'for us' too prominently placed; rectified.

8. The word 'behold' changed into 'we grant,' to suit the strain of these murmurers' reasoning.

9. Lines 3 and 4 in Rous very unpoetical; hence the attempt to improve them.

10. Rous here makes prepositions rhyming words,—a practice not to be followed; and in line 4 he writes 'li'th.' Did 'lies' not occur to him?

11. In Rous has nine syllables. 'Round about,' and 'tabernacles and tents,' pleonastic.

12. In Rous the last three lines unpoetical.

13. Rous's arrangement altered to unite the antecedent 'food' and its relative 'which.'

14. Rous writes 'fattest,' better 'goodliest.'

15. Rous ends the line with 'therefore,' a word accented on the first syllable.

16. 'Consume and waste,' pleonastic.

17. Rous writes 'spake;' should be 'spoke.'

18. Rous has here a syllable wanting, 'per-fi-*di*-ous,' for 'per-fid-yous;' this rectified.

19. Has no rhyme, 'ness,' 'ness.'

20. 'Lives of them;' flat this.

21. This line wants two syllables—has six for eight.

22. Has no rhyme, 'ly,' 'ly'

23. 'Shame perpetual' unmusical; last syllable feeble.

24. Rous, I apprehend, has failed to give the sense.

25. When Rous wrote 'Jehudah,' he must have been sore pushed.

26. Not felicitous.

PSALM LXXIX.—1. Rous confuses the tenses of verbs here; line 1 is a *perfect;* line 4 is what in Greek would be an *aorist.* Yet what is in line 4 must in time be posterior to what is in line 1. In line 4, therefore, Rous's 'they' should be 'they've.'

2. Rous writes 'slain and dead;' flat and pleonastic.

3. Ends in Rous with 'we;' too prominently placed for a pronoun.

4. Rous writes 'keep the same;' unpoetical.

5. Rous writes at the end of this line 'upon,' a word too unimportant for such a place.

6. Rous has here no rhyme; 'ly,' 'lie,' have the same sound.

7. Rous writes 'prevent us;' to an ordinary reader obscure.

8. Rous writes 'design'd to die.' Not clear, as an ordinary reader would suppose that those to whom this word is applied were resolved to die; that death was their intention.

PSALM LXXX.—1. In making the proposed modification of these lines, the meaning, rather than strict letter, of the text was attended to. It is quite plain that Joseph's descendants were meant, from the present tense of the verb *guide* being used.

2. Rous here wants a syllable, 'sal-va-*ti*-on :' rectified.

3. Has in Rous no rhyme, 'safe,' 'safe ;' and this stanza occurring thrice in the Psalm causes three stanzas to be without rhyme. But in these three stanzas Rous has not, I think, fully conveyed the sense. What is mainly objectionable is the use of the word 'safe,' rather than 'saved.' To be safe is one thing, and to be saved is another; the latter, and not the former, is the word used by our translators. To be safe, is to be out of danger; to be saved, is to be delivered from evil felt, not apprehended or feared. But it may be said, Why put in 'afflicted and enslaved?' From vers. 12 and 13 it is clear that those referred to were both afflicted and not in their own power at the time; but persecuted, oppressed, and wronged on all sides.—See Patrick, Horne, and Orton, *in loco*.

4. Rous writes 'laugh and flout,'—of questionable elegance; and in line 2 he has 'round about,'—a pleonasm.

5. Rous writes 'to make *a* room.' The use of the article here is worse than useless. It hurts the sense.

6. Lines 2 and 4 have each seven syllables; rectified.

PSALM LXXXI.—1. Unable to see a good reason for Rous's compressing into eight lines the matter of these four verses, I have in the emendation made the eight become sixteen; properly or improperly is another question. Improper condensation is one extreme; paraphrastical expansion is another : 'in *medio* tutissimus ibis.' In this respect Rous seems at times to go to extremes. In Psalm lxxviii. he allots eight lines to one verse, viz., 55, while here he gives only eight lines to four verses.

2. Rous's arrangement changed.

3. Rous's arrangement seemed not good, in putting 'shalt' after 'thou.'

4. Ungrammatical, by a redundant nominative,—'Israel' and 'he ;' hence the proposed emendation.

5. Rous has here no rhyme, 'ed,' 'ed ;' rectified.

6. In Rous ungrammatical, 'had chose' for 'chosen.' To rectify this is the design of the change.

PSALM LXXXII.—1. In this Psalm, as in Psalm lxxxi., Rous allots only eight lines to the first four verses. In the proposed amendment here, as before, four lines have been given to each verse.

2. Rous writes, 'out of their course are gone ;' prosaic and unmusical.

PSALM LXXXIII.—1. This line has been modified to introduce a dissyllable more among so many monosyllables in this stanza, viz., two.

2. The amendment seemed in phraseology preferable to Rous's rendering.

3. The secrecy of the consultations is so evidently implied, that the addition of 'close' seemed advisable.

4. This stanza has neither rhyme, proper measure, nor elegance of style. It is one of Rous's worst.

5. Very prosaic and flat.

6. In Rous wants a syllable, ' pos-ses-*si*-on.'

PSALM LXXXIV.—1. These two lines are Rous's own. As the matter of ver. 1 is all given in the first two lines, I have modified lines 3 and 4, only to make them grammatical. As given by Rous, they have a redundant nominative, viz., 'they,' line 4.

2. Rous's word, 'purchased,' changed into 'provides.'

3. Rous here must have been in difficulties, when he changed the preposition 'through' into the adjective 'thorough.' In line 2, 'dig,' Rous's word, changed into 'make,' which is quite literal.

PSALM LXXXV.—1. In Rous has a supernumerary syllable.

2. In Rous a rugged line, by 'took'st' and 'turn'dst.'

3. In Rous not well arranged; hence modified.

4. Rous writes 'folk;' obsolete.

5. In Rous this stanza has neither rhyme nor full measure in lines 2 and 4.

PSALM LXXXVI.—1. 'Sith,' obsolete; changed into 'since.'

2. A syllable wanting, 'gra-*ci*-ous.'

3. 'Not any work is *there ;*' this unimportant word too prominent.

4. Rous's word, 'the,' before 'glory,' darkens the meaning.

5. In Rous has no rhyme; and lines 2 and 4 want a syllable each.

PSALM LXXXVII.—1. 'And' of Rous changed into 'but,' as apparently better fitted to bring out the meaning.

PSALM LXXXVIII.—1. Vers. 1-4. Rous has allotted eight lines to these four verses; in the proposed emendation vers. 1 and 4 have each four lines assigned them, making, for the whole four verses, twelve lines.

2. Line 1, and indeed the whole stanza, in Rous seems obscure. To remove this darkness was the design of the proposed amendment. 'Set free,' that is, the *dead man*, set free from the world and the bondage of affliction, referred to ver. 3.

3. In Rous this stanza has in lines 2 and 4 a redundant syllable; this rectified by the emendation.

4. In Rous has a syllable too little, 'af-flic-*ti*-on.'

5. In Rous this stanza has no rhyme, 'ness,' 'ness;' hence the proposed emendation.

6. Rous, by giving to this verse only two lines, writes in line 2, not clearly, in the expression—

'at morn prevent shall thee.'

Lines 3 and 4, in the proposed amendment of ver. 13, bring out, if I mistake not, the meaning with more perspicuity. As Rous gives it, the prayer was to *prevent God ;*

as the emendation gives it, the prayer was to be presented *before* the dawn of morning. *Veniet præ horâ matutinâ.*

7. To improve Rous's style was the object of the modification in this stanza.

8. As the 'and' at the beginning of line 2 couples the words 'friends' and 'him,' it was thought that the construction would be clearer by putting 'friends' at the end of line 1.

PSALM LXXXIX.—1. Rous in this line puts in 'graciously,' not, I think, judiciously, as he was giving the language of the great Jehovah respecting his own doings. In these circumstances the words of the text should by the translator be strictly given, with the least variation possible.

2. Wants in Rous a syllable, 'con-gre-ga-*ti*-on;' rectified.

3. The rhyme rectified.

4. As expositors have no doubt that by the 'sound' in this verse is meant the sound of the trumpets used by the Jewish priests, it seemed preferable to give to the expression the turn in the emendation.

5. By changing Rous's arrangement here, a *hiatus* is avoided, 'they exalted be on high.'

6. Rous writes 'horn *and* power;' changed into 'horn *of* power.'

7. Rous writes 'out of the folk,' changed into 'Judah's tribe;' 'folk' obsolete. In putting 'Judah's tribe,' it was adhering strictly to the fact, if not to the *ipsissima verba*.

8. Rous writes 'exact on him;' obscure.

9. In Rous wants a syllable, 'sal-va-*ti*-on.'

10. Rous writes 'commandements;' altered.

11. Rous writes 'spake;' obsolete.

12. For my authority in giving the 'bow' here, see Horne, *in loco.*

13. Rous writes 'abhor and loathe.' The last two words Rous's own; also 'displeas'd' is Rous's own.

14. Rous writes 'hast broke,' should be 'hast broken.'

15. Rous wants here a syllable, 'in-dig-na-*ti*-on;' rectified.

16. Rous writes 'then, to rhyme with 'Amen;' but the word 'then' is Rous's own, and in the present case seems very inappropriate.

PSALM XC.—1. Rous writes 'again,' unnecessary when the word 'return' is used,—unless it were addressed to a person who had been raised from the dead, and who was about to die a second time.

2. 'Changing grass;' see for this Bishop Horne's rendering of this verse.

3. The 'and' which Rous banished has been replaced in the emendation.

4. The 'and' which Rous put in has in the emendation been put out; for the same reason, the word 'sins' has been put out of the first line, and 'faults' out of the third.

5. Rous writes here 'wrath;' prose version, 'anger.'

6. 'Wherein' twice changed into 'in which;' and at the beginning of line 3, where Rous had added an 'and,' the added word has been displaced, or rather banished.

7. Rous here, as often, makes a preposition a rhyming word; a thing never to be done, if possible to avoid it. This rectified in the proposed emendation.

PSALM XCI.—Rous writes, 'by day, while it is light.' This is apparently not a good line, as 'day' supposes 'light;' but the poet needed a rhyme for 'night.'

2. Rous has here no rhyme, 'ly,' 'ly;' rectified.

3. In Rous the style unpoetical and pleonastic, since 'to look,' and to be a 'beholder,' are similar, if not identical.

4. Wants in Rous a syllable, 'ha-bi-ta-*ti*-on.'

5. By changing Rous's word 'ill' into 'evil,' the style is improved by omitting 'shall,' line 2.

6. Rous's line altered, because it ends with a preposition; and as the whole of this line forms no part of the text, there is the less occasion for hesitation about changing it.

7. Altered for a better rhyme; 'free,' 'high,' not good.

8. Wants in Rous a syllable, 'sal-va-*ti*-on.'

PSALM XCII.—1. Thrice in this one Psalm Rous writes ungrammatically. Of the examples of bad grammar, the first is in this line. Rous writes, 'To render thanks unto the Lord, *it* is,' etc.; the 'it' redundant.

2. Ungrammatical 'each thought of thine how deep *it* is;' the 'it' redundant.

NOTES.

3. Changed, to put out Rous's apocryphal word 'lewd.'
4. Ungrammatical. Where is the verb to the nominative 'those' in line 1? Either 'those,' or 'they,' line 3, is without a verb. These errors amended.

PSALM XCIII.—1. The change was made to lessen the number of monosyllables. In this stanza there are twenty-five.
2. Rous's 'but yet' not in the text.

PSALM XCIV.—1. Rous's arrangement here too Latinized, in making 'Judge' stand after, instead of before, 'earth.'
2. Rous writes 'uttered and told;' unpoetical and pleonastic.
3. Rous writes 'folk,'—obsolete; rectified.
4. The word 'chastise' is accented on the last syllable.
5. In Rous a relative wanting before 'thou.'
6. Rous has here no rhyme, 'ty,' 'ty.'
7. Rous writes 'quit and forsake;' pleonastic.
8. Rous writes 'return again;' pleonastic.
9. Rous's arrangement of 'almost' changed.
10. Lines 2 and 4 have each an expletive, 'do;' rectified.
11. Rous writes 'shall of iniquity the throne.' Latin in arrangement.
12. Rous writes, 'But of my refuge God's the rock.' Latin in arrangement. 'Rock' should precede, not follow, 'refuge.'

PSALM XCV.—1. In Rous a syllable wanting, 'sal-va-ti-on;' rectified.
2. Rous writes, 'the same did make;' unpoetical.
3. Lines 2 and 4.—These two lines want a syllable each; and the rhyme, instead of being in the last syllable, is in the antepenult; rectified.
4. Rous writes, 'tempt'd and prov'd,'—the 'and' omitted.
5. Rous writes 'sware;' obsolete.

PSALM XCVI. 1. These two verses limited by Rous to four lines; in the proposed emendation extended to eight lines. He has allotted four lines to ver. 3, though it is shorter than the first or second.

2. Wants in Rous a syllable, 'na-*ti*-ons.' Rous seems improperly to have put a 'the' before 'people,' line 3. Our translators give it 'all people,' not 'all the people.'

3. Rous writes 'idols dumb.' As the latter clause of this verse refers to God's power in making the heavens, it seemed right to change 'dumb' into 'powerless.'

4. Rous's arrangement too Latinized—'of people ev'ry tribe;' rectified.

5. Rous's word, 'likewise,' tame, and not in the text.

6. Rous has here no rhyme, 'ly,' 'ly;' rectified.

7. Rous writes 'cry out and make a noise;' changed into 'lift up their deafening voice,' because the 'noise' referred to is the roaring of the sea. Rous's line was thought not sufficiently expressive.

8. Why Rous and our translators have rendered the first clause of this verse by the imperative, and the second clause by the indicative mood, it is not easy to see. Junius and Tremellius render it by *exaltabit et cantabunt*, both indicatives; there is here no mixing of moods.

Psalm XCVII.—1. To these two verses Rous assigns four lines; the amendment eight.

2. Rous's arrangement changed; in line 4, 'I say' dropt.

3. Rous writes twice unpoetically in the first four lines of this verse, in putting the relative and its clause before the antecedent and its clause. Both of these rectified.

4. Rous writes 'above all other gods thou art.' The word 'other' is apocryphal, and quite unnecessary. It is not in the prose translation.

5. Rous writes 'all ye,'—'all' apocryphal.

6. Rous ends this line with the word 'upright.' This word being accented on the first syllable, cannot properly end an Iambic line.

7. This stanza has in Rous no rhyme, 'ness,' 'ness;' this rectified.

Psalm XCVIII. 1. In Rous a syllable wanting, 'sal-va-*ti*-on.'

2. The word 'he,' end of the line, too prominent.

Psalm XCIX.— 1. Rous's expletive, 'doth,' got rid of.

2. Rous writes 'for;' apocryphal.

3. Rous's expression, 'the king's strength,' is quite literal, but to an ordinary reader not clear.

4. Rous in this stanza, as frequently, but not judiciously, makes pronouns rhyme, thereby giving them undue prominence.

5. Lines 3 and 4 in Rous badly composed, by wanting the word 'which' after 'testimonies.' These two lines, altogether, are far from tasteful composition. The same observation applies with about equal justness to the composition of stanza 8, especially line 4. To '*have* vengeance,' is not elegant English; 'wouldest' should not be a dissyllable.

Psalm C. (L.M.)—1. Rous writes 'do dwell;' expletive.

2. Rous writes 'mirth.' Since Rous's time, 200 years ago, this word has gradually become less applicable to sacred things.

3. Rous writes 'praise, laud;' tautological.

4. Rous writes 'For why?' obsolete, if ever good.

Psalm C. (C.M.)—1. Rous's measure redundant in lines 2 and 4, 'thithe*r*,' 'togethe*r*.'

Psalm CI.—1. Rous writes, 'To sing mercy,' etc.; our translators write, 'to sing *of* mercy.' I prefer the expression of the latter. *Arma virumque cano*, is good Virgilian Latin; 'I sing arms and the hero,' is not equally good English, though a literal translation of this Latin.

2. Rous writes 'endure;' our translators, 'I will set before mine eyes.' Junius, *proponam*. Rous wrong.

3. Vers. 5-8.—The changes in these verses have for their object some improvement in Rous's style; as, for instance, the flat line, 'who of deceit a worker is,' ver. 7.

Psalm CII. (C.M.)—1. Rous's rhyming words too unimportant for their position.

2. Rous here wants a syllable, 'in-dig-na-*ti*-on.'

3. Rous writes 'dry'd and withered;' pleonastic.

4. Lines 3 and 4.—These two lines pleonastic in Rous, since to 'endure continually,' and to be 'to generations all,' mean the same thing.

5. Rous twice uses the word 'prayer' as a dissyllable; not now done.

6. 'Record' (a substantive) used by Rous as if accented on the second syllable, which is not now the fact.

7. Rous uses the word 'spy,'—a word not sufficiently dignified as applied to God.

8. Rous writes 'strength and force,'—pleonastic; 'force' apocryphal.

PSALM CII. (L.M.)—1. In Rous faulty, by the word 'access,' which is accented on the first syllable, being wrong placed.

2. Rous places the word 'therefore' in a wrong position.

3. Vers. 8, 9.—In Rous not well composed. To improve the style was the object of the changes.

4. Wants in Rous a syllable, 'in-dig-na-*ti*-on.'

5. 'Change and mutation,' tautological.

6. The substantive 'record' cannot end properly this line.

7. Rous has here suppressed the word 'Lord,' for no apparent reason.

8. 'Thy endless years do last for aye,' changed to get rid of 'do' and 'aye;' the former feeble, and the latter obsolete.

PSALM CIII.—1. 'Hath bestow'd,' changed into 'bestows,' and 'which' supplied.

2. Lines 2, 4 want in Rous a syllable each, 'gra-*ci*-ous,' 'plen-*te*-ous.'

3. Rous improperly closes the line with 'alway.'

4. Rous writes 'in heavens firm to stand.' The last three words Rous's own. Rous's word, 'command,' line 4, not appropriate, as applied to 'kingdom.' A general *commands* his army; a kingdom, or king, *rules*.

5. Rous's 'and' here not in the text.

6. Lines 2, 3.—In Rous not well composed; hence the proposed emendation.

PSALM CIV.—1. In Rous a syllable wanting, 'foun-da-*ti*-ons;' this rectified.

2. This line, both in Rous and in the emendation, is not

in the text; but it was thought that line 4, as amended, is more in harmony with line 3 than Rous's fourth line is.

3. Rous writes 'they fled, and would not stay;' pleonastic.

4. Some commentators, among whom Bishop Patrick, explain this as if the 'mountains' rose, and the 'valleys' fell, seemingly forgetful that it is of the 'waters' of these that the inspired writer is speaking.

5. Rous has here a redundant syllable in lines 2 and 4, 'over,' 'cover.' This rectified.

6. Lines 2 and 4 want a syllable.

7. Rous writes by 'fruits and increase;' tautological.

8. Rous's word, 'use,' changed into 'sustenance.'

9. In Rous there is no rhyme, 'ful,' 'full.' This has been rectified by the emendation.

10. Rous evidently places the word 'leviathan' as if it were accented on the penult. Either he was wrong in this, or this word is pronounced differently now.

11. In Rous the reader is led to suppose that those who in the preceding verse are said to 'die,' are in this verse said to be created. The emendation is fitted to clear up this point.

12. In Rous this stanza has in lines 2 and 4 a redundant syllable, 'ever,' 'together.'

PSALM CV.—1. Vers. 1, 2.—Rous has allotted to these two verses only four lines. In the emendation eight lines, yet not paraphrastical.

2. The change in lines 1 and 2 was made to give to them more of the turn of an imperative mood than Rous does.

3. Rous writes 'which admiration breed;' unpoetical.

4. Rous's rhyme here, if rhyme it may be called, is at least very imperfect, 'approven,' 'own;' rectified.

5 In Rous the meaning not clear; it was felt hard to give an emendation quite satisfactory.

6. In Rous neither the rhyme nor the style good.

7. The word 'Canaan', as now pronounced, has only two syllables. Rous here gives it three.

8. Rous has here added more words than he commonly does; such as, 'Yet, notwithstanding,' 'great and strong.'

The emendation is an attempt to improve the stanza in style.

9. Rous's word, 'brake,' changed into 'broke.' In ver. 17, line 1, the arrangement modified, for the purpose of uniting the antecedent 'man' with the relative 'whom.'

10. Rous's construction Latinized, by the word 'charge' being placed long after its regimen.

11. The repetition of the word 'he' is hurtful; the word 'teach' has been changed into 'instruct,' to get rid of the 'he.'

12. Rous's word, 'envy,' cannot well end a line; neither is 'envy,' but 'hate,' the proper word.

13. Rous's word, 'spake,' changed into 'spoke.'

14. Rous writes, 'were none,' ungrammatically. 'None' is 'no one,' and cannot therefore take a plural verb.

15. Vers. 44, 45.—Improvement in the style the object of the changes in these stanzas. Rous's arrangement in ver. 44 not good—too like Latin.

PSALM CVI.—1. Rous's expression, 'that love,' changed into 'the love;' 'that' is neither in the text, nor is it useful.

2. Rous has 'triumph' in a wrong position.

3. Rous here, as often, makes 'power' a word of two syllables; not so used now.

4. Rous writes 'dried up it was;' feeble.

5. Rous writes 'of those,'—text, 'of him.'

6. Rous writes 'But,' etc., not in the text; and as 'But' begins ver. 14, the former 'but' has been omitted. Ver. 13, besides, has no rhyme, 'ly,' 'ly.'

7. As in the verse preceding, Rous has here no rhyme, 'tempt,' 'sent.'

8. Rous writes 'en-*vi*-ous;' wrong now.

9. 'Therefore' in a wrong position; rectified.

10. Rous's word, 'then,' not in the text, and put there to be a rhyme for 'men.'

11. To make the calf was a great sin, and to make it in Horeb was a great aggravation of the sin, a mountain near which the law had so lately been given in alarming majesty, and out of whose rocky foundation miraculous water daily

flowed. On these grounds the word 'very' was put before 'hill.' In the latter clause of ver. 19 there is nothing in the text about the *making*, but only about the *worshipping*, of the image.

12. 'Stood in breach,' unpoetical.

13. 'Therefore' wrong placed; rectified.

14. The change here was made on the assumption that Baal was the god worshipped, and that the hill Peor was the place of his temple. If this assumption be erroneous, the line may be

'With Baal-peor's votaries
they did for worship meet.'

15. Wants a syllable. Line 2 has an obsolete word, 'ire;' and line 4 another obsolete word, 'brake.'

16. Lines 1 and 3 changed, by making 'rose and' become 'rising,' and 'that' become 'this.'

17. In Rous flat and prosaic; hence the attempt to mend it.

18. Rous has here no rhyme, 'ly,' 'ly,'; rectified.

19. 'Canaan,' as now pronounced, has only two syllables; hence the proposed amendment.

20. Rous here wants a syllable, 'in-ven-*ti*-ons.'

21. 'Therefore' cannot end an Iambic line; hence the proposed change.

22. 'Regard,' which is our translators' word, seems here preferable to Rous's word 'beheld.'

23. Rous writes '*of* all those,' better '*by* all,' etc.

24. Rous has a redundant syllable, 'gath*er*;' this has been corrected.

PSALM CVII.—1. Vers. 1-4.—Rous has allotted to these verses only eight lines; in the proposed emendation the number of lines has been doubled. It is not always easy to catch the happy medium between excessive condensation and excessive expansion. In looking at the prose version of this Psalm, ver. 38 has seventeen words; ver. 39 has only twelve words; yet Rous has allotted two lines to the longer of these verses, and four lines to the shorter, which is the very contrary of what one would expect.

2. Vers. 12, 13.—In Rous four lines; in the emendation eight lines given to these two verses.

3. Rous writes 'brake;' obsolete.

4. 'Mighty gates,' changed into 'massive gates;' and 'in sunder,' changed into 'asunder.'

5. In Rous has no rhyme, 'ness,' 'ness;' rectified.

6. 'To swell and rise,' tautological.

7. Rous's arrangement modified, to bring the antecedent 'God' immediately before its relative 'who.'

8. 'Command and will,' pleonastic.

9. In Rous has no rhyme, 'ness,' 'ness;' rectified.

10. To improve the phraseology was the design of the emendation.

11. Rous improperly, I think, translates as an indicative mood what is really a subjunctive mood. He puts a full point at the end of ver. 36, where our translators have only a semicolon. This rectified. For 'stones,' in line 2, read 'stores.'

12. These two lines want a syllable each in Rous; and the stanza has properly no rhyme, at least no proper rhyme.

13. Rous's phraseology modified.

PSALM CVIII.—1. Verses 3, 4.—Rous's four lines to these verses made eight.

2. Rous's arrangement changed.

3. Vers. 7, 9, 10, 11.—See notes on Psalm lx.

PSALM CIX.—1. Rous writes 'false and lying tongue;' tautological.

2. 'Round about,' tautological.

3. Rous writes 'spight,' changed into 'spite.'

4. In Rous this line is prosaic and inharmonious.

5. Rous's arrangement Latinized; rectified.

6. The pronoun 'I' not a good rhyming syllable; for the same reason the word 'me' in line 4 of ver. 25 has been changed. Pronouns so placed are too prominent in position.

7. Rous here places the 'who' too far from its antecedent 'thou.' This rectified.

8. Rous writes 'hast done the same;' unpoetical.

9. Rous's arrangement changed.

10. Rous has in lines 2 and 4 a syllable too much.

11. For the pronoun 'he,' it was thought advisable to put the noun 'God,' as conducive to perspicuity.

PSALM CX.—1. Rous's expression, 'The Lord did say,' changed into 'Jehovah said;' and 'whereon' into 'on which.'

2. In Rous, lines 2 and 4 have each a redundant syllable, 'nev*er*,' 'ev*er*.' This rectified.

3. Slightly changed in lines 2 and 4, by which it was supposed the style would be somewhat improved.

4. The word 'that' changed into 'which.' In lines 3 and 4 Rous's expression, 'for this cause,' changed into 'therefore.'

PSALM CXI.—1. Lines 2, 4.—In Rous these lines have a redundant syllable, 'mea*sure*,' 'plea*sure*;' rectified.

2. Has a syllable too little, 'com-pas-*si*-on;' rectified.

3. Rous here, as frequently, uses 'power' as a dissyllable; not now so used in poetry.

4. Rous writes 'handy-works;' unpoetical.

5. Rous writes 'folk;' obsolete. Lines 2, 3 are in meaning obscure, both in Rous and in the prose version. 'To command a covenant for ever' is not a clear expression. Whether the proposed amendment makes the expression any clearer is another question.

6. Rous writes 'for aye;' antiquated.

PSALM CXII.—1. Rous's 'commandements,' inelegant.

2. In Rous ends with a preposition; changed.

3. 'Riches and wealth.' This is quite literal; but as riches and wealth are of the same meaning, another turn has been given to the phrase in the emendation, without injury, it is hoped, to the sense.

4. 'He' being a pronoun, is not in ordinary cases a word fit for a rhyming syllable.

5. By changing Rous's arrangement, the sound is improved by separating 'him move.'

PSALM CXIII.—1. Vers. 1-4.—In Rous eight lines are allotted to these verses; in the emendation sixteen. Can a good reason be given why in Rous vers. 7, 8 should have each four lines, while the first four verses should have only two lines each?

2. Vers. 5, 6.—Rous's composition in these verses faulty. His expression, 'who can compare?' should be 'who can be compared?' Neither of the relatives, 'that,' in ver. 6, is well placed, especially that in line 2.

3. Rous's 'doth raise' changed into 'raises,' as more elegant. 'Oppress'd with poverty,'—the word to 'oppress' applies better to the conduct of a usurer or of a tyrant than to poverty.

PSALM CXIV.—1. Rous's expression, 'while as,' not good.

PSALM CXV.—1. In Rous a rugged line.

2. Rous, I apprehend, puts here the question wrong, and writes also bad English. The question is not whither God was 'gone,' but where he is. Where is he gone? is not good English, as the 'where' should be 'whither.' Whether the proposed emendation be any improvement, I do not pretend to say.

3. The word 'that,' to be tasteful English, should begin the line.

4. Rous's word, 'them,' seems redundant; or, if not, is not in a right position.

5. Rous's words, 'nor' and 'not,' darken the meaning, and do not, it is likely, convey Rous's meaning.

PSALM CXVI.—1. 'Cords' not in the text. Line 2, in Rous, very tautological.

2. More literally translated in the emendation than in Rous.

3. Rous writes 'lo,'—not in the text.

4. The change in this line was made to make the sense plainer.

5. 'Spoke,' for Rous's 'spake.'

6. Rous's arrangement Latinized,—'of salvation the cup.'

7. Rous writes 'servant sure;' the latter word is not in the text.

PSALM CXVII. 1. In Rous a syllable wanting, 'na-ti-ons.'

2. In Rous the preposition 'toward' awkwardly divided.

Psalm CXVIII.—1. Vers. 1-4.—In Rous all the short lines have a redundant syllable.
2. In Rous the word 'therefore' wrong placed; rectified.
3. In Rous inharmonious from the position of 'better.'
4. Rous writes to 'compass about;' tautological.
5. In Rous unpoetically composed.
6. Rous's 'my' not in the text.
7. In Rous a syllable wanting, 'righ-*te*-ous.'
8. In Rous this stanza has in lines 2 and 4 extra measure.
9. In Rous the relative 'that' is much too far from its antecedent 'he;' this rectified.

Psalm CXIX.—1. 'That' changed into 'who.'
2. Rous writes 'inclined to observe,' etc.,—not literal this.
3. Rous writes 'praise and bless;' pleonastic. In line 3, as 'judgments' governs 'righteousness,' the nearer the former word is to the latter in position the better.
4. Rous here, as frequently, makes a pronoun a rhyming syllable, thereby making it too prominent.
5. Rous's rhyme imperfect, 'fy,' 'be;' this rectified.
6. Rous's arrangement changed for greater harmony.
7. 'Stored' seemed plainer than 'hid,' in giving the sense.
8. In Rous wants a syllable, 'me-di-ta-*ti*-on;' rectified.
9. Rous writes 'with spite,'—not in the text.
10. Rous writes 'commandements;' altered.
11. Rous, in the verb 'remove,' changes the voice, turning the active into the passive. 'To grant law,' obscure: hence the change in lines 3 and 4.
12. Rous writes 'truth and verity;' tautological.
13. As given by Rous objectionable; as unworthy of God.
14. The words, 'of life,' added for greater clearness.
15. Rous has here a redundant syllable.
16. Rous writes 'sight and eyes;' tautological.
17. Rous here wants a syllable, 'sal-va-*ti*-on.'

18. Rous has here no rhyme, 'ly,' 'ly;' this rectified.
19. 'Sith' changed into 'since;' and the word 'that' put out.
20. Rous's arrangement changed on account of 'always.'
21. To 'lift up the hands to commandments,' seeme and obscure expression; hence the change in the stanza.
22. 'Spake,' obsolete; hence the change in this stanza.
23. In Rous a syllable wanting, 'af-flic-*ti*-on.'
24. 'Stuff'd' changed into 'fill'd;' and in line 3 'commandement' rejected.
25. In Rous ungrammatical, 'thou gave' for 'gavest.'
26. This verse seems in Rous obscure, by the vague use of the word 'this;' hence the proposed emendation.
27. Rous's word, 'face,' not in the text.
28. Rous's arrangement changed, to make the word 'teach' more emphatic by its position.
29. The composition in line 1, and the word 'commandement' in line 3, seemed to require improvement.
30. Ungrammatical, by a redundant nominative, 'they.'
31. In Rous this line apocryphal.
32. Rous writes 'sweet delectation.' The expression in the emendation seemed preferable.
33. The amended line more literal than that of Rous.
34. Rous's favourite relative, 'that,' changed into 'which.'
35. In Rous there is here no rhyme, 'cute,' 'cute.'
36. Where in Rous is the antecedent to the relative 'which?'
37. The emendation is an attempt to improve the expression, 'testimony of thy mouth.'
38. In Rous a syllable wanting, 'gen-er-a-*ti*-on.'
39. As the word 'they' is here somewhat vague, the turn given to the thought in the emendation seemed to make the sentence clearer.
40. Rous's expression, 'when as,' objectionable.
41. Rous improperly left out here the 'for' or 'because.'
42. Wants a syllable.
43. Wants a syllable, 'me-di-ta-*ti*-on.'
44. 'Ancient' being now at least a dissyllable, makes this line defective in measure.

NOTES. 345

45. Rous's expression, 'which are pure,' not being in the text, it seemed allowable to substitute another addition, if preferable.

46. In Rous an inharmonious line.

47. In Rous wants a syllable, 'af-flic-*ti*-on.'

48. 'Soul' changed into 'life,' as being plainer.

49. To improve and modernize the style of this stanza was the object of the proposed emendation.

50. Rous is here obscure. 'To perform a statute' is questionable English. We perform a promise, we *obey* a statute.

51. Rous, in line 2, writes 'depart away.' The latter of these two words is useful in supplying a rhyming word; but it is quite useless otherwise, since 'to depart' includes the notion of 'away.'

52. It was thought that these two verses, 118, 119, would be better translated by eight than by four lines, as Rous has done.

53. We do, or administer justice; we do not 'perform justice.'

54. In Rous wants a syllable, 'sal-va-*ti*-on.'

55. Rous writes 'teach and show;' pleonastic.

56. Rous writes, ''Tis time thou work;' 'thou' changed into 'to.'

57. Rous ends this line with 'therefore;' as before, this line cannot properly end an Iambic line.

58. Rous has here no rhyme, 'ly,' 'ly;' rectified.

59. Rous, to obtain the rhyme 'saw,' turned in this stanza present tenses into past. I have restored the present tenses. If it be objected that my fourth line is apocryphal, I may in reply say that it is not more so than the third line of Rous.

60. In Rous no rhyme here, 'right,' 'right.'

61. The wrong position of Rous's word 'therefore' in this line greatly impairs its smoothness; hence changed.

62. Rous's words, 'found and,' apocryphal.

63. Rous ends with 'alway,'—improperly; rectified.

64. Rous wants here a syllable, 'ex-pec-ta-*ti*-on.'

65. Rous's word, 'revive,' not in the text.

66. In Rous obscure and ill arranged. The emendation seems somewhat clearer, if equally textual.

67. A syllable wanting; rectified.
68. Rous's arrangement changed.
69. In Rous has no rhyme, 'ly,' 'ly;' rectified.
70. Wants a syllable, 'commandements.'
71. A syllable wanting, 'gra-*ci*-ous;' rectified.

Psalm CXX.—1. It seems doubtful, at least, whether, by the word 'strong' here, Rous meant the powerful Jehovah. Rous's line is obscure.

2. In Rous here no rhyme, 'long,' 'long;' rectified.

Psalm CXXI.—1. In Rous ungrammatical, by a redundant nominative, 'he.' The 'he' in the preceding line is the nominative to the verbs 'slumbers' and 'sleeps.' Hence a reason for trying to amend this line.

Psalm CXXII.—1. In lines 2 and 4 Rous gives redundant measure, in 'toge*ther*' and 'thi*ther*;' this rectified.

2. This verse, as rendered by Rous, seems both incorrect and unpoetical; incorrect, by the unhappy use of the word 'for.' There were two reasons for the tribes going to Jerusalem, one to perform their duty to God, another to attend to the courts of law for the settlement of important cases. The first of these reasons is given in the end of ver. 4, the second in ver. 5. Had Rous, in commencing ver. 5, said, 'and because,' thereby connecting the former with the latter reason, his meaning would have been clear. The verse is unpoetical also, by his tamely telling us that David's thrones of judgment 'stay' at Jerusalem.

3. In Rous no rhyme, 'ty,' 'ty.'

Psalm CXXIII.—1. Rous's 'do look' changed into 'attend.'

2. In Rous a syllable wanting, 'gra-*ci*-ous.'

Psalm CXXIV.—1. The word 'quick,' which Rous probably uses not adverbially, but as an adjective denoting 'alive,' is now in that sense obsolete, or nearly so. Rous's rhyme also in this stanza is imperfect, 'flame,' 'stream;' hence the proposed amendment.

2. In Rous prosaic and inelegant, 'waters make way over the soul.'

3. Unmusical in Rous; hence the proposed change.

PSALM CXXV.—1. By turning the verb 'trust' into its participle, we avoid the inelegance of a separated antecedent and relative, 'they,' 'that.'
2. Rous's word 'folk,' obsolete; changed into 'people.'
3. In Rous unmusical; hence the change.

PSALM CXXVI.—1. 'That dream'd,' changed into 'who dream.'
2. Rous writes, 'They among the heathen.' This is literal; but the expression is obscure, as it may mean the Jews living among the heathen, or it may, and I think does, mean the heathen.
3. Ungrammatical in line 3, by a redundant 'he.'

PSALM CXXVII.—1. 'Builders lose their pain,' should be 'pains' to be good English.
2. 'So gives,' the word 'so' seems obscure. Whether the proposed amendment removes any part of the obscurity I dare not be sure.
3. Rous's word, 'those,' which should be 'these,' objectionable; but he needed a rhyme for foes; hence the proposed change.

PSALM CXXVIII.—1. In Rous no rhyme, 'ways,' 'ways;' rectified.
2. In Rous has a redundant 'he,' as the word 'Behold' does not govern the word 'man,' but is to be considered an interjection.

PSALM CXXIX.—1. In lines 1, 3, as given by Rous, the words are all monosyllables, and consequently less musical.
2. Rous wants here a syllable, 'con-fu-*si*-on.'
3. 'Whereof' changed into 'of which,' more modern.
4. Rous has here an expletive, 'do;' rectified.

PSALM CXXX.—1. 'That' changed into 'who.'
2. In Rous, line 4 wants two syllables, 'and plent-*e*-ous re-demp-*ti*-on.' This has been rectified.

PSALM CXXXI.—1. Rous, in line 4, makes a pronoun rhyme; altered.

2. Rous contracts into one syllable the word 'spirit,' not a good practice in the view of harmony.

3. Rous's style here improvable.

PSALM CXXXII.— 1. 'Within my house,' better 'in my house.'

2. Rous wants in line 3 a syllable, in the word, 'ha-ta-*ti*-on;' this rectified.

3. In the proposed emendation of this stanza 1 have followed the paraphrase of Bishop Patrick, which is adopted by Bishop Horne also.

4. Has in Rous a redundant syllable.

5. In Rous this stanza has no rhyme, 'ness,' 'ness.'

6. Rous's expression, 'to turn away the face,' obscure. To make it clearer is the object of the change.

7. In Rous ends with the pronoun 'it,' making that little word too prominent.

PSALM CXXXIII.—1. Rous in translating this verse has omitted an important idea given by the inspired poet, namely, the pleasantness of dwelling in unity, a motive to concord far too important to be passed over, when addressing men who are naturally so fond of what is pleasant.

2. 'That,' as a relative, in three instances, changed into 'which.'

PSALM CXXXIV.—1. Rous here, as often elsewhere, puts the word 'even' apocryphally; probably when he needs a syllable, as a poet sometimes does. In the emendation 'even' is omitted.

2. Rous here, as often, thrusts inelegantly some word between the antecedent and its relative, 'Lord thee bless that.' The emendation rectifies this; or it may be rectified otherwise in the following way:—

  'Your hands within God's holy place,
   lift up, and praise his name;
  Thee bless from Sion hill the Lord,
   who heav'n and earth did frame.'

PSALM CXXXV.— 1. Verses 1, 2.—These two verses in Rous have only four lines; in the proposed emendation eight, which do not seem paraphrastical.

2. In Rous redundant measure here, 'plea*sure*,' 'trea-*sure*;' this rectified.

3. Rous inconsistent here, in combining 'things,' which is a plural word, and 'that,' which is singular; this rectified.

4. Rous writes, 'who smote.' This is quite literal, and would do, had he been able to place the 'who' before 'Egypt's,' but not well otherwise.

5. The word 'folk' obsolete. Rous's word, 'pleasant,' and his word 'chosen,' in this stanza, not in the text.

6. Rous has here no rhyme, 'all,' 'all;' rectified.

7. In this stanza lines 1 and 4 want each a syllable.

8. The object of the proposed emendation in this stanza was to reduce the number of *theys* and *haves*, and to give more fluency and variety to the style.

9. Rous has here no rhyme, 'ly,' 'ly.' I have so frequently occasion to repeat this, that it must by this time be to the reader wearisome. But I deem it right to mention it always, as a reason for my attempting to correct this fault of the stanza.

PSALM CXXXVI.—1. In making the above changes in Psalm cxxxvi., no attention was paid to the preservation of Rous's double rhyme. In attempting the more difficult task of double rhyme, both in this Psalm, and in others, Rous has injured both his poetry and his English. See for an instance and proof of this the second version of this Psalm.

PSALM CXXXVII.—1. Rous has in this stanza no rhyme, 'on,' 'on.' Line 3 is also obscure in Rous—'In midst hereof.' In the midst of what? Is it in the midst of Babel? or of the streams? or of the willows? Rous gives quite a literal translation; but still the expression is not at all a clear one. The emendation makes no pretension to clear away the darkness referred to. Bishop Patrick gives in this no help. Does it mean Babel, through the midst of which ran the Euphrates?

2. Defective in measure, 'foun-da-*ti*-on,' 'de-struc-*ti*-on.'

PSALM CXXXVIII.—1. Rous makes 'above' a rhyming word; not properly.

2. Rous's arrangement changed, to bring the relative to its place; and 'when as' changed into 'what time.'

3. Has in Rous no rhyme, 'sing,' 'reign;' rectified.

4. The change here made was to move the 'he' from the end of the line.

PSALM CXXXIX.—1. In Rous there is in this stanza no rhyme, 'ways,' 'ways;' also bad English, 'thou art acquaint,' for 'acquainted.' The proposed emendation was intended to rectify these two points.

2. 'When as,' in Rous, changed into 'what time.'

3. In Rous the eight lines of this verse are neither perspicuous nor poetical, though, taking the Psalm as a whole, it is well done.

4. Rous's word, 'there,' seems wrong. The word 'there' is only used when the verb is put before its nominative; as, There was a man, etc.

PSALM CXL.—1. 'And froward,' not in the text.

2. In Rous lines 2 and 4 have a redundant syllable.

3. Rous writes 'underneath;' not now used.

4. In Rous wants a syllable, 'sup-pli-ca-*ti*-ons.'

5. In Rous has neither rhyme nor full measure; rhyme, 'on,' 'on,'—measure, in line 2, 'sal-va-*ti*-on.'

6. In Rous not well composed; to 'compass about,' and the unnecessary word 'even,' put in to fill up a line.

7. 'Throw in flame,' bad English; should be 'into.'

8. Rous's line, to be good English, should either have the word 'that' placed after 'know,' or have the arrangement changed, as in the emendation. Rous places the word 'upright' in a wrong position.

PSALM CXLI.—'Prayer,' in Rous, a dissyllable; not now so used in poetry.

2. Rous's thought and expression somewhat modified in the whole of this verse. Room is wanting to say why.

3. Rous writes 'time shall fall,'—unpoetical; but a rhyme was needed for 'shall.'

4. 'When as' changed into 'what time;' and 'stony'

changed into 'rocky,' as it is supposed to refer to what is related in 1 Sam. xxiv. 2, 3, etc.

5. By the slight change in this line the expletive 'do' got rid of.

6. 'Help' changed into 'support.' As the word 'help' is apocryphal, there was no scruple to change it for a word of nearly similar meaning, when by the change the style is improved by the want of the 'do,' a great favourite with our translator.

PSALM CXLII.—1. Vers. 1, 2.—In Rous these two verses have four lines; in the proposed amendment eight.

2. Rous writes, 'none were;' should be 'was,' *none* being singular—the contracted form of *no one*. The word 'all' in line 3 apocryphal.

3. Deficient in measure, 'por-*ti*-on;' rectified.

4. In the emendation the word 'for,' omitted by Rous, has been restored.

5. To this long verse Rous has given four lines: the emendation eight lines.

PSALM CXLIII.—1. Rous does not happily connect the clauses of this verse; the 'and' beginning line 4 comes in awkwardly; hence the attempt to improve it.

2. Rous's English here very exceptionable, 'the enemy hath tread my life to the ground.' Why not 'trodden?' A rhyme was needed for 'dead.' To make the verse passable English, I have been under the necessity of using a little liberty with the tenses of its verbs, turning past into present tenses.

3. This stanza in Rous, besides having no rhyme, has in line 4 been, if I mistake not, greatly mistranslated in the expression 'amazed wondrously.'

4. Vers. 7-9.—The object of the change in these stanzas was improvement in the phraseology of these verses.

PSALM CXLIV.- 1. Rous writes 'strength and might;' pleonastic.

2. Vers. 8 and 11. Rous's word, 'their,' changed into 'whose.' Rous's word, 'their,' is quite literal; but as in both verses the word 'whose' is used in the immediately preceding line, and as 'whose' and 'their' apply to the

very same persons, it seemed advisable to make this change, as conducive to the perspicuity and elegance of the expression.

3. Wants a syllable, 'sal-va-ti-on.'

4. Rous obscure here, as it is not evident whether his relative 'that' refers to 'sons' or to 'plants.'

5. For Rous's word, 'streets,' we have 'sheep-walks;' it being uncommon to find in 'streets' lambs in 'ten thousands.'

PSALM CXLV. (C.M.)—1. Rous ends the line with 'always,' although accented on the first syllable.

2. In Rous a syllable wanting, 'gra-ci-ous.'

3. Rous's word, 'other,' not in the text ; and it is at least questionable whether the use of the word 'other,' as here used, is defensible as good English.

4. Rous's arrangement is here too Latinised.

5. In point of correct expression, I would prefer to these two lines the following version:—

'The Lord upholds the bow'd down all,
upraises all who fall.'

6. In Rous grammatically objectionable, in the phrase 'them gives,' which should be 'gives ;' but the translator needed a rhyme for 'lives,' so that here, as in some former instances, he sacrifices grammar to sound.

7. In Rous redundant in measure, 'never,' 'ever.'

PSALM CXLV. (L.M.)—1. In ver. 21 of the preceding version, Rous has a syllable too much, here he has one too little, 'plen-te-ous.' His expression, 'wrath and anger,' tautological ; only one of them is in the text.

2. In Rous very awkwardly composed, hence the attempt to improve it. When Rous, as here, attempts verse with double rhyme—a difficult attempt for most poets—his style invariably falls below its usual standard.

3. Rous writes 'name end ;' 'name' not used when the substantive to which it refers is expressed.

4. In Rous the first two lines not well composed, by the awkward position of the relative 'that' in line 2 ; and in lines 2 and 4 there is no rhyme, 'live,' 'lieve.' For these reasons a reconstruction of the stanza was attempted. If

is be asked why is the verb 'loves' singular, and the verb 'wait' plural? the reply is, that the nominative is one of that class of words which authorizes the composer to use either number, as circumstances might require.

Psalm CXLVI.—1. Verses 3, 4.—To these verses Rous assigns four lines; the emendation eight.

2. Rous here, as occasionally elsewhere, when at a loss to fill up a line, calls to his aid a synonym passing two such words. Here we have 'happy' and 'blest;' in Psalm cxliv. 1 we have 'strength' and 'might.'

3. Rous writes 'within the same;' unpoetical.

4. It was thought that these lines, as given in the emendation, would in point of style be an improvement.

5. In Rous wants a syllable, 'gen-er-a-ti-on.'

Psalm CXLVII.—1. In Rous ungrammatical; he there writes, 'to praise, it is a comely thing;' rectified by leaving out 'it.' The line may be thus, 'it a becoming thing.'

2. The emendation in these lines is grounded on the opinion entertained by commentators, that this Psalm was composed about the time when Israel was restored from the Babylonish captivity; and as this restoration was not effected all at once, but at different periods, we may see in a Psalm then composed the propriety of the word 'gathering.'

3. Rous writes 'his'—the word 'God' is in the text.

4. Rous's word, 'nor,' changed into 'not.' The word 'not' cannot properly, as here, be placed before 'doth he.' 'His pleasure not doth he.' This arrangement is at variance with almost every, if it be even otherwise. In the emendation the sentence stands thus,—'His pleasure neither in horses' strength, nor,' etc.

5. Our translators render this line, 'Praise thy God, O Sion;' Rous renders it, 'Sion, thy God confess.' To praise God, and to confess God, are synonymous. It seemed therefore proper to modify Rous's translation, as in the emendation of ver. 12. Rous was probably led to render ver. 12 as the way in which he has done it to find a rhyme to 'confess' to suit 'bless,' line 4.

Psalm CXLVIII.—1. As the second 'ye' in this line appeared quite uncalled for, it has in the emendation been omitted.

2. Rous writes, 'all the creatures;' apocryphal this. 'Let them,' is the expression in the text. Such an addition as that above, if allowable at all, would have come in with a much better grace at or near the end of the Psalm, after the long enumeration of creatures referred to had been finished. To introduce so early into this Psalm so comprehensive an addition without a warrant from the text, was injudicious.

3. Rous's expression, 'for all times to come,' appearing somewhat vague, the expression in the emendation was preferred as more clear and definite.

Psalm CXLIX.—1. In Rous a syllable wanting.

2. 'That' changed into 'who.'

3. 'Above the firmament,'—in Rous, 'in the firmament.' This part of the exhortation Bishop Patrick supposes to be addressed to the inhabitants of heaven; hence the reason for changing 'in' into 'above.'

NOTES.

I HAVE not attempted to make any amendment in Rous's *peculiar* metres, in Psalms cxxiv., cxxxvi., cxliii., and cxlviii.

To say nothing of the inferiority of their style to that of his *common* metre Psalms, I cannot see that these peculiar metres are of the least value. At no time, either in public or private worship, have I during life seen one of these versions used. The value of the Psalms would not be at all diminished by excluding from our psalmody these four peculiar metres.

In their place it might be advisable to introduce a few additional long metre versions. We have at present only four or thereby. It is quite conceivable that it may be possible to render some Psalms both more accurately and more elegantly in long than in common metre, provided the translator did not bind himself with the inconvenient and harassing shackles of double rhymes in the same stanza, as Rous does.

www.ingramcontent.com/pod-product-compliance
Lightning Source LLC
Chambersburg PA
CBHW020324240426
43673CB00039B/907